Praise for Julie Morgenstern's **SHED** program

"Lays out a plan for clearing out both physical and sentimental clutter . . . a handy little guide to Dumpstering your way into a state of Zen."   —*Time*

"Morgenstern is the queen of helping people put their lives in order."
—*USA Today*

"If you want to, need to, or are being forced to make a big life change, it's probably a good time to check out [this book]."   —*Detroit Free Press*

"[Julie Morgenstern] is gifted at explaining organizing techniques and systems and isn't afraid to speak from personal experience. . . . The goal of her system is impressive. Who among us wouldn't want to have more energy, insight, and clarity? Sign me up for a hefty dose of those three things!"
—*Realsimple.com*

"Picks up where other de-cluttering books fall short. Morgenstern doesn't pass judgment or implore readers to 'live with less'—rather, she uses the process of letting go as a catalyst for finding your unique voice and creating a meaningful, fully engaged life."
—Stephen R. Covey, author of *The 7 Habits of Highly Effective People* and *The 8th Habit: From Effectiveness to Greatness*

"No matter what your age or life stage, Julie Morgenstern shows how the power of **SHED** can bring more happiness into your life."
—Marci Shimoff, #1 *New York Times* bestselling author of *Happy for No Reason*, coauthor of *Chicken Soup for the Woman's Soul*, and featured teacher in *The Secret*

"Goes right to the heart of why it's hard to let go of physical and emotional clutter, offering inspired solutions that really work."

—Barbara Sher, author of *I Could Do Anything If I Only Knew What It Was*

"**SHED** shows you what is underneath all the reasons why people do what they do, and helps people get to the heart of their issues."

—Jean Chatzky, author of *Make Money, Not Excuses*

"The simple **SHED** model teaches a tactical, practical approach to getting one's arms around the psychological, behavioral and physical aspects of change so that it can finally happen."

—Julie Jansen, author of *I Don't Know What I Want, but I Know It's Not This*

"A clear guide to uncovering your innermost desires by examining your 'stuff,' this book is full of wisdom, insight, and practical advice. The stories and Julie's own confessions draw you in and keep you there to work through your own clutter."

—Laura Berman Fortgang, author of *Now What? 90 Days to a New Life Direction* and *Take Yourself to the Top*

"Perfect for anyone whose current life isn't working anymore but who doesn't know which way to head next."

—Margaret Lobenstine, author of *The Renaissance Soul: Life Design for People with Too Many Passions to Pick Just One*

"Here's a practical 'guide' on how to take control of your stuff and set yourself free!"

—Barbara Corcoran

"Julie's wise words and sage advice lead you to surprise yourself . . . about yourself."

—Nate Berkus, author of *Home Rules*

ALSO BY JULIE MORGENSTERN

Never Check E-Mail in the Morning
(previously published as *Making Work Work*)

Organizing from the Inside Out

Time Management from the Inside Out

Organizing from the Inside Out for Teens

JULIE MORGENSTERN

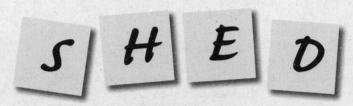

Your Stuff,
Change Your Life

A FOUR-STEP
GUIDE TO
GETTING
UNSTUCK

A FIRESIDE BOOK
Published by Simon & Schuster
New York   London   Toronto   Sydney

Fireside
A Division of Simon & Schuster, Inc.
1230 Avenue of the Americas
New York, NY 10020

First Fireside trade paperback edition March 2009

FIRESIDE and colophon are registered trademarks of Simon & Schuster, Inc.

For information about special discounts for bulk purchases,
please contact Simon & Schuster Special Sales at 1-800-456-6798
or business@simonandschuster.com.

Designed by Jan Pisciotta

Manufactured in the United States of America

10   9   8   7   6   5   4   3   2   1

The Library of Congress has cataloged the hardcover edition as follows:
Morgenstern, Julie.
    When organizing isn't enough : SHED your stuff, change your life / Julie Morgenstern.
        p.   m.
    "A Fireside book."
    1. House cleaning. 2. Orderliness. I. Title.
TX324 .M66 2008
648—dc22   2008299736

ISBN-13: 978-0-7432-5089-4
ISBN-10:   0-7432-5089-3
ISBN-13: 978-0-7432-5090-0 (pbk)
ISBN-10:   0-7432-5090-7 (pbk)

Originally published as *When Organizing Isn't Enough* in 2008 by Fireside

To Dad and Pepper

for their loving and remarkable
help with this book

Contents

Step 4

DRIVE YOURSELF FORWARD   211

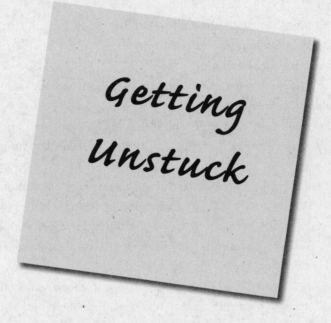

Whatever you can do, or dream you can, begin it.
Boldness has genius, power and magic in it.

—Goethe

Ever felt stuck?

Like there's something more, but you don't know what it is?

You know:

lead-footed.

tongue-tied.

paralyzed.

Eager to make a change, shake things up, try something different, or get back to normal, find your passion, be happy.

But you're not sure how.

Or you're not sure whatever you've dreamed up is worthy of pursuit, or even possible to pull off.

Or maybe you've already experienced that big change (marriage, divorce, empty nest, retirement, new career, new house), but are having a difficult time adjusting.

I don't believe that any book (including this one) is a fix-all, magic pill. I won't promise this book will solve your problems, help you find peace or reveal the secret of life. It won't. What I will promise, however, is that reading this book will dislodge you from your current state of paralysis and help you move forward with optimism and confidence.

The theory behind **SHED** (the process you will learn about in this book) is that by releasing your attachment to obsolete, tangible items in your space and schedule, you will gain the energy, insight, and clarity to make decisions about the big stuff. **SHED**ing creates the space to think; it fortifies your identity and eliminates old, unhealthy belief systems.

I developed the **SHED** process over several years of working with clients who needed something more than the organizing and time management services I usually provided. I also have personal experience with **SHED**. It helped me navigate a difficult transition from the life of a day-to-day parent to life as an empty nester (in a brand-new home), and from the solitary existence and singular focus of a business owner and single mom to building a vibrant social life and engaging more fully in expanded business and personal relationships.

In my experience, there are three common characteristics that define people who are ready to **SHED**. See if you recognize yourself in the descriptions below:

- **There is a specter of a better future in your mind.** You are gripped by the feeling that there's something more, but you don't know what it is.

You're not sure exactly what you want, but there is a glimmer of a future in your mind that is pulling you forward. It may be hard to articulate, but it's a deep-seated wish, a hope, a dream that's been rattling around inside.

- **You don't know if you'll be able to do "it."** Whatever you are hoping for feels potentially out of reach, and you wonder if you can actually pull "it" off. You ask yourself questions like, Is now the time? What if it doesn't work out? Is this the right decision? and Do I deserve this happiness?

- **You're feeling weighed down by something that's preventing you from moving forward.** It could be old habits, too many obligations that don't fuel you, a behavior that's getting in your way, or piles of paper and belongings that are obsolete but hard to detach from. Whatever the anchor, it's hard to move forward or even think clearly when you feel crushed under its weight.

It takes courage and a little bit of faith to release the past and fling yourself toward a better (if ambiguous) future, but the rewards are effective and profound.

The good news is, as stumped, paralyzed, stuck, or frustrated you may currently feel, the answers are deep inside you. **SHED**ing is a catalyst and companion on the journey to self-development, and a richer, more connected life.

SHED will get you unstuck by enabling you to:

- **Create the space to think and move**. It's hard to visualize the future when the present is so full. You invest a lot of time and energy analyzing and criticizing the old stuff, fighting against it, and beating yourself up over it. It's difficult to change or move into a new place in your life or career when you are consumed with things that distract you and steal focus and mental space.

- **Fortify your identity**. We often use objects, activities, roles, and habits to define ourselves—which leaves us feeling lost and vulnerable if those things disappear. We wonder, "Who am I without my objects?" "My busyness?" "My role as caretaker?" Breakthrough occurs when you realize it's not about the stuff—it's about you. You disengage your identity from the stuff, and recognize that you are who you are wherever you go, regardless of your possessions, habits, or roles. Each of those things is an external manifestation of your inner self, and you can create new ones anytime you want.

- **Eliminate old belief systems**. Contained in the defunct behavior, and submerged in that pile of stuff, is an old, no longer relevant belief system that you are still holding on to for some reason. The belief is usually so old and habitual that you are barely aware of its presence. All of the stagnant objects and behaviors in our lives represent something to us—someone we used to be, or wanted to become, something we once believed about ourselves or the world, or a different time in our lives. The clutter becomes a very literal clue to that old belief system: something tangible you can examine and expunge.

Remember the old adage "The only certainty in life is that things will change?" Somehow we don't seem to handle transition consciously (or very well). We don't have a process, we skip steps, we resist. **SHED** provides a framework to manage any transition with grace, verve, and mindfulness.

How to Use This Book

This book is organized into five sections that are meant to be read and applied in order.

Preparation, Getting Unstuck, consists of the next three chapters: What Is **SHED**?, Name Your Theme, and Inventory What's Weighing You Down. These chapters will explain how the **SHED** process works, guide you in charting a general direction to your **SHED**, and help you identify what's weighing you down by quantifying all the opportunities in your life to free up space for something more interesting and relevant. This section should be read by everyone, regardless of the type of clutter you are **SHED**ing.

Steps 1 and 2, Separate the Treasures and Heave the Trash, enable you to confidently identify the gems worth hanging on to when you **SHED** and then completely release the "trash" you have decided no longer fits into your life. Each of these sections is broken down into three chapters, one for each type of clutter the book addresses: Physical, Time, and Habit clutter. You may find it helpful to read all six chapters as an initial overview, but once you are ready to take action, you should focus just on the chapter pairs related to the area you are **SHED**ing at the moment. In other words, read and apply in conjunction with each other:

chapter 4, Finding Physical Treasures, and chapter 7, Heaving Physical
Attachments
chapter 5, Finding Time Treasures, and chapter 8, Heaving Time
Attachments
chapter 6, Finding Habit Treasures, and chapter 9, Heaving Habit
Attachments

Step 3, Embrace Your Identity, is designed to fortify your self-confidence in those first days/weeks after you've initially **SHED** the old and familiar and before you've filled the empty space with something new. Consisting of three chapters—Trust Yourself, The Five Disciplines, and Savor the Moment—this section should be read by everyone, and read repeatedly, each time you **SHED** any kind of clutter. Each read through will give you more insight, self-confidence, and strength to embrace the open space you've created rather than run from it.

Step 4, Drive Yourself Forward, provides a very specific series of activities to help you explore the direction of your dreams, and stay on track post-**SHED**, until you arrive at your new destination. All three chapters—Break Your Mold, Experiment with Your Theme, and Beware the 30 Percent Slip—will guide you throughout the course of your transition, and are meant to be read over and over, as needed, until you land in the place that provides you with a sense of fulfillment and satisfaction.

All in all, keep in mind that **SHED** is a fluid process: once you begin **SHED**ing one area of clutter, others begin to emerge that you tackle next. The steps begin to cascade in order—you could be Separating the Treasures in one pocket of clutter, while already on to Embrace and Drive from earlier pockets of clutter you have already released. The whole process develops a flow that every client and reader has described as exhilarating and invigorating and energizing. So, come on. Are you ready to **SHED**? Let's get to it.

Chapter 1

What Is **SHED**?

*Go confidently in the direction of your dreams. Live the life
you've imagined.*

—Henry David Thoreau

As an organizing and time management guru, my work over the past
twenty years has been dedicated to delivering practical and insightful solutions that transform the way people and companies function. My "inside-
out" philosophy lies at the heart of my mission—building systems around the
unique personality, style, and goals of each individual and company so that
they can make their greatest contributions to the world.

Organizing is the process of arranging your home, office, and schedule so
that it reflects and encourages who you are, what you want, and where you are
going. Simply put, organizing is about designing systems that improve your
efficiency and enable you to achieve your goals.

But what happens when organizing isn't enough?

Dear Julie,

I am stuck, paralyzed, before my own future. I've been opening doors
and closing them, unable to confront the task that awaits me—getting
my so-called empty nest ready to sell.

Brooke, 53, public relations consultant

I'm unhappy in my job, but am stumped whether to stay or go. I've been
spinning my wheels for years and I have no idea where to go from here.

Greg, 36, financial analyst

On the outside, my life looks good—nice house, great family, good
job. I look so accomplished. But it's an empty shell. I've felt my whole life
that there is something unexpressed in me.

Olivia, 47, real estate agent

I read your organizing books, and they make utter sense, but change is hard. I can't seem to part with my old ways.

Adam, 62, architect

Organizing works when you know where you are going but don't know how to get there. But when you are feeling stuck in your life, when you are in transition and unsure of where you're going next . . . *organizing is not enough*.

Here's a little more from Brooke's letter to me:

Before spring vacation I had made a list of things to do based on putting the house on the market this spring. It included shopping for improvements—French doors to separate the front hall from my computer room—and lots of sorting tasks to pare down the nineteen years' worth of stuff that is stored all over this big house.

But at the end of spring break the only task I had accomplished was loading and using Turbo Tax! I still can't believe that with nothing to do I was unable to face that list. Spring vacation is my get-it-done time. I clean, I sort, I organize. What is *wrong* with me?!

Brooke

When I read Brooke's note it seemed clear to me that the issue she was struggling with was *not* how to get *organized*. She sounded like a "get-it-done" person who was good at making lists and tackling her to-dos ("I clean, I sort, I organize"). Our follow-up conversation confirmed my hunches:

A public relations professional and a divorced single mom, Brooke, 53, woke up one morning to find herself an empty nester. "With no actual kids under my roof, everyone—including me—thinks I ought to consider moving on," she said. "Plus, it is ridiculous. I have over 2,600 square feet of house, and I spend most of it camped out on my bed, surrounded by novels, magazines, and crossword puzzles, happily munching on my dinner like a kid in a tent." Brooke was wrestling with a major change.

Brooke's house was not messy or disorganized—it was a lovingly designed and arranged work of art, a symbol of love and family. She felt attached to it, although she knew that attachment was weighing her down. She had always known her children would grow up, go to college, find jobs, and live on their own, but the moment had arrived all too soon, and she felt unprepared. She was not quite sure where she would go from here. She didn't need a better system; she needed something more. In Brooke's state of paralysis, simply getting organized wasn't the solution.

In my experience, people who are ready to get organized *always* have a clear vision of their destination—they have their eyes on a bigger goal. They want to save their job or start a business, strengthen their marriage or take better care of their children. In other words, no matter how high the piles, or packed the schedule, breakthrough comes when someone sees something that they desperately want on the *other side* of the clutter. By the time a client calls for my services, he or she already knows where they are going, is clear on their goals, and just needs help laying out a path to get there.

But when you don't know exactly where you are going or what you want (even though where you *are* isn't working), organizing isn't enough.

When you need or want to change something about your life, when you are going through a transition and are struggling to relinquish something that represents the past, you don't need to get organized—you need to **SHED**.

What Is **SHED**?

SHED is a transformative process for letting go of things that represent the past so you can grow and move forward. The four steps of **SHED** (*S*eparate the Treasures, *H*eave the Trash, *E*mbrace Your Identity, *D*rive Yourself Forward) provide a framework for proactively managing change, transition, and the feeling of being stuck and unsure. By releasing the defunct, extraneous, and burdensome objects and obligations that are weighing you down, you create the space to discover what's next and gather the energy and courage to move forward. By understanding and releasing your emotional attachments to tangible areas (like your space and time), **SHED** enables you to release intangible burdens including unhealthy beliefs and limiting thoughts.

SHED is not only about throwing things away (though that is a piece). **SHED**ing converts the process of letting go into an opportunity for self-discovery and healthy growth. It is a catalyst and companion on the journey to living a richer, more connected life. The ultimate payoff? Clarity, lightness of being, authenticity, and living as your most genuine, fully engaged self.

Is **SHED** for You?

SHED can be used by anyone who is feeling stuck in their lives. This book helps people gracefully and optimistically manage all kinds of change, including those prompted by:

- Natural life transitions: moving, retiring, graduating, marriage, promotion, new baby, empty nest, new business
- Sudden shift in life circumstances: job loss, company merger/management change, health crisis, divorce, threat of eviction, unexpected gain (financial windfall, new relationship)
- Internal drive for self-fulfillment and improvement: a desire for improved relationships with others, oneself, and the world

This book treats all change as an opportunity to grow. It provides a framework to positively manage change and converts the transition process—usually considered the most intolerable part of change—into a vital, vibrant adventure. **SHED** can be used to help you gain clarity no matter what stage of a transition you are in, although there are typically three points along the change continuum that trigger the process. You could be feeling ready to **SHED** if:

- You're on the brink of change—having thought about it for years—and now you're ready to take action
- You've already made a change but are still feeling stuck in the past
- You're being forced to make a change, whether you like it or not, and are feeling resistant

Let me give you a few examples.

I've been brewing about making a change for years

Caroline, 41, had worked in investment banking for years and did not want for money, comfort, or prestige. Yet, despite her outward success, something wasn't quite right; she was unhappy. On the fast track to becoming a senior managing partner, Caroline was extremely organized, productive, and efficient in her behind-the-scenes job crunching numbers, prepping deals, and crafting mergers. But something about the work had always felt hollow and mechanical; there was a social part of her personality that craved deeper, more sustainable relationships with clients and peers. Caroline's unhappiness intensified over eighteen months and she finally decided to make a change. She stepped off the fast track and accepted a new position in training and development, a more visible role within the company. Leaving the comfort and safety of her behind-the-scenes role was scary, but she felt incomplete and knew she couldn't stay where she was a moment longer.

I've already made a change but am still feeling stuck in the past

Jay, 32, grew up in the foster care system, and had battled physical chaos in his life for as long as he could remember. Having switched homes many times throughout his childhood, he never successfully set up a space for himself. He'd gone on to college (where he lived in the dorms) and then postcollege to a house share with some friends. No place ever really felt like home. In every abode, his room was cluttered and stifling. He moved into his first real, grown-up apartment four years ago—a contemporary one-bedroom flat with a brand-new kitchen, beautiful wood floors, and renovated bath. Yet he'd never fully unpacked, and when I first met him, he was still living out of boxes and bags. "The one thing every single living thing on this earth has is a home," Jay told me. "A place it calls its nest, its cave, its hole. These little animals go through the hassle of moving rocks and clearing out the dirt to make a space their own. When you don't have that element in your life, you feel lost."

Jay had a dog-eared copy of my book *Organizing from the Inside Out,* spine broken, facedown on his coffee table, peeking out from under a mountain of clutter. He'd been studying the book for years, and loved everything it said, but was unable to sustain any order he created or to make any progress. The stifling state of his home kept him feeling isolated and lonely; unable to fully engage in life. He wasn't able to invite friends or dates over, and his creativity was stalled.

In finally finding his own place, Jay had hoped to put down roots and create a nurturing place of his own. But some old belief system was holding him back. "As I compromised with this problem and learned to live with it, it's gotten worse and worse," Jay said.

I wasn't ready for this change

Max, 60, was a devoted department head and beloved faculty member for more than thirty years, when the health care crisis forced him to consider an early retirement. One afternoon, the university suddenly announced that, for faculty fifty-five and over, the only way to save their health care coverage was to take an early retirement the following year. His first reaction was outrage. How could the employer he'd been so loyal to act with such callous indifference? Yet after the initial rage subsided, in quiet moments of reflection he could detect the tiniest impulse of excitement from deep within himself. His whole career he'd had the persistent feeling that there was something else he was meant to do. He hadn't known what, nor had he ever taken the time to determine what that might be. He'd simply waited for a sign. He'd always maintained a love-hate relationship with the bureaucracy of education. Years had passed. Max felt that perhaps this forced retirement was the sign he needed.

Everyone going through any sort of transition is encountering an opportunity to **SHED**. The impulse to leave the obsolete or broken or irrelevant behind in order to pursue something new is universal. If your current situation sounds similar to one of the above, or if you are going through any kind of career, relationship, or lifestyle change, it's likely that you, too, are a candidate for **SHED**.

SHED Is Not a De-cluttering Crusade

Readers of my earlier books—*Organizing from the Inside Out, Time Management from the Inside Out,* and *Never Check E-Mail in the Morning*—are familiar with my belief that organizing is not about getting rid of things. Organizing is about identifying what's important to you and giving yourself access to it. While streamlining your belongings can sometimes be a *by-product* of getting organized, it's certainly not required. No matter how much you own, if you can find what you need when you need it, and are comfortable in your space, then you are organized. Similarly, no matter how full your schedule, if your days feel efficient and productive; if you are able to keep track of everything you need to do and accomplish what you'd planned, then you are organized.

Yet conventional wisdom constantly confuses "organizing" and "decluttering." Most people believe organizing = throwing things out. Decluttering is a very different process, with a very different purpose. Getting rid of things will *not* get you organized. But it *will* get you unstuck when you are feeling stagnant in your life and craving a positive change. Organizing is what you do to settle down. Decluttering is what you do to grow. Each process is important, and it's essential to know the difference—because we need different things at different times in our lives.

Our popular culture feeds into our misperceptions—with a large portion of the organizing makeovers on television and in print focused on how to get rid of things. Equally misleading is the common belief that decluttering is something you need to be "forced" to do through some sort of tough love. You know the crusade-like messages I'm talking about—available in full supply from genuinely well-meaning friends, family, professionals, and even from inside your own head: "Don't think, don't hesitate, put it in the garbage! Just say no! It's time to move on! What good is it doing you?! Throw it all away!" People who are coerced into throwing things away will comply in the moment, but they will feel sick to their stomach the entire time and will quickly refill their barren spaces, ending up right back where they started. Cavalierly tossing things from your home, office, or schedule (due to shame or pressure) never provides a lasting solution.

The unique promise of this book is that it will help you clear the clutter for good, by taking a very different approach to the process. **SHED** goes far beyond just "throwing things away" and helps you avoid the most common pitfalls of decluttering. How?

1. By ensuring you are doing it for the right reason—"to get unstuck" rather than to get organized
2. By teaching you what you do *before* and *after* getting rid of things to make sure your efforts last
3. By changing your view of clutter from "just junk" to what I call a Point of Entry—an opportunity for real transformation

SHED takes an activity usually approached like ripping off a Band-Aid and converts it into a positive, nurturing experience that you will savor. The objects or activities in your life (however stagnant or obsolete they may be today) served you at some point . . . or you wouldn't have them in the first place. And they still have some meaning . . . or you wouldn't be holding on to them. Studying the clutter and understanding its value to you before you toss it creates an opportunity for self-discovery, transformation, and a more meaningful and liberating change. And in this sense **SHED** is a uniquely personal process.

So, do you need to get organized or to **SHED**? There are times we clearly need one or the other, but it's altogether feasible that someone may require a bit of both. For example, when you are working through a major transition (new job, new relationship, new city, retirement, etc.), you will benefit from **SHED**ing the stagnant areas in your home or office. At the same time, however, there might be a few areas (your briefcase, linen closet, kitchen cabinets) that don't necessarily feel stagnant—they just need to be organized. Which do you need? Log on to the free community at www.juliemorgenstern.com and take the online assessment called **Do You Need to Organize or Do You Need to SHED?** The shaded box below also summarizes the differences to help you figure out what you need.

The Difference between SHEDing and Organizing

Think of it this way: if organizing is dropping anchor once you know what you want, **SHED**ing is lifting anchor so you can go someplace new. Here are the differences in a nutshell:

1. You organize to become more efficient. You **SHED** to get un-stuck.

2. Organizing involves designing systems for your space and time so you can function better where you are. **SHED** involves eliminating the obsolete so you have room to grow.

3. Organizing gives you *access* to what's most important to you. **SHED**ing is a process for *discovering* what's most important to you.

4. Something that's entirely organized but no longer relevant can be a candidate for **SHED**ing. For example, a perfectly organized closet filled with items you never use can be **SHED**.

5. It's possible to get organized without throwing anything away—purging is the one step you can skip. It's impossible, however, to **SHED** without letting things go.

6. While organizing has a clearly defined finish point (i.e., you can organize your garage or home office in a weekend), **SHED** is an ongoing process that generates movement and fuels transformation, which means the finish line is harder to define. You measure success by the feeling of being settled in a new place, as well as the subsequent energy, authenticity, and excitement about your life that ensue.

How **SHED** Works

SHED involves four steps for methodically releasing the objects and activities that represent the past so you can mobilize in the face of change. By breaking the process down into practical, nameable steps, you can move forward at a pace that is most comfortable for you; kind of like driving a car, you can speed up or slow down whenever you want.

This book is organized into five parts. This first section, called Getting Unstuck, helps you prepare to **SHED** by defining the process, and then walking you through two important steps, Name Your Theme and Inventory What's Weighing You Down, which help you prepare for a successful **SHED**. Name Your Theme will help you articulate your vision for the future, no matter how vague it feels right now, and Inventory What's Weighing You Down will help you find the best opportunities to begin.

The next four parts of the book are designed to take you through each step of the process:

- **Step 1: S**eparate the treasures. Slow down and take time to understand the emotional attachment you have to the clutter. Then identify and unearth the gems that energize you and have true value for the next chapter of your life.
- **Step 2: H**eave the trash. Once you have selected the items worth saving, completely relinquish that which represents the past by letting go of everything that is no longer relevant. This includes a radical release of any activity or object that depletes you rather than energizes you, and creates a large opening of time and energy.

- **Step 3: E**mbrace your identity. Recognize that you are who you are *without* your stuff. This is your opportunity to reconnect to your most authentic self and pull your identity from within.
- **Step 4: D**rive yourself forward. Experiment with filling your space and schedule with activities, experiences, and items related to your theme for the future, until you settle on the ones that feel right for you.

The four steps of **SHED** enable you to manage your way through change optimistically so that your transition is mindful, complete, and rewarding. In my experience helping clients through change, I've found that most of us blindly find our way through transitions, as we are driven by fear, confusion, and guesswork. Working without a framework, people often default to one or two parts of the process, while skipping other steps entirely. When you miss a step, or go through them out of order, you miss the opportunity to use each transition as a way to grow and nurture your most authentic self.

Take Your Online **SHED** Profile

Log on to the free juliemorgenstern.com community and get your personalized **SHED** profile. The diagnostic should take you approximately ten minutes to complete. The results will be a personalized **SHED** profile report, which is an analysis of your strengths and weaknesses in regard to each **SHED** step and a personalized guide to how to make the most of this book.

Your personalized report will tell you exactly which parts of the **SHED** process will come easily to you and which ones will be more challenging. And it will provide advice on which chapters you should make sure to pay special attention to in order to ensure your success.

When you **SHED**, it's natural to stumble along the way, losing steam or speeding through steps you find particularly challenging. If you fast-forward steps or go out of order, you will shortchange the decluttering process and your transition won't be nearly as transformative or fulfilling.

For example, if you think of every object or activity as a "treasure" and can't bring yourself to "heave," you won't free any space for growth. If you value nothing from the past and always jump straight to "heave," you'll end up leaving some wonderful gems behind and always feel empty. When you don't "embrace your identity," it's easy to get caught up in someone else's vision of who you are. And if you're afraid to "drive yourself forward," you'll stagnate in the present, limiting your ability (and opportunity) to achieve the change you seek.

SHED is a holistic process that works best when you give equal weight to each step along the path. Use your **SHED** profile to guide your reading, avoiding any of your own personal pitfalls and keeping yourself on track.

From Theater Director to Professional Organizer

I fell in love with the theater sometime in the third grade and never looked back. I dedicated myself to community theater growing up, majored in theater in college, and moved to Chicago to pursue graduate studies in theater direction. My life, from age eight on, was about honing my creativity. After grad school, I landed in New York City and made steady progress for the first few years, with footholds in off-Broadway theater companies, television, and film. I was realizing my dream to beat the odds and "make it."

Then I got divorced. I was 29 at the time and suddenly a single mom (my daughter Jessi was three). The late-night casting calls and marathon rehearsal weekends didn't fit my new circumstances; and the nominal pay I received for the work I loved didn't provide enough income to support myself, let alone raise my daughter.

For the first six months after my divorce, I did a little bit of everything just to keep things together. I waitressed at a '50s-themed diner (where my nametag read "Trixie"); I tried temping and read scripts. My rousing (if half-hearted) rendition of "Shout" (by the Isley Brothers) one February afternoon atop a sea of empty tables in my Trixie outfit only cemented my hunch that these were strange and uncertain times.

When I was in graduate school, I'd always wished there was a "rent-a-mom" service available for frazzled people like myself—you know, someone to organize your closets and make sure you weren't subsisting on a diet of Dr. Pepper and ramen noodles. The idea came back to me one night over a plate of lasagna with my old theater friend Walt (who, at the time, looked like he'd been living on a stage manager's diet of cigarettes and Diet Coke himself). Walt agreed that a rent-a-mom service was a great business idea. He desperately needed the service himself and thought I should go for it. But I didn't know the first thing about business, plus there was no way I could ever imagine trading in my peasant skirts for pinstripe suits, or my playbills for *The Wall Street Journal.*

As the months rolled on, I realized I had to do something because clearly life as Trixie wasn't the answer. So I called Ric, my old friend and mentor, to ask for his advice. I told him about my divorce and single motherhood, about Trixie and the failed temp assignments, and my rent-a-mom business idea. I confessed to being excited about the idea and told him that I might actually be able to pull it off—but I was afraid to pursue it for fear of what it said about me: that I was just another hapless theater dreamer that couldn't cut it, a failure, a slouch.

In his soothing, insightful way, Ric gave me permission to relinquish that identity. He said there was nothing wrong with wanting a more stable life for my family—it was a valid sacrifice and a wonderful gift to Jessi. He pointed out that he'd made a similar choice when he became an administrator so that he could support his family and provide a stable life.

I felt an immediate sense of relief. With that burden of shame lifted from my shoulders, I barreled ahead. I was able to reconcile what I perceived as a noncreative profession with the idea that it would help me provide a better life for my daughter. I marched myself to SCORE (Counselors to America's Small Business), bought books on working from home and picked friends' brains for advice. I stopped thinking I knew nothing about business once I realized my lifelong experience as a consumer would guide me well. Pretty soon, my new rent-a-mom business, Task Masters, took off.

A More Thorough **SHED**

About three years later, Task Masters was doing well, but I could feel the business beginning to plateau. I could only make as much as the hours I worked and couldn't figure out how to expand. At the time, Jessi and I were still living in a small Brooklyn apartment. Like most New York City apartment dwellers, we didn't have enough storage space, so I was storing about six boxes of my old theater production books underneath my dining room table. I'd meant to go through those boxes for years but hadn't had the heart. I knew letting go of those books would mean I was permanently out of the theater and never going back. One lazy Sunday afternoon, realizing how ridiculously unattractive it was to eyeball those boxes every time we sat down for a meal, I finally mustered the courage to go through them. I heaved everything but the books from my two best productions.

Within two months Task Masters soared to the next level. It was as if the chains holding the business back had been released. I hired people to work on my team, and we increased client billings and started to generate great publicity for the business. Suddenly there was no stopping me.

As committed as I thought I had been to start the business, it's now clear to me that I hadn't had both feet in the saddle for the first few years. I hadn't fully **SHED** my theater identity. Half of me was still tied to the theater world I'd chosen to leave several years before. By releasing those production books, I sent a mental and physical signal to myself that my business was now my core focus, and it took off. The feeling of mobilization was palpable.

The fact that I held on to those production books for so long indicated that my original transition wasn't complete, and that's what I think makes my story universal. We've all felt lost struggling to make a change—afraid and hesitant to let go of the past. That transition was one of the most difficult of my life. But in order to move fully into the next phase of my life as a parent and provider, I had to **SHED** my old skin.

Throughout **SHED** you will follow the stories of many clients (whose identities have been changed to protect their privacy) to learn from their transformational experiences. In particular, four clients—Brooke, Jay, Caroline, and Max—have generously agreed to share their **SHED** stories, providing you with an intimate glimpse into a very personal process. I hope following their journeys will give you comfort, insight, and inspiration for your own:

Brooke, 53, divorced mother of two, public relations professional. Brooke was a reluctant empty nester. Once her children moved out, she grieved the end of her parenting years and was lost as to what the next chapter of her life would be about.

Jay, 32, single, professional musician/composer. Jay had been struggling to get his apartment and life together for years. Living in perpetual clutter, he was having trouble letting go of the deeply buried belief "I'll never have a welcoming home."

Max, 60, married, retired theater professor. Max worked in academia for more than thirty years before being forced to consider an early retirement due to the health care crisis. Faced with an unexpected blank slate, he bravely began an adventure to reinvent himself.

Caroline, 41, single, career investment. banker. Caroline knew she looked powerful on paper, but in reality she felt hollow and mechanical. She was like a production machine, crunching numbers, cranking out reports, developing policies. Caroline craved human interaction, connections with others, and the opportunity to make a meaningful difference through her work.

Shedding is defined by the National Geographic Association as "a natural process that must occur in order for growth to be achieved." Birds molt, snakes slough, and lobsters shed their exoskeletons. Shedding is an ongoing process that mammals, arthropods, reptiles, and birds are engaged in most, if not all, of the time. In each case, the animal emerges from its shed fresh, lighter, and renewed.

Transformation is as pervasive in our lives as it is in the animal kingdom, but the human shedding experience (at least the one we pay attention to) is more ethereal in nature. Yet by making it tangible, we put ourselves more in control. **SHED** is about experiencing a transition that transforms us in some way. And though this process is not always pleasant or easy, without it life gets stalled. Clinging to the old, the irrelevant and stagnant will bog you down, hold you back and make you feel stuck. It can confine you to a space that no longer fits, denying you the opportunity to be your truest best self.

So let's go quietly through your old attachments, releasing the stagnant and creating the space for transformation. I promise it will be a vibrant and fulfilling journey toward your destination. Take your time. Enjoy the ride.

Chapter 2

Name Your Theme

*Your vision will become clear only when you look into your
heart. Who looks outside, dreams. Who looks inside, awakens.*

—Carl Jung

In reality no one lets go into a vacuum. In other words, no one lets go of
anything without reaching for something else.

Whether you came to this change of your own volition or didn't have a
choice, you are probably sifting through a sea of possibilities with no way of
knowing what's right.

Do I learn to work with this difficult new boss or search for a new job?
Do we stay in the suburbs or move to the city?
Do I stick with my industry or go back to school?
What about my marriage or relationship—does it stay or go?

When something about your life stops working, you can get paralyzed if you
aren't sure what to do next. It's human nature to freeze until we know exactly
what we want next. The problem is you can't figure out what you want if your
mind is so full of the past.

The solution? Stop thinking about your immediate options (or lack
thereof) and concentrate instead on the bigger picture. Instead of worrying
about the specifics of your next step, I'd like you to come up with a theme, a
vision, for your future. What is a theme in the context of **SHED**? A broad
goal or feeling; an overarching simple expression of the adventure you'd like
to be on. You probably have a deep intuitive sense of what you want, even if
you don't have the words to articulate it or are afraid to. There's a part of you
craving expression, a feeling that you want to create a better future.

As you begin to meditate on the spectre of your own future, think in terms
of a word or a phrase—a simple statement that summarizes the feeling you are
seeking. It's not what you want to *do* . . . it's how you want to *feel* or the part

of you that you want to express next. What are you hoping to create or learn next? Giving that deep-seated impulse a name will help dislodge you from your current state of paralysis—it's your "out," your exit plan. There is a great sense of hope and optimism in knowing that you are moving in the right direction without being required to make any *specific* decisions. Ultimately, your theme will be your beacon, focus, and filter, paving the way for your **SHED**.

We met Max in chapter 1. At 60, he had a reputation as one of the most gifted theater professors in the United States, and he had a cadre of successful students (many current superstars in theater and film) whose lives had been changed through their study with him. His work was invigorating, creative, and influential, yet he was consistently nagged by a sense that there were more untapped goals he wanted to achieve. His journal describes the ambiguity.

 Max

I am plagued by the notion that there is some potential in me that is both unrealized and unrecognized—a nagging sense that comes with no names, no ideas.

I could force the situation by inserting some ideas of my own, based on past experience. For example, I love to bake and I could develop those skills as a professional baker; I remember early morning walks in Greece and Italy, smelling the morning's yield of local bakeries. It seemed a wonderful life. Or bookbinding was an art that always appealed to me—I dabbled in it years ago and, again, it seemed an attractive way to work.

In the end, however, these ideas seem romantic, something of a fantasy and, most of all, artificial solutions to a feeling that has its own integrity. Moreover, I feel I will know the truth of a solution when and if it arrives. And that is my feeling—something will "arrive." There is no choice but to wait for something that feels authentic. I have faith that somehow clarity will emerge.

With a forced retirement on the horizon, Max was initially paralyzed with options, afraid of making the wrong choice. What ultimately mobilized him a sense of calm was realizing on the deepest level that he didn't have to decide yet whether he wanted to be a bookbinder or a baker, but simply that he could declare a phase of exploration. As a professor, his last thirty-five years had been devoted to helping others discover and unearth their talents. This next phase for Max—his theme—would be about *self-discovery*.

Finding True North

I believe we feel most alive when we are learning, discovering, or creating something. And regardless of what triggers change, most of us sense that the transition we are experiencing is an opportunity for growth.

Sometimes we hesitate to articulate our deepest wishes because we are afraid of failing. We are halted by our own insecurities and have grown accustomed to ignoring that quiet voice. Other times we stumble when asked to chart our own path because society, other people (parents, bosses, teachers, advisors), and institutions (school, company) have always defined a path for us. Maybe your focus in high school was to be accepted to a Top Ten university, so you took AP classes, played sports, and did community service. Once you graduated from college, your focus switched from getting good grades to landing a job with a well-respected company. Once there, you relied on your boss to chart the appropriate milestones: research associate, junior analyst, senior manager, vice president, partner.

This is an opportunity for *you* to decide what *you* want.

Remember Brooke from chapter 1?

When I first met Brooke, she struck me as extremely warm, expressive and upbeat on the outside, but I could tell something was churning inside her. It didn't take long to get to the heart of her confusion. She wrote in her journal:

 Brooke

When I first met Julie Morgenstern, I was really jazzed. I appreciated how she was able to get at organization by dealing with it on an emotional level first. What I was not prepared for was the gift she gave me.

I have a feeling Julie could tell that behind my cheerful exterior I was struggling. Ordinarily, I would not have been so forthcoming to someone I just met. She sat down, like someone I have known forever, and asked how I was doing. I could hardly stop from telling her how I had been opening doors to rooms and then closing them, unable to confront the task associated with moving out of my so-called empty nest. I couldn't decide what to keep and what to get rid of; whether or how to decide about 19 years' and 5 bedrooms' worth of furniture, what was important and what wasn't. I didn't even know if I should be moving out of the house.

For several years, Brooke said she had been playing with the possibility of selling her house, but she hesitated, finding one excuse after another to postpone her decision. At first she would tell herself—quite logically—that the housing market was terrible, and that she might as well wait for things to improve. Then it was winter, never a good time to sell. But then the market seemed to have leveled off, and property values were never going to be where they had been when she'd refinanced her place. And truthfully the issue was never about housing values.

Brooke's journal read: "Before I could elaborate, Julie was able to describe my problem for me. She knew exactly what I was going through: the protectiveness I felt over this 'structure' I had built for my family. Most important, she knew what I should do."

What you need, I explained to Brooke, is a theme for the next phase in your life. I explained that it is not about what house she will move into or where she will live; it is about focusing on the theme. A theme would give her a context for making decisions about the house and furnishings. Anything that will support her theme should be kept. The rest can go.

Brooke visibly relaxed, the tension melting out of her body and face. And then she lit up, delighted at the prospect of getting to decide the focus of the next chapter of her life, for herself.

I was personally able to relate to Brooke's situation because four years ago, I went through my own experience as a single mom facing an empty nest. For eighteen years, I had poured my energy into raising my only daughter and building my business. I loved being a mom, I loved being able to create a warm, inviting home where we had everything we needed, and I loved the structure and focus being a mom gave to my life. With Jessi graduating high school and moving out in the fall, I was on the verge of a big identity shift. And quite literally a very big opening in my schedule. What would I fill that space with? How would I figure out what's next? I was tortured with questions such as: Do I stay in this apartment or do I move elsewhere? Would keeping this apartment be helpful to Jessi? If I move, do I stay in this neighborhood where I have a great community of friends, or should I move into Manhattan? Do I invest all my energy in my business—and if so, what do I do from here? Or do I pour it into my personal and social life? If so, what shape does that take?

In anticipation of all these changes, I felt ready to connect to the world in a more complete and sustained way. Always one to give themes to years and phases of my life, I decided that this new stage of my life was about *Connections*. Having that theme not only gave me a great deal of excitement about the next phase of my life, but it also gave me a filter through which I would make decisions about everything—from where to live to how to grow my business to what to wear.

 Brooke

So, what's my theme? Wow. My whole life so far, other people, or life, have prescribed my decisions. Education. Marriage. Kids. Career. The idea that now I get to choose what's next—from *within*—that is so exhilarating. So liberating!

The first theme to cross my mind was a theme of *creativity*. I have been longing to write more. With the gazillion things I have going on, writing is always the last thing I get to do.

But, as I think about my desire to write more, I realize it's not that I want to write more from a quantity standpoint. It's about variety. Exploring my voice across different vehicles.

I have been writing poetry, and what I really want to explore is writing essays. Perhaps a column. Fiction. Kids books. I want to express myself across more genres, and connect to a wider and richer audience. This came to me with such clarity, I felt giddy.

Brooke's theme: *Expand my audience*

Brooke's experience was typical; a theme for the future provides just a hint of clarity to dislodge you from your current state of paralysis—it gives you a grand view, the motivation, and a broad context from which you can make all the specific decisions about what stays and goes during your **SHED**.

Below are five techniques for coming up with a new theme or focus for your future. Try one or more until you find the one that works.

Technique 1: Compare to Your Current Chapter

One of the best ways to figure out your new theme is to compare and contrast it to what the current chapter of your life has been about.

The richness of life and complexity of our beings necessitate that we focus on developing different aspects of ourselves at different points in our lives. During some phases we zero in on developing our knowledge, achievement, or social selves, while in other years we focus on finding love, caring for others, or finding inner peace. We pay attention to one set of interests or challenges when we are young, and others as we get older. As psychologist Abraham Maslow's "hierarchy of needs" theory of human motivation argues, we are, ideally, in a constant state of evolution and self-actualization.

Consider the time frame since the last big transition you went through; whether it was when you got married, started your current career or business, when you graduated, or had your first child. What's been your main focus for this chapter of your life? What has been your driving impulse, motivation, big-picture goal?

I want you to take the most positive spin on describing the current chapter of your life. What were you trying to accomplish? What is the "pure" and "healthy" impulse of your current phase? What have you gained? Was it wisdom, responsibility, love, insight, self-expression? If you were writing a book and needed a title for the current chapter of your life, what would you call it?

Kate, 45, got married at 28 to fulfill her family's image of what "life should be like." She married a successful young stockbroker, and they built a life together based on country club memberships and ambition. But, Kate's life never felt like "Kate." There was a part of her that aspired to conform, but in the process she muffled the more artistic, social, down-to-earth parts of her soul. Her marriage was unfulfilling and loveless, but she had always been able to adapt to any circumstance, adjusting her needs to accommodate others. She'd thought so many times of leaving but kept choosing to stay, to play within the "rules" and avoid the outside judgment for "giving up" on her marriage.

Her discontent escalated as she and her husband grew more distant. Things finally came to a crescendo after a particularly nasty argument one afternoon. After several months of contemplation she decided to file for divorce.

What her new life will look like in specific terms is unclear. But what she knows for sure is that she will finally be in the position to decide for herself what she wants and go for it. What Kate craves more than anything else is the freedom to be her truest self. If Kate were to sum up what the last chapter of life was about, she'd say *Tradition*. Her next chapter is about *Freedom*.

Here are a few brief character profiles and their themes:

Remember Jay from the introduction—the young man looking for love and a place to call home? His previous chapter was about *Finding his place*; his next is about *Putting down roots*.

- Sophia, 43   Type of change: just married
  Last chapter: Proving my independence
  Next chapter: Healthy interdependence

- Ben, 36   Type of change: new career
  Last chapter: Instant gratification
  Next chapter: Complete gratification

- Cory, 52   Type of change: recently divorced
  Last chapter: Fulfilling others' expectations
  Next chapter: Expressing myself

- Malik, 48   Type of change: new entrepreneur
  Last chapter: Making a living
  Next chapter: Building a life

These simple, powerful statements gave each client a renewed sense of excitement and focus; latching onto the hope of an idea was enough to get them moving forward. Released from the pressure of having a specific plan, they felt mobilized to **SHED** the stagnant from their lives in order to make space for new ideas related to their theme.

What would you say the current phase of your life has been about?

Name your current chapter here: _____

Next chapter: _____

Technique 2: Find an Inspiring Phrase

There are an unlimited number of ways you can define each chapter of your life, depending on what interests you, challenges you, and makes you happy. To think all of life's details can be encapsulated by a single word is, perhaps, unreasonable. Life is too complex. So it could be a sentence or a phrase. But think as all-encompassing as you can. Think of this simple statement as a top-level, broad-strokes way of describing what you next want to focus on in your life. What aspect of yourself has not been given enough attention so far. What do you next want to express or explore. Don't get hung up on trying to pick the "right" or "best" thing, just pay attention to the most visible and loudest voice. You'll recognize your theme by the excitement you feel.

Here are some examples of common themes to spur your imagination. Do any inspire you to action?

Common Themes

- Connections
- Creativity
- Freedom
- Mobility
- Self-expression
- Developing wisdom
- Calmness
- Inner peace
- Embracing my power
- Fun
- Discovery
- Expanding my horizons

- Education and enrichment
- Career excellence
- Health
- Adventure
- Self-discovery
- Authenticity
- Courage
- Honesty
- Vibrant health
- Finding deep love
- Creating a nuturing home

The future belongs to those who believe in the beauty of their dreams.

—Eleanor Roosevelt

Three Rules for Naming Your Theme

As you begin to come up with your own theme, here are three rules to consider:

1. **Your theme should be broad enough to impact all the different buckets of your life.** By definition, a theme will apply to all the facets of your life. It should be able to color every interaction you have—at home, at work, in your marriage, with your children, and your friends. However, if you are only feeling a need for career change or relationship change, it's fine to come up with a theme specific to that area. My experience is that whatever you choose will spill over in a positive way to all the areas of your life.

2. **Keep it simple.** Remember that theme or vision is only what you want to *express* or how you want to *feel*, not necessarily exactly what you want to *do*. And feelings are subjective and apt to change. The theme is meant to be a tool, a lens through which you will experience the **SHED** process. If you get halfway through and decide "This isn't actually what I want," no problem. You can change it. But push yourself now to come up with something that feels like it can dislodge you, something that excites you, even if it changes later.

3. **Give yourself permission to say what you *actually* want, not what you *should* want.** Don't edit your dreams. Imposing any sort of "shoulds" or "should-nots" onto this process defeats the purpose. It's not uncommon to feel shy or embarrassed about your most intimate hopes, even in the privacy of your own thoughts. But now's your chance to give yourself permission simply to say what you want. Ask yourself "If no one is watching and there is nothing holding me back, what do I really want my life to look like?" Write it down on a piece of paper that only you will see. Answer this honestly: If anything were possible, if there were no obstacles, what do I want the next phase of my life to be about?

The discussion so far may have prompted you to identify your theme already. If so, good for you. If not, no worries. There are a variety of ways to help pinpoint your new theme. Try one or all of the following techniques to uncover the words to your theme.

Technique 3: Listen for the Quiet Knock

As children, we are each a body of interesting and varied possibilities and potential. As we get older, we edit ourselves; burying past interests in order to feel content with our current lives.

It's hard to become an athlete, a musician, and an economist all at once. It's difficult to develop your artistic, intellectual, and social selves with equal attention. Various career and relationship choices bring out certain aspects of our beings and ignore others. The point is that there are many facets to yourself still buried deep inside, just waiting to come out.

Have the courage to get quiet with yourself and see what unexpressed aspects of your personality or being you can pull out to give voice to. What dreams have you so far been unable to pursue due to life choices and circumstances? What parts of yourself have felt like they've been shyly hiding deep inside, just waiting for you to invite them out? What interests did you used to enjoy but have not had a chance to do for years? What challenges you in a joyful way?

By the time I did my first consult with Caroline, she had already made the big decision to step off the fast track at her company, taking an internal role with less monetary reward, but more meaning and personal impact. Caroline, 41, was the mid-career single woman we met in the introduction. Her new position required her to move across the country, from Boston to San Francisco. Over dinner in London, I asked her if she was afraid of this big move. "I've done this before," she confessed. "Every several years since high school, I've completely reinvented myself, throwing everything away and starting new. New job, new country, new friends. I kind of excel at starting over and thriving in new situations." Caroline struck me as a Heaver.

This time I wanted to be sure that Caroline's bravery paid off. Instead of her leaping headlong into the unknown, I encouraged her to think in terms of a theme. I wanted Caroline to go into her new life with a focus, something that would serve as an internal compass at her new destination, to guide the decision and growth she was after. What was she hoping to gain from this big change? What would the next phase of her life be about?

Here's what she wrote in her journal.

 Caroline

It had been surprisingly easy to forget myself—the person who loved to draw and write poetry, volunteer, hang out with kids, ponder the mysteries of the universe with friends, skydive, and frequently fall in love. It was surprisingly easy to look back on all those things that used to define me and accept that they were in the past. Truth was that person wasn't gone; I just couldn't fit her into my work schedule. I am ready to reclaim that person. I need to find myself, but that is an ambiguous concept and although I have a sense of what I am looking for in myself, I needed a theme. I am willing to take a chance on being a powerful woman—I am ready to be me.

Caroline's theme: *Embrace my personal power*

Open yourself up to the notion that what you *really want* has been there all along.

Technique 4: Look to Your Past for Clues

A quick search through a few old boxes of memorabilia from your youth is another great way to reconnect to dreams yet to be expressed. Don't worry if your boxes aren't organized—just go through one random box at a time, with a keen eye for clues about yourself. Old boxes of photos, high school awards, college papers and yearbooks are a virtual treasure trove.

I started working with Matthew about six months before he decided to make a major career move. He'd worked in a law firm for several years and had made it his mission to become a partner in his firm. After twelve years he finally made partner, but once there, he admitted his new status wasn't quite as fulfilling as he thought it would be. His role as a partner now mandated that he do more "advising" than "doing," and he was growing more cognizant of a desire for a role that was more "hands on." Furthermore, the lifestyle sacrifices required by the firm were difficult. He traveled globally, frequently worked fourteen-hour days and often missed major events in the lives of his friends and family: high school reunions, weddings, eightieth-birthday parties. The thrill of anticipating a client's every need was gone; he wanted to redirect that energy back into his family and friends. Matthew was fully aware of the things he'd had to let go.

Last chapter's theme: *Proving my competence*
Next chapter: *Fulfilling personal commitments*

 Matthew

There are elements of your past that you may have "edited out" in order to succeed in one professional environment, but often those things really are what make you a unique person. What was knocking at my door? A desire to build something? I came across a box in my mother's attic of memorabilia from my high school years. Looking through that box allowed me to remember parts of myself I'd left by the roadside.

Matthew's theme: *Fulfilling personal commitments*

What lost parts of yourself can you rediscover through your memorabilia?

Technique 5: Study Your Present for Clues

If you're still having trouble pinpointing a singular theme, pay attention to current changes and activities in your life and see if you can connect the dots to discover what you may already be moving toward. Your theme might be manifesting itself in different seemingly unconnected ways.

Rebecca, 47, was a computer network teacher whose company had recently been bought and restructured by a larger firm. New management reassigned Rebecca from the classroom to a behind-the-scenes technical job. She hung in for a few months, but ultimately found her new desk job profoundly boring. Rebecca decided to use the change as an opportunity to consider her next career move. As much as she'd loved teaching, she'd always had a sense that there was more to her core self yet to be discovered. We talked through several possibilities and studied recent changes in her life. We were looking for clues about the direction she was moving toward.

Rebecca had a variety of interests and talents. Ostensibly this is a benefit, but for her that mostly resulted in a checkerboard resume, which left her feeling lost. She's a born entrepreneur, but none of the six small businesses she'd started had ever turned a profit. She'd always had a knack for science and technology, but had never more than dabbled in computer science. She found power and joy in the classroom but never appreciated the bureaucracy of education. What she liked best about teaching was tuning into the collective needs of the classroom, then expertly weaving in the information in a way that was relevant to her students.

Rebecca was also experiencing several other intriguing shifts in her life. She'd always been extremely messy and disorganized, without much regard for her physical environment, yet for the past eight months she'd been craving a more aesthetically beautiful home. She'd developed a desire to travel more, driven by an appreciation for the food, sights, sounds, and aromas of new cultures. She also had a burgeoning interest in all things beautiful (art, music, fashion, etc.).

We looked at what all of the joyful elements and experiences in her life had in common and realized that all of these experiences had to do with tuning into the senses: art, teaching, travel, home decorating.

The previous chapters of her life had all been about *intellectual development*. Whether teaching, or doing research, mastering computer skills, or even starting her own businesses, her emphasis has always been on taking a very cerebral approach to every job and activity. The small voice deep inside, long buried and now clawing its way out, had to do with tuning into her senses. She wanted to connect with the world on an intuitive level.

Last chapter: *Developing intellect*
Next chapter: *Connecting intuitively*

Think through what is new and interesting in your life. What new activities or objects are starting to appeal to you, perhaps for the first time ever? What clues do they give you about your future theme? Observe whatever's been knocking quietly at the door, past themes, and any new interests, and connect the dots.

What do you want the next phase of your life to be about?
Name your theme:_____

Still Stuck? Overcoming the Obstacles

There are three common obstacles to naming your theme, even after you've followed the steps outlined above: (1) you only know what you *don't* want; (2) you *can't* want what you want; and (3) you want what you *had*. If any of these apply, use the tips below to keep you moving forward.

First obstacle: I only know what I *don't* want.

Sometimes it's much easier to articulate what you don't want than to articulate what you do want. When someone is profoundly unhappy, dissatisfied, or restless, they might be so focused on how "wrong" their current situation feels, that they have a difficult time saying what could make it "right." That's OK; it's actually a good starting point.

Esther was a perfect example of this dilemma. From the outside her life looked full—married, two kids (a 27-year-old daughter and a 17-year-old son), beautiful home, adoring husband—but on the inside she felt empty and unsatisfied. She'd been feeling dissatisfied for a few years, but now that manageable dissatisfaction had given way to desperation. Talking about her feelings, even briefly, brought tears to her eyes. "My life is missing adventure," she said. "This life, this safe little suburban life, with all the same friends, all the same conversations, all the same activities, it all feels so safe." Her explanation sounded like a passage from *The Feminine Mystique*. She was confused—was it her marriage? Was it her attitude? Was it their neighborhood?

She could barely find the words to articulate her hope: "I can tell you what I *don't* want," she sighed. "I don't want this. I don't want to feel so empty. All I can think is that even though I tried not to become my mother, somehow I did—always following her advice to 'be safe.' I'm so sick of it. I don't want to 'be safe' anymore."

Using what she didn't want (safety) as a starting point, we did something a little unexpected—I reached for my trusty J. I. Rodale's *Synonym Finder* (a must-have book for all writers). We looked up the word "safety" and found the following synonyms: guarded, sheltered, defended, riskless, cautious, timid, under lock and key. This exercise confirmed Esther's definition of her current life. Next, we checked out the antonyms: brave, daring, courageous, bold, intrepid, gallant, valiant, confident, forward, brash, forthright, self-assured.

"Yes," she nodded, "brave, courageous. Those are traits I aspire to be." But these antonyms didn't make her feel energized or liberated. In fact, they made her feel discouraged. The word "brave" kept her trapped in the old place reinforced by her mother's messages of fear.

So, if bravery and courage didn't feel like the opposite of safety to Esther, what would?

I asked Esther to think about a time in her life when she felt similar to the way she wished she could feel; in essence, the opposite of the life she has built for herself. Without hesitation, she reminisced about her time at overnight camp, every summer from ages 12 to 15 (as a camper) and 16 to 21 (as a counselor). She described the excitement of discovering a new world and lifestyles different from her own. The thrill of discovery made her feel alive.

Esther's antonym (and antidote) for "safety" was "discovery." From that revised perspective, finding happiness and fulfillment seemed possible again.

Last chapter: *Safety*
Next chapter: *Discovery*

Go to the thesaurus and look up the word that you don't want. Play with that word, talk it out with a friend or think it through on your own. Go through the process of articulating what you don't want and free-associate until you can articulate a theme for what you *do* want.

Second obstacle: I *can't* want what I want.

If you feel like you can't want what you want, the first question is, why not? Beyond uncontrollable life circumstances, the thing that makes it hard for people to name their desire is self-doubt (in one form or another). You are afraid of failing, so you find a way to write it off: "It's not practical"; "It's too big a risk"; "I have to make a living"; "It would be impossible to pull off"; "I don't deserve this chance." My advice? Don't allow self-doubt to silence your desire. It hasn't worked so far anyway. Ignoring the voice, the desire, has not made it go away. Try just giving it a name, and let's see what happens. The act of coming up with a theme is the beginning of getting dislodged, the first step toward pursuing your dream. If you censor yourself from the get-go, you'll never be able to see your options.

 Max

Taking up acting again was taking up a challenge that I had enjoyed in my youth; nonetheless, it was a challenge I had never fully met. Even more, it was taking up the issue of self-doubt that had, over the years, grown around the subject. In essence: I had come to doubt that I was able to do what I was meant to do; I had come to doubt my own potency as a human being. I would have to unlock a chamber inside myself and run the risk of finding it empty.

Max's theme: *Self-discovery*

Third obstacle: I want what I *had*—and resent this change.

If change was thrust upon you and you weren't ready for it, you may still be so focused on what you've lost that you can't picture wanting anything else. Without the regular relationships and routines in our lives, it's natural to feel discombobulated. How do you develop a theme for the next phase of your life when you were perfectly content with the way things were?

We have all experienced an unexpected or unwanted change (forced move due to spouse's job change, death of a loved one, job loss, change in management, divorce, the end of a relationship, empty nest) or at least the threat of one, at some point in our lives. In many ways forced change is the most difficult place from which to develop a theme.

- After Mel's husband left her for another woman, she knew rationally that she needed to move on but was so hurt and shocked that she wasn't sure where to start.

- The executive board of Robert's apartment building threatened him with eviction unless he tossed half the items from his three-bedroom apartment (which they considered a fire hazard).
- Vicky loved her job and home but had to move to the Midwest because her company was relocating.

These scenarios don't inspire enthusiasm and motivation: they draw our defiance. We think, Who do you think *you* are to tell *me* how to live?

Give yourself the time to process the change, and don't feel pressured to rush ahead just because other people have told you it's time to move on. Try to separate your resentment or shock at the unexpected change from your ability to move forward. You can't always control what life throws at you, but you can control your response. Take the ownership back; decide what *you* want next. *Only you* have the power to imagine the next phase of your life.

What is quietly knocking at your door? We've all heard the "little voice" in the back of our heads. Can you articulate what it is saying? What opportunity is buried underneath this misfortune?

Write your new theme here: _____

Let It Sink In

You know you've got a good and useful theme if it makes you feel good about yourself and excited to move forward. You'll feel energized, hopeful, and ready to clear out the things that are weighing you down and holding you back.

Once you've come up with a theme, give yourself a few days to let it sink in and see if it continues to feel right to you. Even test it out—when you wake up each morning, put your theme in mind, then go about your day. Do you feel energized, excited, ready to reinvent yourself? As you ponder the items on your schedule, to-do list, and desk, interpret everything you encounter through the lens of your theme. Do you suddenly see that certain tasks and objects are candidates for heaving? No longer feel so attached to them? Your perspective is likely to shift through this new lens. You'll also experience a sense of relief—you might not have a specific goal or end point yet, but at least you'll be able to tell if the direction of your future feels right. No one lets go into a vacuum. Your theme fills that void and energizes you.

As you tackle each stage of **SHED**, I'll ask you to picture your theme very vividly, because it will help you make decisions all along the way. Your theme will be your beacon and filter throughout the entire **SHED** process.

- Keeping your theme prominently in your mind makes it easier to decide what stays and what goes. As you look through old piles of clothes, or stacks of long-abandoned to-dos, for example, if your theme is "freedom" or "self-expression" you'll be able to quickly determine how that old sweatshirt or incomplete CD inventory supports or detracts from your vision for your future.
- A theme dislodges you because it gives you something positive to move toward—something that excites you that you are looking forward to making real.

With your theme or vision as your road map, more specifics about your future will emerge as you continue through the process. When you feel confused or discouraged, or encounter any challenging moments while **SHED**-ing, reconnect with the powerful discoveries you've made in this chapter to keep yourself grounded. Think theme, and you'll find new energy.

With your new theme prominently in mind, your next step will be to inventory the things in your life that are weighing you down, preventing you from feeling free to move forward to the life you are craving.

Chapter 3

Inventory What's Weighing You Down

They say that time changes things, but you actually have to change them yourself.

—Andy Warhol

What Is Clutter?

A well-known Zen parable tells of a wanderer on a lonely road who came upon a torrential stream that had washed out the bridge. He couldn't swim and was afraid to wade across, so he had to spend several days cutting down trees and vines with his small knife to build a raft. The raft he built was solid, and the heavy raft carried him safely across the flood. On the other side of the bank he thought, "This is a good raft—if there's another stream ahead, I can use it." And so, he carried the raft for the rest of his life.

Take a moment to think about the meaning of this story. How often do we hang onto things that served us well at one point in our lives but are no longer relevant or useful? And while our attachment to these items makes sense on a certain level, by continuing to carry them around we limit our ability to invite new and more relevant experiences, opportunities, and growth. The best way to get unstuck is to free up your space and time of the things that are no longer relevant. The purpose of this chapter is to identify the "rafts" in your life—the objects, commitments, and behaviors which you acquired that have become burdens, taking up space and energy, while no longer providing real value. These burdens will become the focus of your **SHED**, offering opportunities to get unstuck so that you can move in the direction of your theme.

We each have a certain quantity of belongings and activities that anchor us. Some of us prefer to fill our homes and offices with tons of stuff and to keep a very full schedule; others prefer more streamlined closets and calendars. Regardless of what your ideal equilibrium is, there are times when the volume of objects or activities expands to an untenable degree, exceeding your comfort level. You suddenly feel weighed down, stagnant, suffocated. When you feel the driving impulse to **SHED**, it's because some portion of what is filling your schedule and/or space no longer feels healthy or vibrant. You are ready to change your equilibrium, preparing to lift anchor, releasing the deadweight, so you can move forward.

The word *clutter* is often associated with chaos, disorganization, and mess. But in this book, I am using a slightly modified definition that does not necessarily include disorganization. Clutter in this book is defined *as any obsolete object, space, commitment, or behavior that weighs you down, distracts you, or depletes your energy.* Clutter, in the context of **SHED**ing, is symbolic of your attachment to something from the past that must be released in order to make room for change.

Something doesn't have to be disorganized to be clutter. A perfectly arranged dresser drawer filled with clothes you haven't worn in years is still clutter. Likewise, a perfectly efficient weekend routine of errands, chores, and housework can also be clutter, if it's a draining, mindless, outdated use of your time that prevents you from doing activities you enjoy. Clutter is anything that no longer serves you. And whether that clutter is located in your space, schedule, or everyday habits, the most telling characteristic is a feeling of stagnancy.

We will call these stagnant areas "points of entry." Points of entry present opportunities to move in the direction of your theme. Each point of entry acts as a doorway to opportunity and insight, allowing you to open up space and energy, confront an old belief system, and fortify your identity.

A point of entry can be anything from a barely used room to a specific cabinet; from an old filing system to the entire left side of your garage; a bad habit (procrastination, for example) or a PTA commitment you (secretly) wish would just vanish from your schedule.

In this chapter you will identify the objects, obligations, and behaviors that are like the raft in the Zen story, weighing you down, taking up space that could be opened to provide room for something new, relevant, and valuable.

Your job in this chapter is twofold. First, you will locate the opportunities to free up space and energy by inventorying the points of entry (i.e., stagnant areas) in your space and schedule that contain clutter. This involves going on a tour to measure the potential space gain for each point of entry. Second, you will pick the best point of entry to start your **SHED**. You will leave this chapter not only with your starting point but also with a whole list of additional points of entry you can select from as you continue your **SHED**.

By the end of this process, your space and schedule will be filled only with things that are relevant and vibrant, those which energize, fuel, and inspire who are you and where you are going. But first we have to figure out what is holding you back (is in the way). Creating an inventory of these points of entry is the final preparation step before you are ready to **SHED**.

Where to Find the Clutter: Searching for Rafts

There are three tangible realms in your life to look for old attachments that you can **SHED**. First up is your physical space, which can include anything from your whole house, to just a few specific rooms, or to a particular collection of belongings (bookshelves, filing system, photo albums). The second realm is your time, including very specific activities, obligations, commitments, and tasks that are already on your calendar or sitting in your backlog of to-dos. The third realm is bad habits. These are time-hogging behaviors that continuously add distracting demands to your schedule no matter how fast you clear it off.

The next few pages describe each realm more fully and indicate very common points of entry in your physical space, time, and habits where you are likely to find old attachments.

Look over each list and consider where opportunities to open up space exist for you. You are likely to find "clutter culprits" in all three realms. Don't let that overwhelm you. After you've done your inventory, I will help you decide the best realm to start with. For now, the purpose of the lists is to raise your awareness of the many possible points of entry you have available to you.

Physical Points of Entry

Most people could probably stand to release something from their physical space. Think about the following categories of belongings and put a check next to those you consider suspiciously dormant. Remember that just because something is organized doesn't mean it's active and dynamic in supporting your theme. In this inventory, you are looking for collections of items that are generally immobile, unused, excessive, those that bring up negative feelings or no longer feel relevant. Some common points of entry in your physical space include old magazines, newspapers and books, useless papers and files, unwearable clothing, unloved furniture and décor, excessive memorabilia, housewares or supplies, and overstuffed storage areas.

Sample Physical Burdens

- Any minimally used room or office
- Unread books, magazines, newspapers
- Stacks of unused recipes/clippings
- Rarely worn clothing
- Excessive memorabilia
- Unloved furniture
- Stagnant piles of paper
- Dysfunctional filing system
- Overstuffed handbags, briefcases, and suitcases
- Stuff that belonged to someone else

Time Points of Entry

As we move from the physical realm to the time realm, we cross a tiny boundary. We are going a little deeper, moving closer to our feelings and our hearts. It's one thing to identify an old collection of books when you only have to contend with your own sentimentality in doing so, but it's entirely another issue to name tasks or activities you find depleting when they involve commitments we made to others.

Put a check on any point of entry below that you suspect is particularly draining. Points of entry in the time realm usually include unfinished projects and to-dos, unfulfilled obligations, burdensome commitments, and cumbersome roles. The time these activities currently occupy in your schedule would be better used for something else because they bog you down, make you feel bad about yourself, de-energize and deplete you. These activities may have energized you at some point, or perhaps they've always been a burden. In either case they no longer serve you now.

Sample Time Burdens

- Responsibilities that belong to someone else
- Assignments whose scope has expanded out of control
- Committee work that is less rewarding than anticipated
- Roles that you cannot adequately fulfill
- Meetings with little value
- Projects you started and can't finish
- Unfulfilled promises/obligations
- Excessive number of incomplete to-dos

Habit Points of Entry

Bad habits are a form of clutter that are related to time points of entry, but with their own unique characteristics. While time clutter refers to measurable commitments you've already taken on, habit clutter refers to the unconscious behavior that often produces time clutter. Issues such as perfectionism, procrastination, chronic lateness, mindless escapes, and workaholism often drive us to take on more than we can chew, say yes when we mean no, or mindlessly pad our schedules with activities that provide little or no value. Habit clutter has a way of pilfering energy without our realizing it. Bad habits steal hours every day, not only from time lost but also from the energy we spend beating ourselves up over them.

Think back to the raft story at the beginning of this section. It's safe to say that we acquired our bad habits at some point in our lives because, in fact, they served us well at the time. Bad habits are adaptive, a way of coping with challenges we encountered at earlier points in our lives. Getting to the root of those original motivations will allow us to expunge the bad habit and replace the healthy need with a more beneficial solution.

Of all the forms of clutter we address in this book, **SHED**ing habits is the toughest of all. Which is why I recommend tackling habits after you have cleared out some physical and time clutter. You'll need extra energy, confidence, and clarity to take these on. Yet they are among the most powerful forms of clutter to **SHED**. By nipping your bad habits in the bud, you will solve one of the core problems of your overburdened schedule. I have addressed some of these habits in previous books, offering insight into what causes these behaviors. In this book, I will give you guidance on permanently expunging these destructive behaviors from your schedule, creating a larger possibility of freedom to move forward.

Sample Habit Burdens

- Mindless escapes (TV, email, internet, video game, shopping)
- Chronic lateness
- Procrastination
- Workaholism
- Perfectionism

Which Realm First: Physical, Time, or Habit?

If you are like most people, you will find points of entry in each realm. Please understand that you do not need to conquer *all* the clutter in your life in order to get unstuck and move in the direction of your theme.

It is impossible to tackle every stagnant area in your life at the same time. My recommendation is that you approach these in the order presented by the book—first **SHED**ing in the physical realm, then time, and finally habit. Physical clutter is an excellent starting point, because it is so tangible. You'll see the results of clearing out physical clutter very vividly, which gives you a good foundation for navigating the less tactile forms of clutter in your schedule and habits.

Time clutter, aside from being less visible, can be slightly more challenging than physical clutter because it often requires dealing with other people's attachments to your activities, in addition to your own. Still, time clutter remains easier to work with than habits, because targeting a commitment such as a particular meeting or responsibility is more tactile than the unconscious behavior that drives habits.

This order of inventory is simply a suggestion. If you feel that there are no big "rafts" occupying your physical space, by all means feel free to skip ahead to **SHED**ing a time burden. And if your time doesn't feel weighed down by non-fueling obligations, but you have a time-wasting habit that is boring down heavily on your back, go ahead and start there.

My experience is that all three realms provide tremendous benefits, and the victories you experience in one area fuel your capacity to take on the additional challenges of the next.

The Cascading Effect of **SHED**ing

There is a remarkable cascading effect to the **SHED** process. The simple act of creating space in any one area fuels your ability to clear out space across many realms. You begin with a few points of entry in your physical space (let's say your entryway, old magazines, and the desk in your study at home), which frees up the mental space to think, resulting in the energy to continue your discovery and exploration. Pretty soon, less obvious areas of clutter reveal themselves to you (another physical space, a burdensome commitment, a role, or a bad habit), which you can tackle next. You begin to move easily between the physical, schedule, and habit realms. Eventually, the process spills from one area to the next, until you've addressed every point of entry.

Much of the difficulty in **SHED**ing is simply getting started. Once you see how energizing this process is, you become like a kid in a candy shop, sampling the malted milk balls, tasting the gummy bears—you are empowered to keep going until you've cleared enough space to start experimenting with your theme.

By completing each point of entry in sequence, you will systematically clear the clutter, providing yourself with space and energy to address the points of entry that remain.

Where do you intend to start your **SHED**? Physical, time, or habit?

Once you begin a point of entry, be sure to study the separate and heave chapters that pertain to the realm in which you are currently working. For physical space, read chapters 4 and 7; for time, chapters 5 and 8; and for habits, chapters 6 and 9 in sequence.

Measure the Potential Space Gained

Now that you have chosen which realm to start with, you will tour your space or schedule to measure the potential space gain by **SHED**ing. This is a very motivating stage of the process which accomplishes several goals: first, it gives you the opportunity to quantify the amount of space that can be opened up by addressing each point of entry; second, it helps you root out old attachments in your life that you've become so accustomed to that you no longer realize they are there; and third, it will allow you to control the degree of speed in your own transition/transformation. In a nutshell, doing a reality tour enables you to preview the benefits of trading tangible objects (items, activity) for intangible rewards (space to think, energy, insights).

There are always items lurking in our spaces and schedules beyond the obvious that have gone stale. These smaller pockets of clutter are sometimes so far in the recesses of our home (or office) or so habitually buried into our schedules that we are not conscious of their presence. Everyone has a junk drawer or a messy closet he barely even notices. Or it could be a habit, like absentmindedly turning on the TV when you walk in the door, or checking your email every time you sit down to work.

However invisible this nonfunctional clutter may be, it runs rampant through your subconscious. Somewhere in the background, you sense that something negative and unresolved is taking up space and weighing you down, just waiting for you to move it forward or eliminate it from your life. Until you identify and eliminate those specific areas, you are literally and metaphorically weighed down.

As you inventory each point of entry consider:

- **The size of the point of entry:** A point of entry could be enormous (e.g., your attic) or tiny (e.g., a junk drawer). No matter how small or large your particular point of entry, addressing each one will result in empty space and energy gained; it's just a matter of *how much* space or time. Categorize each point of entry as small, medium, or large.

- **What percentage of each point of entry is obsolete:** How much space or time would you free up if you were to release the obsolete items in each stagnant area? For example, if you determined that the bookcase in your living room is a point of entry in your physical space, what percentage of books in that bookcase are obsolete? If 75 percent of the items in the bookshelf are obsolete, it means 75 percent of that bookshelf can be opened up.

- **Your level of attachment:** How difficult would it be to let go of the obsolete items (physical objects or activities in your schedule or habits)? In other words, how much do you really care? Obviously, the more emotionally attached you are to something, the harder it will be to remove it from your life. Rate each point of entry on a three-point scale:

easy (you won't miss an item or activity at all); so-so (there will be some level of remorse when letting it go); or hard (this item or activity has been around for so long that it's difficult to imagine your life without it, even if it does qualify as stagnant).

Keeping these questions in mind will ultimately help you determine which point of entry to tackle first—the bigger the point of entry, the more space you can pry open. You may not be able to think of every single thing that is cluttered in your life, and that's okay. Once you start the process, you'll continue to discover additional stagnant areas. This chapter will help you recognize how rich the possibilities for **SHED**ing are once you start to pay attention.

The following pages will show you how to conduct an effective and enlightening reality tour for each realm. The techniques will vary slightly for each realm. And you only have to study the instructions for the realm you are going to tackle first. Therefore, by starting in the physical realm, you only need to read the instructions for Touring Your Physical Space. When you are ready to **SHED** a time or habit point of entry, you can come back and read the instructions for that realm.

Remember Your Theme

Before you go on your tour, make sure you get the theme or vision you named in the previous chapter solidly in your mind. That theme will serve as a litmus test to keep you on track, helping you quickly distinguish what's clutter from what isn't. If an object, commitment, or habit supports your theme, it's a candidate to treasure (at least for now); if it doesn't, it becomes a candidate to heave.

Measuring *Physical* Clutter

Going room by room, like a beachcomber with a metal detector searching the sands for gold, you are going to take a "tour" of your space, systematically searching for areas of stagnation. Some areas will be obvious—you knew it was a "trouble spot"—but you'll also find pockets of clutter that you never noticed before. Keep a running list of the points of entry in your physical space, noting what percentage of each area is stagnant, how big a space you would create by releasing the clutter there, and the strength of your emotional attachment to each object. You will eventually use that information to determine which point of entry to tackle first. Every point of entry presents an opportunity for transformation: by relinquishing even one attachment, you will create the space to move forward.

For example, Brooke's house was 2,600 square feet—five bedrooms, a living, dining and family room, a screened-in porch, a breakfast room, a study, a front hall, and a big backyard, all perfectly appointed with nineteen years' worth of beautifully organized belongings and memories. "It took me years to actually furnish all these rooms!" she said.

During our first consultation, Brooke had come up with the theme *Expand my audience*, which fueled her with a sense of enthusiasm and excitement to move forward. Keeping her new theme in mind, I asked her to now inventory the categories of belongings that felt like they were weighing her down, keeping her too anchored. During her tour she identified the following points of entry.

Point of Entry	Overall Quantity of Space	Percent Obsolete	Level of Attachment
Books	Large (As an English literature professor, books were her life)	40–60	Strong
Grown children's belongings	Large (Several items all over the house)	90	Moderate
Household furniture	Large (5 bedrooms' worth)	60	Light
Glass-fronted kitchen cupboards	Medium (several pieces of earthenware, artistically arranged)	80	To be determined
Perennial garden	Medium	100?	So-so
Household files	Medium	80	So-so

There may well have been other areas of stagnancy in her home, but these were the six areas that were weighing heaviest on Brooke's mind. This inventory at least gave her a few different options to get started; she could always add more things to this list as they occurred to her.

Here's another example. Marisa's biggest de-energizing area was her wardrobe, and we found many specific points of entry within that area. Marisa's first words to me during our consultation were, "Seriously, I can't take my home. It used to be fine, but now I'm buried beneath all this stuff. I can't live like this." Fifty-three and single, Marisa expressed a mild dissatisfaction with her life, as if it were coated in a gravy of ambivalence. She worked in merchandising for a large retailer and no longer felt challenged by her work, and her romantic life was just "eh" (she'd been involved with two men, off and on, for the past eighteen months). The theme for the next chapter of her life was *Fulfillment*. She wanted to feel passionate again about her work and personal relationships.

Marisa told me that she'd always had a lot of stuff, but until recently it had been organized and reasonable. It was only after her ex-husband moved out that the scales tipped. She started to pile on top of her systems and the stuff started to take over. She was so embarrassed about the state of excess that she stopped having guests. She wanted to get back to the essentials.

In her closet, Marisa found several categories of stagnant items:

Point of Entry	Overall Quantity of Space	Percent Obsolete	Level of Attachment
Work clothes	Medium	40	Moderate
Casual clothes	Small	60	Moderate
Dressy clothes	Large (several dozen evening gowns)	70	Strong
Handbags	Large (at least 200 handbags)	75	Light
Shoes	Large (350 pairs)	80	Moderate
Belts	Small	30	Moderate

Marisa opted to focus her efforts, at first, on these wardrobe categories, which had basically swelled beyond their assigned home (the closet) to invade the rest of her space. In comparison to her wardrobe, other areas of her home (the garage, paper files) didn't feel so oppressive, or so negatively symbolic of old attachments.

Measuring *Time* Clutter

Points of entry in your physical space are fairly easy to identify because they are visible. Points of entry in the time realm are trickier precisely because they are not visible. Time clutter is usually connected to our perceived sense of duty, obligation, and responsibility to other people.

There are two places we are going to hunt for burdensome commitments—your calendar and your to-do list, if that is a separate tool from your planner. Gather two weeks of your calendar (either a paper planner or printed pages from an electronic-based system) and a copy of your most recent to-do list. Sit down with a highlighter, a pencil, and a calculator. Keeping your theme very clear in your mind, go through every hour of your schedule and item on your to-do list, highlighting any task, project, meeting, or activity that feels like it's weighing you down in some way. You should highlight every activity that feels draining, irrelevant, and uninspired and doesn't connect to your theme for the future. You may have decided, for example, that any home maintenance project (that doesn't require your expertise) is time clutter. On your to-do list, you would highlight the specific projects that fit into that category. Or you may realize that the half day spent weekly updating the status of each of your work activities leaves you feeling drained.

Note: As you go on your time tour try not to confuse time effectiveness challenges (being more productive, managing your time efficiently) with identifying the stagnant areas in your schedule. Here's the difference: you are not looking for things you could be doing more efficiently—you are looking for things you *should not be doing at all*.

Once you've highlighted every bit of time clutter, look at the visual snapshot of the percentage of your schedule that is highlighted. How much of your schedule or to-do list is stagnant? Is it 20 percent, 40 percent, 80 percent? Next, put a time estimate beside each highlighted *to-do* item, indicating honestly how much time you think each would take to complete, from a fifteen-minute call to a four-hour project. Then, add it all up, calculating how much time you would free up by releasing some (if not all) of those energy drainers.

Trevor had recently been promoted to the executive team at his computer software company. In his new role as a product director, he supervised several people at the product manager level (a position he'd held for the previous twenty of his twenty-five years at the firm). About eleven months into this transition, Trevor felt stuck. He was excited by his new job but felt like he was crushed under an oppressive workload. He suspected he had not made the shift very well.

The first thing I asked Trevor to do was to picture his new theme, *Be an inspiring leader.* I asked him to come up with a list of things that he felt might be holding him back. He didn't have any trouble coming up with an answer: "I spend way too much time doing my staff's work."

We came up with the following list of broad categories of time clutter.

Point of Entry	Overall Quantity of Time	Percent Obsolete	Level of Attachment
Any task that was his staff's job and not his own	Large	70	Strong
Work product that is *good enough* (and didn't absolutely require his attention)	Small	40	Moderate
Meetings where he did not have a distinct role besides training or support purposes	Medium	50	Moderate

We then looked at the nitty-gritty in his schedule and to-do lists to quantify how many hours he could open up by releasing each one. Trevor tracked everything (meetings, to-dos, personal errands, etc.) in Microsoft Outlook. We discovered that a significant number of the items (13 out of 20 items) on his to-do list were actually his *staff's* projects, not his own. Those tasks occupied about two and a half hours every day. And the three weekly meetings he attended with his staff were costing him 10 more hours a week—a combined 40 percent of his schedule!

When doing this exercise, it's not unusual to discover that you might be spending almost *half* your time on activities that *used* to be important to you instead of activities that are important to you *now*!

Where Paper Meets Time

If you are someone who doesn't write everything down on your to-do list or schedule, you can quantify the time gain by measuring the backlog of to-dos sitting on your desk or kitchen countertop. Your backlog of to-dos is where physical clutter meets time clutter. Anything that's been sitting on your desk for months is probably stagnant in some way, otherwise why would you neglect it?

Pick up each paper and slap on a post-it note indicating what action is required from this piece of paper and an honest estimate of how long it will take. Make two piles. Place the tasks that feel relevant, vital, and connected to your vision in one stack. Tasks that feel disconnected and distracting go in the other pile. At the end, take out your calculator and add up the hours you could open up by eliminating the tasks from the second pile.

Measuring *Habit* Clutter

When it comes to quantifying how much time your insidious bad habits are eating up, the best way to measure the volume is to track your time for a couple of days. Every morning, picture your new theme vividly in your mind, then be on the lookout throughout the day for every time your bad habit rears its ugly head—whether it's in the form of actual time spent on the habit (overcomplicating tasks, incessantly checking email), or time spent beating yourself up over the choices you made. Either in a notebook or on a printed-out version of your calendar, note every time the habit holds you back.

As you are tracking your time, also make note of any routine activities you find yourself doing that zone you out and put you on automatic pilot. Do you feel resentful or annoyed that you have to do them? Then they are mindless and non-fueling clutter.

For example, Dana was worried that up to 40 percent of her time was eaten up by two bad habits: an inability to say no and procrastination. She was 39, married and the mother of two children in elementary school. She'd built a successful career in the media industry and continued to love working, but in recent years she had become more interested in spending time with her family than pushing the pace at the office. Dana had no intention of giving up her career, though she was starting to explore more flexible work options (telecommuting, part-time hours, etc.) to have more hours at home. Her vision for the next phase of her life was *Balance*.

Below is one of Dana's journal pages.

6:30 A.M.	About to get on treadmill. Zach asked for last-minute help reviewing math homework. How to say no? Gave feedback. Ran out of time to exercise.	−30 min lost
9:00 A.M.	Sat down to work on PowerPoint presentation due by tomorrow morning. Staffer came in with work-related worry. Couldn't say no.	−45 min lost
9:45 A.M.	Checked email (25 new messages). Saw question from colleague. Stopped to read proposal and craft a helpful reply. Then called her to make sure she knew I sent back comments, and got caught in chitchat. Poor use of time!	−30 min lost
11:00 A.M.	Thought about starting PowerPoint again, but instead skimmed *Washington Post* articles but didn't finish one. Useless procrastination!	−25 min lost
12 P.M.	Checked email (7 new messages).	−5 min lost
2–3 P.M.	Attended meeting. Didn't absorb a thing because distracted with guilt that PowerPoint wasn't done yet. Why did I waste the day?	−1 hour lost
5:00 P.M.	Colleague came in to share news of her engagement. Stopped what I was doing and listened (albeit half-heartedly) with smile on my face. Couldn't say no.	−20 min lost
8:00 P.M.	Got home too late and hungry to make a nice dinner. Crabby at family, hurt some feelings, had to do damage control with kids and husband.	−1 hour lost

Dana totaled the amount of time she lost at work to her procrastination and inability to say no. It came to about four and a half hours each day—almost twenty-three hours a week! Releasing those stagnating, unproductive habits would open up the same amount of time, which she could then fill with activities more related to her vision of *Balance*. The beauty of keeping a journal like this is that it enables you to make tangible what is usually hard to see or know for sure—where your time goes. That knowledge puts you in a better position to take the confident action you need to **SHED** your bad habits.

Now it's your turn. Take this opportunity to fill out a chart for yourself. This becomes your personal à la carte **SHED** menu—you can pick and choose which point of entry you want to tackle, depending on your energy level, the time you have available to devote to the task and what you want to accomplish.

Point of Entry	Overall Quantity of Space/Time	Percent Obsolete	Level of Attachment

Pick Your Point of Entry

When you have completed your reality tour for each realm that you are currently addressing—physical, time, and habit—you'll have a comprehensive inventory of the stagnant, irrelevant areas. Use the information you gathered (the size of the space or time, the percent obsolete in each area, and your level of attachment), in combination with your energy and time available for the job, to choose your starting point of entry. Aim for an easy win.

Often the most dramatic kickoff is choosing an area that would free up a lot of space, but to which you have a light or moderate level of attachment. The energy you feel from that victory will inspire you to tackle an area with a stronger degree of attachment. If you are feeling cautious and prefer to dip your toe in the water, start with a smaller point of entry with a light degree of attachment. For a bold move that will take less time, choose a small area with a high degree of attachment. Anything you choose will provide more of an opportunity to release an old, unhealthy belief system. The key is to start in an area you will be able to complete in a three- to four-hour session. You can opt for something big or small, something especially challenging or relatively easy. The beauty of the **SHED**ing process is that any amount of clutter you release will help you get unstuck and move you forward.

Here's what Brooke, Marisa, Trevor, and Dana decided.

- **BROOKE:** Looking at the list she'd made during her inventory, Brooke decided to start with household furniture. Because she was considering selling her home, she was most concerned about the amount of physical space that releasing the clutter would open up in each area. She was looking for the biggest potential gain—in physical space and in the relief that gain would provide. It was clearly a stagnant category, but she didn't think it would be as emotionally taxing (or complex) as, say, her books would be. Going through her furniture first gave Brooke a chance to grab an easy win on space. (In fact, any area that will free up a large quantity of space with minimal emotional expenditure is a great place to start.) Working in this way, one area at a time, she could work at her own speed in her own time frame and release the pressure to tackle everything at once.

- **MARISA:** She wanted to make a big enough dent in the clutter so that she could start having guests over again. After taking inventory, she decided that, relatively speaking, her clothing was the biggest challenge—it took up the most space and elicited her strongest emotional attachment. Her father had been a costume maker in Hollywood's heyday in the 1950s and many of the pieces she'd identified as "stagnant" were gifts from him. A less emotionally taxing area was her shoes—many didn't fit, some required repair, and even more were out of style. The hundreds of pairs also occupied tremendous amounts of space in her bedroom, front-hall closet, and along her second-floor hallway.

- **TREVOR:** After he had estimated the "withdrawal factor" he and his team would experience, Trevor figured that weaning his staff (and himself) off the spontaneous problem-solving sessions he was having with them would result in the most immediate gain of free time. Like Brooke's furniture, it was a relatively easy "win." No more than 5 to 10 percent of the issues his staff brought to him were true emergencies anyway, so it wouldn't be that difficult. "Babysitting" vendor calls, meetings, and internal written communications were next on his list. Trevor just had to fight his own temptation to jump in and rework the easy stuff.

- **DANA:** A piece of Dana loved being the hero, throwing everything aside to help her kids with a last-minute request or help a coworker solve a tough problem. But by never saying no she wasn't giving herself a fair shot at achieving the balance she wanted. I suggested that Dana look back through her journal and try to measure the impact that her saying no would have had on other people. It's much harder to say no to someone in a crisis, for example, than it is to say no to someone just casually seeking help (and not necessarily thinking about what the time spent helping them is costing you). She could gradually release her attachment to saying yes all the time by picking and choosing her spots based on how desperately someone needed her help, thereby seeing more free time in her schedule more quickly.

Now it's your turn. Which point of entry will you start with?

Armed with your very first point of entry (and an à la carte **SHED** menu for the next round), you are ready to move on to Separate the Treasures. Keep your inventory on hand—when you don't feel like you're opening up enough space, or you just want to propel the project forward, pick something else from your list. You can determine the speed and intensity of this process.

Are you excited? Have more energy? Feel less paralyzed than you did before? That maybe you can actually do this? You can. You are ready to **SHED**.

separate the Treasures

Anything that has real and lasting value is always a gift from within.

—Franz Kafka

What to Pack?

We've all packed a suitcase before, whether it's for a trip to Grandma's house or a European vacation. There are essentials you just don't leave home without: a pair of jeans, comfortable shoes, underwear, a toothbrush, maybe your camera, or a good book. And if you are like the majority of people, packing happens in a tear, the final items shoved in your bag just minutes before departure. The mad rush to get out the door often leads to a 50-pound suitcase full of stuff you don't need or empty of scores of forgotten items—ever found yourself away from home with ten shirts and only one pair of pants?

The first step of **SHED**, Separate the Treasures, is like packing for a long trip—only instead of a bathing suit and dress slacks you bring your most valuable belongings, behaviors, and lessons into the next phase of your life. By the end of this section, you'll be able to answer the question, What do I want to preserve from the past as I move into my future?

When faced with a big, bold change—like divorce, a new job, or a move—people typically have one of two responses. The first is to clutch fast to the familiar and dig in their heels, slowing the inevitable process and making it more difficult or traumatic than it need be. The second is to leap headlong into the future, tossing everything and starting over (there is something appealing, heroic even, in the innocence and excitement of starting anew). But neither of those responses is ideal.

Going through a transition (big or small) always requires you to release your attachment to an old way of doing things. But it's a careful balance: hang on to too much, and you won't create enough space for change; get rid of too much and you might have to start from scratch unnecessarily. Consciously evaluating what's truly valuable and what's not forces you to connect to what's relevant and vital to you as you move forward into the next phase.

In this section you will determine which objects, activities, and habits you want to preserve from your past to bring with you into your future. Using the inventory built in chapter 3 you will go through each point of entry and pluck the treasures from the stagnant areas. It's so easy to hold on to the negative images of the clutter and go for a clean sweep, but I challenge you to keep looking beyond the negative in the clutter and find the treasure inside. In many ways the "treasures" are a reflection of what is unique about you. It's an opportunity to examine and celebrate your life so far.

What's a Treasure?

When it comes to selecting the treasures, there are two basic types, practical and meaningful.

1. **Practical treasures** are pragmatic objects, activities, skills, or life lessons that will be useful to you or could contribute to your ability to fulfill your new theme.
2. **Meaningful treasures** are symbolic or sentimental objects or activities that bring you pure and unambiguous joy, energy, and inspiration, and as such, reflect your core self.

With both types, the value of identifying the true treasures is to bring forth the gems from your past that support your truest self and your future goals, rather than criticize or call your truest self into question. These objects and activities are well worth the space and time they occupy in your life.

For each point of entry in your inventory, you should aim to keep only 10 to 20 percent or a handful of items at most—these are the true treasures. If you hang on to more than that, you won't be able to create enough space for objects and activities that support your new theme. This is the moment you decide whether the value an object once had to you is still valid, relevant, and useful in the context of your new direction. If it is, you'll keep it. If it isn't, you'll toss it during the second step of **SHED**, Heave.

Whether a treasure is a physical object, an activity in your schedule, or a daily habit, as a general rule your treasures will:

- give you energy rather than deplete you;
- inspire you;
- be useful to you (in a physical sense or otherwise) in the next phase of your life;
- serve as the best reminder of an event, a relationship, or a particular time in your life;
- symbolize life lessons that make you a better person;
- support your vision or theme for the future.

A sample of a "physical" treasure could be the perfect pair of jeans you find hiding in the back of a cluttered closet or a beloved gift that acts as the best reminder of an important person or event from your past.

A sample of a "time" treasure could be any activity that is healthy and productive, rather than negative and energy draining. It could be a weekly check-in meeting with your boss, the ability to deliver on a deadline, or a spin class every Thursday night.

A sample of a "habit" treasure could be the mental break you get from procrastinating after an exhausting week, or the feeling of connection you attain from constantly emailing.

Separating the treasures will fortify you and make you feel safe to move forward in a healthy way toward the change that you seek. The next three chapters will guide you in selecting the treasures from each of the realms—physical, time, and habit points of entry. Once you have selected the gems, you will be ready to heave the defunct and archaic holding you back, confident that you've got the *best* from your current life tucked safely in your backpack.

Finding Physical Treasures

*May your walls know joy; may every room hold laughter and
every window open to great possibility.*
　　　　　　　　　　—Maryann Radmacher-Hershey

In chapter 3, you came up with an inventory of the things in your physical space that are weighing you down, stagnant points of entry in your home or office that present an opportunity to open up space. Physical belongings come into our lives in any number of ways—conscious acquisition, mindless accumulation, gifts, and hand-me-downs. Other times, belongings just seem to grow like weeds. Some of your objects have practical or emotional value, while others are no longer useful, but sorting one from the other can be confusing.

While the popular advice from friends, family, and even many clutter experts might be "Just toss it, let it go, time to move on," I am going to suggest that you slow down a minute. Don't be so quick to reenact the Boston Tea Party. Instead, I want you to study the contents of each point of entry before launching them all overboard.

Contained in the clutter are clues that present you with an opportunity to gain powerful insights into who you are, what makes you tick, and what is vital to you. Taking the time to separate the treasures positions you to make a more complete transformation, rather than a temporary fix. In this chapter, we'll go through a two-part examination of each physical point of entry. First, you will explore and discover what your attachment to this stuff is. Second, you will decide which items are worth saving; these are your treasures.

What Is Your Attachment?

In my experience, buried beneath even the most oppressive clutter was a good, healthy impulse; it's just not always obvious what that good, healthy impulse was. Many of the stagnant objects and activities in our spaces actually represent an old belief system—someone we used to be or wanted to become; something we once believed about ourselves or the world. Maybe you have been accepting subtle, false ideas: "My only value is through my work" or "I do not deserve love," or "Life is supposed to be difficult." Whatever those preconceived notions may be, this kind of negative, habitual thinking is one of the most menacing things holding you back from making the big change in your life because it's invisible. You are barely aware of its presence. In this respect, your clutter actually helps you. By providing a very tangible clue to that old belief system, it's something you can examine, evaluate, and expunge.

Understanding Your Attachment

The easiest way to find value in the clutter is to go backward before going forward. Pinpointing precisely when something became obselete, and then finding the pure impulse or value in it, allows you to separate your identity from your stuff. By visualizing a time when the stuff wasn't weighing you down, you can picture life without it again. This is an opportunity to reconnect with the most authentic version of yourself. Wouldn't you love to remember who you were before you attached your identity to the stuff?

Sometimes clutter represents old insecurities; we didn't feel quite good enough without the stuff. Or it validated who we were or what we had achieved. Sometimes our stuff represents things or people we weren't ready to relinquish; other times it represents emotions we can't articulate. Clutter can fill a void, and in its own way provide a level of companionship by always being present as a focus for our thoughts and energies.

The following client examples highlight the most common value people find in their clutter and the importance of slowing down to discover it. Once clients understood the root of their attachments, they were able to address their legitimate needs in a healthier way.

1. Physical Clutter Can Represent Obsolete Goals

Jessica, 53, sidled up to me after an organizing presentation I delivered a few years ago. Wearing a downtrodden expression, she carried the unmistakable air of someone paralyzed by a heavy burden. She divulged that her home was buried under so much paper that it was treacherous to walk. Not even her bed was safe—she'd been carving out a sliver of mattress to sleep on each night. And while her mess had been a source of marital conflict for years, now her husband was threatening divorce. She needed a magic pill. She wanted to rein in her piles, but had no idea where to start. She felt utterly clueless, stuck, tied in a knot.

I asked Jessica what was in the piles. She explained that they consisted mostly of reading materials—several years' worth of newspapers, magazines, and books that she still had every intention of reading. When I respectfully pointed out that she'd never be able to get through all that material, even if she read ten hours a day, seven days a week, her face went pale. "I'd feel like such a failure if I didn't get to it," she said.

It would've been easy to discount her comment as unrealistic and implore her, "Don't be ridiculous! Just dump the junk!" But I was struck by her attachment to this clearly impossible task. The trick was to find the time when the mess didn't exist. So I asked her how long she'd had these piles. "Ever since we moved into our new house eight years ago," Jessica said. "I didn't want to move. I think I let things go because I never liked it here. I just haven't cared."

I then asked Jessica if there had been piles in her previous home. "Well, yes," she confessed, "it was pretty bad there, too." Within seconds, her eyes lit up in an epiphany: "The piles *must* be an act of rebellion against my husband!" she exclaimed. "He's always harassed me so much about my mess, it just makes me dig my heels in even more." But I wasn't convinced. Jessica was so quick to blame her husband, but it seemed like a distraction to me. The cause of our clutter is never someone else. It's inside ourselves; we own it. So I prodded a bit further and asked about the state of her home *before* she met her husband. Dead silence. "Yes," she said with quiet recognition, "the piles were there as well."

With a little more probing, we finally traced the origin of the stacks all the way back to her teenage years. Her father, a brilliant journalist for a major daily paper, had a critical and demanding disposition. Growing up, she'd been on a never-ending campaign to impress him with her own intellect and win his approval.

At the root of that insurmountable mound of reading material was Jessica's belief that she could only prove her value by achieving the impossible. The insurmountable stacks of reading material represented Jessica's human need for recognition—a very pure and healthy impulse. If I had pushed Jessica to just throw it all away, she would have missed out on the opportunity to discover a very vital need of hers and uncover a healthier view of her situation. In no time at all, she would have missed those piles and re-created them to fill whatever need they were serving. By uncovering the original value, she could hold on to her natural impulse—the need for recognition—but get rid of its unhealthy manifestation, the mountain of reading material.

2. Physical Clutter Can Symbolize Our Insecurity

Earlier in the book, you met Matthew, 44. After fifteen successful years at the same law firm, he decided to explore a different career, one that would allow him to focus more on his personal life. The theme for the next phase of his life was *Fulfilling personal commitments*.

Matthew knew it was time to leave his firm about five months before he announced his resignation and decided what his next career move would be. He used that time to ruminate about the type of company and position he would pursue next. During that period of ambiguity, he successfully tackled every point of entry in his home, cleaning out closets and cabinets, bookcases and drawers, CD shelves and kitchen countertops. He spent weekends and evenings clearing out the garage, the attic, and the stuff in the barn at his country home. This was a man on a mission to reinvent himself, and he left almost no point of entry unturned. The space it cleared mentally allowed him to think through who he was, and what he wanted, separate and apart from his career. It was a tremendous process of self-discovery, and it helped him clarify what type of position he wanted. Within six more months, he landed a job he could feel passionate about.

Yet as good as he'd been about clearing out most of the points of entry in his life, the one stagnant area where Matthew became paralyzed was his office at the firm. Every time he walked into his office to start cleaning it out he froze, turned around, and wandered away. He'd spend the rest of the day roaming the halls at the firm, dropping in on colleagues to see if they needed help on small projects.

Was his attachment to his office sentimental? Maybe. It's easy to say we hold on to things for sentimental reasons (which is sometimes the case), but there's usually more to the story—sentimentality signals a more significant belief, need, or insecurity. Saying your attachment to something is only sentimental discounts other emotions. As we talked it through, Matthew realized there was a certain insecurity at the heart of his attachment. That office was the final remaining symbol of the goal he had strived to reach for so long— to make partner at his firm. Even though he was confident in his decision to leave the firm where he'd been so successful for fifteen years, to start over somewhere new was like making the shift from being a high school senior (where you are the king of mountain) to being a freshman in college (where you know nothing). The value in Matthew's clutter (his office) was that it provided a symbol of everything he had achieved in his professional life.

3. Physical Clutter Can Keep Us Company

In its own maddening way, having a blanket of general clutter can be a comfort. Our musician/composer Jay experienced this phenomenon. My first conversation with Jay happened over the airwaves, when he happened to call in to a radio show that had me on as a guest. I'll never forget his question, which came at the end of the broadcast: "Sometimes, when I clean up and get rid of things," he confided, "I feel lonely." He asked me if that made sense. It did. Very often the clutter occupies your thoughts and energy to such a degree that you really don't know what you would do without it. It can act as a distraction, keeping you from fully engaging in life.

In my work, I do not impose judgment on the quantity of stuff people want to own. If the amount of stuff you own feels right to you, let it be. But if you are reading **SHED**, it's because your volume of belongings no longer feels comfortable. You have reached a tipping point, as Jay did, and are feeling more suffocated than nourished by your belongings.

Owning a large volume of stuff can fill a void, creating fullness where there might otherwise be emptiness. In these cases, people can feel more tethered to the *volume* of stuff they have accumulated, rather than any specific objects.

My first phone consultation with Janice, 41, the mother of two boys, 5 and 12, was punctuated by a litany of self-deprecating remarks: "My mother's house was always perfect . . . except for my room." "My husband gets so mad at me—we must own eighteen nail clippers and I can never find a single pair." "Before I met my husband's parents for the first time when we were dating, he took me to Lowe's to buy shelves and we spent two days organizing."

When Janice emailed me photos of her home as part of our consultation, her modern, three-bedroom ranch looked pristine and spare: clean surfaces, orderly shelves, uniform containers and bins. "My house *looks* organized on the surface, but it's chaos underneath," she said. "Trust me: I own every container known to man, I just don't know what's in them."

We peeked inside three of the several 20-gallon Rubbermaid tubs lining the floor of her master bedroom closet. The miscellaneous, haphazard contents of each bin told the story of someone frantically trying to hide her mess. Bin 1: Unopened sheet set. Colored folders. Blank VHS tapes. Incomplete cross-stitching project. Bin 2: Papers. Afghan. Hooked on phonics CD. Wrapped package of party napkins. Playtex nurser she'd meant to return. Bin 3: High school yearbook. Items to sell on eBay. Cookbook she's been working on for her best friend. Computer cords. "I just wasn't ready to decide or deal with any of this stuff," she said.

Janice was embarrassed and ashamed of her behavior. When she was growing up, her mother was intolerant of clutter, and now as an adult, her husband also was critical. Feeling pressure from each of them, Janice's solution for any mess was to scoop it up and put a lid on it. Unfortunately, practical household items (like the eighteen nail clippers) and important papers (like her sons' Little League registration forms) were often lost in the shuffle.

The chaos lurking below the surface haunted Janice daily. She wanted to get rid of it and felt she had no excuse for living like this. She'd been this way for as long as she could remember and was angry with herself. "Why can't I just let this stuff go?" she kept goading herself.

When Janice gave me her background, she mentioned casually that her father had passed away when she was 14. So I asked, "Did you struggle with this issue when your dad was alive?" WHAM. Dead silence. "No," she said in that same quiet voice Jessica had used. "In fact, my room was always very organized—my clothes, school papers, and record collection existed in perfect order. Isn't that weird?" she asked.

It didn't sound weird to me at all. When her dad died, it would have been natural for Janice to feel a huge emptiness inside. And accumulating lots of stuff to fill the void would have made perfect sense, even if she hadn't been conscious of what she was doing. The value in her clutter was the sense of comfort and fullness it provided. Yet because she hadn't understood it, Janice never even had the opportunity to savor the abundance she had created by her over-accumulation. Once she understood what was at its root, she was able to look at her clutter with less judgment and continue the process of lightening her load.

I instructed Janice to embrace the abundance by giving her belongings a place—basically, a holding room to display her stuff. After less than a month of celebrating her wares, Janice was ready to choose the true treasures, and let the rest go.

Going Backward Before Moving Forward

Use the series of questions below to trace the clutter back to when you first acquired it and uncover its original value to you. Ask yourself these questions for each point of entry in the physical realm, one area at a time.

Point of entry (physical): _____
- *How long* has this area been stagnant? _____
- Was there ever a time when it was fully vibrant and relevant? A positive source of energy? _____
- *What changed* in my life to cause it to go stale? _____
- Is my reason for owning this still *valid* right now? _____
- If I were to get rid of this clutter, what would I miss? _____
- *What* is my attachment to this object (or this mess?) _____

The most important thing when answering these questions is to think past the obvious and push yourself until you find the answer that rings true. During this process, be on the lookout for common traps that block insight: extreme self-criticism, blaming others, and discounting your attachment as simple sentimentality. Be kind to yourself. I guarantee there is a *good* reason for the *bad* behavior. And once you find that reason, you'll experience a sense of relief and liberation, which will help you let go of the things that are no longer serving you and empower you to meet your needs in a healthier, more productive way.

What If There's No Attachment at All

You won't necessarily feel an attachment to every point of entry identified in your physical space. In some cases, the only reason items are
still hanging around is that you were too busy or distracted to notice
their presence. This might include a drawer or supply closet filled with
a box of rusty nails, expired coupons, old cans of paint, or a predeces-
sor's files at the office. It could even include a wedding gift you never
got around to returning or hand-me-downs from your parents' attic
that don't quite fit your personal style. Invest a few minutes thinking
through the reason you have failed to toss them in the past. Even
those seemingly innocuous and useless objects might have a hidden
leash on them representing some past goal—to be the fixit guy, the
penny saver, the responsible new employee, or the dutiful child.

How Do You Know It's a Treasure?

One of my favorite kitchen gadgets of all time is the egg separator. A nifty
little contraption that perfectly separates the egg white from the egg yolk, I'm
told it's an absolute essential for any serious baker (though, admittedly, I'm no
Julia Child). Your task now, like an egg separator, is to separate the treasures
from the clutter.

At the risk of mixing my metaphors (for the benefit of you non-baking
readers), selecting the treasures is akin to choosing which photos belong in
your wedding album, picking a good basket of berries at the grocery store, or
the plays that make ESPN web gems every night at 11 P.M. In each case, you
want only the best. It's not time to throw anything away just yet, but you will
cherry-pick which items should under *no* circumstance be tossed.

Developing your list of treasure guidelines is similar to preparing a packing list for a long vacation, or a shopping list before going to the supermarket.
This pen to paper exercise will ensure that you stay focused and pluck only
the true treasures. If you've ever shopped without a list, you know how full
your cart can get, only to arrive home without butter and paper towels, the
two items you went to the grocery store for in the first place. To create your

guidelines it will help to do a quick scan through the physical point of entry to get a sense of what there is and trigger your imagination.

Samples of Treasure Guidelines

Brooke, for example, felt attached to the family-filing system she built when her children were young even though she no longer used it. It was an awesome system; she could get her hands on any piece of information in ten seconds flat. From annual camp application forms to report cards, the church directory to financial files, it was fast, efficient, and based on rapid and easy retrieval. But now, with her kids grown and out of the house, most of its contents were irrelevant—it was clutter by **SHED** standards—yet there were gems worth saving.

As she considered her new theme, *Expand my audience,* Brooke wrote down the categories of information that would make sense in her new life. She then identified several broad categories of paper treasures among her files:

Brooke's Treasure Guidelines
- Correspondence that contributes to a journal-like sense of her life
- Papers that capture the essence of her children's lives: some to be packaged and turned over to them
- Medical records (immunizations, not old bills)
- Genealogical records (her ancestors came over on the *William and Mary*)
- Exceptionally well done graduate work she was proud of, but no more course stuff from doctoral work in the '90s
- Up-to-date product information and household data (e.g., paint colors that are still actually on her walls)

Brooke didn't try to identify specific items as treasures, so much as establish a few simple, yet very specific, categories. Once she dug into the actual files, she would have greater clarity on what specific papers to keep. Items that didn't match up to the treasure categories established in her guidelines were candidates to heave (in the next section of the book).

Jessica's theme was *Self-appreciation.* To tackle her mounds of reading material, she came up with the following guidelines to preserve information that would be helpful to her as she went back to work and attended to her health and marriage.

Jessica's Treasure Guidelines

- Top 5 career, fitness, and relationship books
- Classic novels she has read
- Book club novels recommended by a friend (i.e., no novels she randomly picked up in a bookstore without a recommendation)
- Latest two versions of any monthly or weekly magazines
- Any banking or other financial documents that may be buried under those stacks

Janice used her treasure guidelines to distinguish items that were actually important in a practical or meaningful way from those that were there purely for the abundance they created. She involved her family by asking her husband and kids to give her a list of items they needed as well.

Janice's Treasure Guidelines

- Practical household items—as requested by family members
- Important papers that are still current (e.g., Little League registration forms for upcoming season)
- Incomplete projects that are truly precious (cookbook for her best friend) and will bring her joy to complete (as opposed to something she dreads or just feels guilty about—like selling items on eBay)
- One-of-a-kind memorabilia (e.g., high school yearbook)

As you develop your treasure guidelines and begin physically to select the treasures, you'll begin to notice that each treasure means something different. Some might remind you of a happy memory or accomplishment, while others serve as clues to your most authentic self. As you read the client examples below, consider what your treasures mean to you.

Treasures Define You

Sometimes our treasures serve to reinforce what is important to us; they become guideposts leading the way toward our goals. Separating our treasures can also work as a tool to help us figure out what our priorities are by illustrating our values and helping us weigh the importance of each item.

Matthew's new position was the director of human resources for a company with a strong commitment to innovation. His company was in transition and Matthew was going to build a new division and staff it with the right people. His "treasure" criteria included practical knowledge from his fifteen years at the law firm that would be helpful in his new role, as well as significant memorabilia that inspired and reminded him of the best of his work and achievements with his old firm.

Matthew's Treasure Guidelines

- Staff evaluation forms
- Training materials
- Network of people in any form (business cards, directories, etc.)
- Framed piece of artwork given to him from his mentor when he won an intercompany promotion
- Stuffed giraffe—a gift he received just prior to making partner as a symbol of the lesson: "Reach for the top"
- A few key documents he authored that had major impact on clients and coworkers
- A Keith Haring print that symbolized his leadership philosophy

The Keith Haring print featured four different figures in four separate squares—a person doing a backbend, someone dancing on water, Siamese twins, and a figure with a heart. Matthew believed these images summed up his approach to supporting his colleagues, an approach he intended to bring with him to his new role. The figures expressed his philosophy: I will bend over backward to help you, but please understand that I can't walk on water, and I sometimes feel pulled in two directions at once. But I'll do everything I can to come through for you anyway, because it comes from the heart.

A treasure does not generate mixed feelings—if there's even a little negative energy mixed in, the item should stay with the trash. Matthew initially considered a series of hand-drawn caricatures created by his company's graphic design department (after the completion of every major client project) as possible treasures. They were one-of-a-kind pieces and, consequently, the natural inclination was to think of them as priceless. Upon further reflection, however, Matthew realized that there were as many bad memories as good ones associated with each of those projects—and while he'd loved working with some people on each job, there were many other characters he'd rather have forgotten. Since he had mixed emotions about them, the cartoons didn't make it into his 10 to 20 percent.

Bottom line, be sure you keep only the one or two best reminders of life lessons, people you knew, or favorite projects. If you keep too many, you won't create enough space for new adventures, possibilities, and growth.

Treasures Empower You

Jay's theme for the future was *Putting down roots*. The clutter in Jay's apartment was symbolic of his rootless childhood in the foster care system, a period when he never had a place to call home. He was so sick of the mess, he was ready to abandon it all and start over somewhere else. But I believed there were items buried in that mess that would give Jay a palpable sense of his roots, identity, and character. Those "treasures" would provide the tangible affirmation of his ability to love and be loved.

Because Jay was convinced there were no valuable objects in his piles, plucking the treasures was one of the most moving experiences he had during his **SHED**.

 Jay

At first I didn't think going through all my stuff was worth it, because I was just ready to throw everything away. Then I found this one thing— a little figurine from my eighth-grade music teacher. That figurine was actually the thing that inspired me to major in music—just this little itty-bitty thing buried under all this stuff on my desk. It's what helped me find my passion in life, and I forgot it even existed.

Jay's theme: *Putting down roots*

The guidelines for Jay's treasures were very simple—keep objects that were a testament to his ability to connect with others, build a home, and establish roots.

To further support his selections, Jay also imagined that every object in his piles of clutter was a person. For anything that was ambiguous, he'd pick it up and sit with it for a moment ("Just feeling it," he said). If an item felt like a member of his immediate circle (mom, dad, siblings, grandparents, best friend), it stayed; if it felt more like a distant cousin or one-time acquaintance, it went to the Heave pile.

Jay's Treasure Guidelines

- The best mementos from childhood: gift from his eighth-grade music teacher, high school yearbook, etc.
- Critical documents: birth certificate, adoption records, Social Security records (Jay discovered he had two Social Security numbers through a glitch in the foster care system)
- Special gifts and collections: a set of books from a favorite foster mother (who passed away), an antique book collection, etc.
- Keepsakes from past romantic relationships and friends

Treasures Connect You to Your Life's Passions

Alice, an 83-year-old former debutante, was living under threat of eviction from the co-op board of her apartment building. She is a regal, elegant woman with an impeccable sense of old-world style and wit, and no one could have imagined the state of her apartment. When I visited her for our first appointment, there was no clear walkway amid the clutter. Her commanding presence stood in great contrast to her uninhabitable environment.

Alice explained that she had started hoarding things in response to a misdiagnosis of Alzheimer's disease about four years earlier. She had massive quantities of purchases, clothing, kitchen supplies, books, papers, CDs, and records. Upon hearing the original diagnosis, Alice had given up. Having figured she would lose her memory, along with her ability to enjoy the things that she was most passionate about (music and reading), she'd created a blanket of clutter to act as a protective barrier between herself and the world. She'd indulged herself with everything in her power to preserve her memory and her passions by surrounding herself with as much stuff as her three-bedroom apartment would fit.

Two years after the diagnosis, she didn't have any symptoms; and four years later, she was still fine. She made appointments with a series of doctors who proved the original diagnosis wrong.

As much as she wanted to dig out, the job of reclaiming her apartment was so daunting that she couldn't do it alone. Unless she could clear up enough space to pass a fire code inspection, Alice was in danger of losing her home. To move forward, she had to release the idea that her life was over—she was going to be okay. Her theme for the future was *Reclaiming my life*.

Alice's Treasure Guidelines

- CDs and records. Music had always been one of Alice's loves, so we saved her favorite albums and a few recordings she'd received as gifts
- Books. Reading was another passion of Alice's prior to the diagnosis. We preserved every hardcover book and book-on-tape
- Tiffany lamps. Of her literally hundreds of purchases (linens, housewares, clothing, exercise equipment), the things that brought her utter delight were several Tiffany lamps. Of the twenty she had purchased, she chose four as treasures to display in her living room
- Clothing. We saved items that were currently in style and looked great on her, as well as several '20s-era coats given to Alice by her mother
- Key financial records—investment statements, tax papers, and current bills
- Heirloom furniture and art objects

Working through the clutter room by room, we used these guidelines to help Alice take back her life. There was a beautiful home beneath the clutter, with 20-foot ceilings and deep crimson walls, antique furniture and exotic art. One of the most rewarding moments of our work together was when I stopped by her place to check in on how she was doing near the end of the project. Alice was practically floating as she toured me through her gorgeous home. She shared treasure after treasure, showcasing beautiful antiques on her tabletops, opening an ancient trunk filled with linens handed down from her great-grandmother. The sparkle in Alice's eyes and voice as she shared her home with me was unforgettable. Unearthing the treasures made Alice feel alive again.

Diamonds in the Rough

There are instances when something you identified as clutter is actually more treasure than trash. Almost everyone has at least a few of these "diamonds in the rough"—treasures you might mistake for clutter if you don't slow down. There are vital parts of yourself you'd put on hold.

Brooke initially identified her perennial garden as a point of entry, because as she thought about her theme, she felt bad about letting the tending of her garden consume so much of her time. She spent at least an hour every weekday weeding and watering, and typically devoted one full day on the weekend to new plantings and maintenance (at least during the spring, summer, and early fall). "I just spend too much time out there . . . I could be writing, or teaching, or exercising, or, I don't know, doing *anything* besides getting dirty," she argued.

If she decided to move, Brooke planned to buy a home without the space for a garden. In the meantime, she planned to dismantle her perennial gardens and grow a tiny herb garden instead, which she would situate just outside her kitchen window (so she could snip basil and chives for dinner). She planned to hire a landscaper to handle everything else. "I'm too old to be wandering around the backyard with a weed whacker," she said with a hint of sarcasm.

But her description of the pure happiness she felt while working in her garden sounded like a clear treasure to me. My guess was that she had always gained this kind of joy from being outdoors, and yet in her effort to **SHED**, she was seriously considering sacrificing one of the very things that fueled her—a serious mistake.

About ten days later, just as Brooke was gearing up to gut her perennials, I received a panicked email. It seemed she, too, had misgivings about giving up her hobby: "I realize that although I like to rest at the end of the day, I feel better relaxing when I have accomplished something, and the physical work in the yard is rather immediate in its reward—I can see an improvement right away. I don't know what could replace those experiences, exactly. I think I should keep the perennials. And I still want to add the herb garden. Does this mean I'm regressing?"

I told Brooke to listen to her instincts and make sure that any new living situation (if she chose to move) included a garden. Tending to those perennials buoyed Brooke's spirit. As she adds more activities to her life that directly support her theme, she may end up spending less time in the garden, but laboring in the dirt is an activity that is essential to her being.

If you don't pay attention to what truly brings you joy and just get rid of everything in one swipe of the hatchet, you run the risk of tossing the baby out with the bathwater—throwing away mementos symbolic of who you are and eliminating of activities and habits that energize you.

Create Your Treasure Guidelines

If you step back and look at Brooke, Jessica, Janice, Matthew, Jay, and Alice's treasure guidelines and/or lists, you see how each one purely reflects back the individual essence of the list maker. Now it's your turn.

Get your theme vividly in your mind and think about the point of entry you've chosen to tackle first. What practical and meaningful items might be buried in those stagnant areas? Use the space below to write down your treasure guidelines for the stagnant area you are tackling.

Treasure Guidelines

Point of Entry: _____

What types of items would be practical and/or meaningful as I move toward my theme?

My Treasure Guidelines

-
-
-
-

Dive In to Select the Gems

With your guidelines in hand, you are ready to go on a treasure hunt in your chosen point of entry. Dig into the clutter, seeking to pluck the gems you will save. Give yourself a few hours per area or room to sort through the contents and select the gems. Think of yourself on a treasure hunt with a limited amount of time to rescue the items of true value.

It can be helpful to have a friend or family member keep you company as you sort through the clutter—to keep you from getting lost in the small decisions, and even to share some of the memories and help with the choosing. This can be a fun process.

As you go through the piles, most of the treasures you pull from a stagnant area will be obvious to you; it'll be like coming home from a long trip. You might say to yourself, "Hey, what's that doing in there? I love that thing!" If an object or activity is totally unambiguous in a *good* way, great. You know it's valuable and you'll be sure to put it to use in the next phase of your life.

In preparation for the moments when an object is not so obviously a gem, it's helpful to have a series of questions to help you objectively evaluate each thing's importance to you. The following questions will help you distinguish the "true" treasures from the "maybes" when you see them:

1. What practical value does this item provide?
2. If I just got rid of it, what would I miss about it?
3. If it was taken away, would I try to re-create it?
4. Is it invigorating to my life right now?
5. As I think about my theme, does it vibrate with relevance?
6. What's worth more—this object or the opportunity to achieve my vision?

Beware of the temptation to think of everything as a treasure. If you do, you won't open up enough space for objects and activities that fuel you now to come into your life . . . and you'll never fully appreciate how magnificent your "true" treasures are. Stick to the 10 to 20 percent rule.

The Most Complete Picture of Who You Are

Your treasures help to provide the most complete picture of who you are so far. With these tangible representations of who you are you can move confidently into the future knowing that you have your best stuff along with you.

As one last stop before you move on to Heave, look at your treasures and see what they say about you:

- Who are you?
- What makes you unique?
- Do you see a pattern in treasures? What's consistent about them?
- Did you find an unexpected treasure? What is it?

Now that you have analyzed their value and selected your physical treasures, you can jump ahead to chapter 7, Heaving Physical Attachments, fully prepared to eliminate the remaining objects that no longer feel relevant to your life. You are poised to make some space and surge forward toward your theme.

Chapter 5

Finding Time Treasures

Until you value yourself, you won't value your time. Until you value your time, you will not do anything with it.

—M. Scott Peck

In chapter 3, you identified one or more burdensome commitments in your schedule that are weighing you down, taking up considerable space and energy that could be used for something new, vibrant, and more relevant to your vision for the future. You even calculated how much time you would free up if you were to release those roles, responsibilities, commitments, and tasks that are depleting your energy rather than fueling it.

Yet, instead of suggesting that you immediately march around with a "Just Say No" sign, I will ask you once again to step on the brakes for a moment. Before you release *any* of the obligations in your schedule (even if you've already decided they are no longer a good use of your time), you have to understand why you made those commitments in the first place. Unless you understand the root cause of the burdensome activities in your life (just as it is important to understand the root cause of your physical clutter), you run the risk of unconsciously refilling your schedule with the same de-energizing activities or unsustainable level of "busy-ness."

What Is Your Attachment?

In this chapter, you will study each point of entry in your schedule and cherry-pick the treasures to bring into the next phase of your life. Finding the treasures in your time clutter is significantly trickier than in your physical clutter because time clutter is less tangible and, in most cases, the commitments and obligations on our calendars involve other people. You will not only be dealing with your own attachment to the time clutter but also the attachment others may have to your activities and responsibilities. We often make incorrect assumptions about what people actually expect from us and confuse our own need to be liked or accepted with others' needs or wants. Many people are paralyzed with fear of disappointing their boss, spouse, friends, coworkers, or kids, only to discover that the other party is shockingly OK with their decision to release a non-fueling obligation.

Once you have clearly identified your own attachment to the points of entry in your schedule, you are in a better position to manage and understand other people's attachments. As a reminder points of entry in the time realm are measurable commitments that come in the form of:

1. Backlog of to-dos. Unfinished tasks and projects you told yourself or someone else you'd complete
2. Calendar commitments, such as meetings and events you dread attending
3. Roles and responsibilities that deplete and distract you

Time commitments cut deep into our sense of responsibility, identity, and determination. Because we often develop very conflicted feelings about the obligations on our time—and even forget why they are on our schedules to begin with—taking time to analyze each commitment to understand its original value to us is the surest way to create lasting transformation.

Sheer Volume of Busy-ness

Before we examine your attachment to *individual* time commitments, it's worth taking a look at how we can get attached to the *sheer volume* of our to-do lists. If you think about it, most people always keep the same basic quantity of to-dos on their backlog—in other words, are constantly behind by the same amount of time—be it a day or a week or a couple of weeks, no matter what the particular items on the list are. Imagine for a moment if you didn't have a ton of to-dos always waiting for you. Stomach clutch? Neck tighten? Even though we never get to that pile of unfinished intentions, we keep our backlogs full for any variety of reasons. To feel important. For comfort. To avoid time to think. In case we run out of things to do. To stave off anxiety. What would you do with yourself if you didn't have your typical 8 or 12 or 40 hours' worth of to-dos waiting for you? Picture the energy you'd feel if you freed up that time.

Maintaining a huge backlog of to-dos and unfinished projects weighs you down. In chapter 3, you totaled the number of hours in your backlog (by measuring the tasks piled on your desk, counters, and to-do lists). For most people, we get accustomed to a certain "quantity" of hours in our backlog, and the goal is to shrink that. If you choose your backlog as a Point of Entry, your **SHED**ing job is to reduce that number by 80 percent on a permanent basis. So let's say you add up your backlog and the total is 40 hours of tasks. Reducing it measurably would mean that you would go from being someone who usually has 40 hours of backlog to someone who never has more than 8 hours of backlog. If your starting point is 10 hours of backlog, after this exercise, you should lower your maximum backlog to no more than 2 hours. Reducing your backlog by 80 percent will get you unstuck.

That shift in what is waiting for you is the permanent space we are clearing out. You'd be surprised at how liberating and perhaps disorienting it will feel to have that space opened. Think about when you get ready to go on vacation. It's amazing how the piles of items that have been ignored for months suddenly get done—because you need the mental freedom to go on your vacation without those burdens weighing on your mind. That's the feeling we are trying to create on a permanent basis. Nothing hanging over your head, so you are dislodged, free, ready for new adventures and opportunities.

Backlog of Tasks and To-dos and Unfinished Projects

So first let's analyze what's on your backlog. They are usually old intentions you have not yet gotten to that have lost their relevance. Tasks that you'd planned to do but upon reflection do not make sense in relation to your theme—unfinished projects that you realize represent the past. In addition, there are things that you simply never got to for one reason or another. They often infuse us with guilt.

Most items on our backlog fall into one of the following categories:

Promised favors. Make an introduction, send some information, write a letter of recommendation. Depending on their scope, they would make you feel better if you got them done.

Personal contact. Plans to send thank-yous; place a call to say "hi," check in, or show concern, express gratitude, maintain a connection (phone, email, letter)—could be personal or business.

Large, ambitious projects. Write a book or a cookbook, assemble a photo album or scrapbook, make an afghan for someone, remodel your kitchen, paint your house.

Repairs, research, or errands. Hang pictures, get locks changed, have dress copied, backup computer files, or update address book.

Financial paperwork. Complete taxes, mortgage application, loan application, reconcile bank statement, or pay bills.

Left undone, these tasks are burdens, weighing heavily on our minds and distracting us from having the freedom to move forward. Getting them done or letting them go clears them off our minds and schedules.

When it comes to what is on your backlog of tasks, not all but most tend to be promises to yourself—you have only yourself to contend with. Yet backlogged tasks, even those that don't require a long conversation with someone, can be surprisingly hard to let go, because of what they represent to us. Failed intentions. Dissapointment in ourselves. A lot of judgment. But that's only one level of attachment. Having a large backlog can represent so much more.

In identifying the treasures, we can talk about the specifics in your backlog today—and how to get rid of each item—but remember that your goal is not simply to get this set of items done and to replace those items with others. It's to clear out that quantity of mental and physical burden for good so that you have space to think and move toward your goal. (This is like cleaning out a storage closet. You want to empty it as much as possible and leave the open space—don't put anything back inside.)

Take a moment to think about the sheer volume of your backlog.

So let's look at a sample backlog list—this from Eleanor, a client who always had about three week's too much to do. How did she know? At the end of every month, no matter how productive she had been, she could total what she'd *not* gotten to, and it always added up to about three week's worth of unfinished tasks. Here was a sample list. Take a breath.

☐ Get house painted 22 hrs
☐ Respond to old friend's baby announcement from 18 months ago 2 hrs
☐ Make appointment for annual dental checkup 15 min
☐ Get door to front hall closet repaired 3 hrs
☐ Track down Aunt Sheila's discontinued perfume 2–3 hrs
☐ Gather tax receipts and paperwork for last year's tax returns 8 hrs
☐ Read last 3 issues of magazine subscribed to 3 hrs
☐ Shred 6 months' worth of junk mail in recycling bin 3–4 hrs
☐ Weed out overstuffed file from recently completed project 2 hrs
☐ Write letter of recommendation for someone 4 hrs
☐ Call George with name of carpenter he asked for 30 min
☐ Return one-year-old phone message from an old friend 1 hr
☐ Have housewarming party 12 hrs
☐ Clean up credit report 6 hrs
☐ Research and register for continuing education course 3 hrs
☐ Organize all photos onto computer 24 hrs
☐ Update addresses into database or address book 4–5 hrs
☐ Return faulty toaster bought 3 months ago 3 hrs
☐ Follow up on 36 business cards from conference last year 9 hrs
☐ Get sketches purchased in Paris framed and hung <u>4 hrs</u>

almost 119 hrs

Needless to say, when we did the math and calculated how much was on her to-do list, Eleanor was a little overwhelmed. Shocked. I asked her what was her attachment to her list, saying, "If I waved a magic wand and this list disappeared (with everything done), how would you feel?" Her response: "Directionless." Her list gave her focus. A sense of purpose. Of being in control. There was always something to do. Without all these tasks awaiting her, she felt unanchored and vulnerable. Empty. Worried. Her list gave her a sense of importance. Her giant backlog meant she'd always have something to focus on even if the tasks themselves weren't very meaningful.

She thought of her theme, Freedom, and realized her backlog was also weighing her down. By always being focused on her list of preassigned to-dos, she was unavailable to receive new opportunities. To be spontaneous. To accept new adventures and things to do.

So we came up with a list of treasure guidelines. She'd keep anything that would keep her out of financial trouble and anything related to a promise to someone else. The promises to herself—the big projects that represented time clutter—she would release.

If the goal were to identify what to keep, what could treasure guidelines be for a list like this? Practical treasures would be things that you must do to keep yourself out of trouble financially. Other treasures are things that would make you feel better to get done.

Practical treasures (anything related to financial or physical health):

- ☐ Gather tax receipts and paperwork for last year's tax returns   8 hrs
- ☐ Clean up credit report   6 hrs
- ☐ Make appointment for annual dental checkup   15 min

Meaningful treasures (anything related to promises to people):

- ☐ Respond to old friend's baby announcement from 18 months ago   2 hrs
- ☐ Return one-year-old phone message from an old friend   1 hr
- ☐ Write letter of recommendation for someone   4 hrs
- ☐ Call George with name of carpenter he asked for   <u>30 min</u>

                almost 22 hrs

Understanding Your Attachment

The key to understanding your attachment to each point of entry in your schedule is to think back to the moment when you acquired the commitment. By figuring out what that "thing" is doing on your calendar (in other words, how it got there and the purpose it once served), you are in a better position ultimately to remove it for good.

Burdensome commitments make their way onto our calendars and to-do lists in three ways:

Obsolete need. Sometimes we chose to take on responsibilities or assignments because it was the sensible thing to do at the time. An activity or commitment may have addressed a legitimate need at the time you acquired it, but it has since lost its relevance.

Right impulse, wrong activity. In other instances, we felt pressured into taking on a responsibility by an employer, client, family member, or friend unable to summon the word "no." Yet the reality is, we said "yes" because it filled some need of our own. Volunteering to chair the annual company retreat or family reunion may come from a desire to make a contribution (a healthy impulse), but if the activity is more draining than enriching, more routine than inspired, it's probably time to look for a different way to contribute.

Insecurity. Finally, we sometimes take on obligations, commitments, and even roles because of our own insecurities—being excessively busy or being the go-to person for every single thing can make us feel important and valued. This availability may have filled some other aspect of our identity we are now ready to leave behind. Study the following client examples to start exploring the underlying value of the clutter in your own schedule.

1. Time Clutter Can Represent How We Want to See Ourselves

The Zen wanderer in chapter 3 built his heavy raft out of true necessity— he'd encountered a raging river and needed to build a way to cross it safely. But twenty years later, he was still carrying that raft, even though he never encountered another raging river. His original reason for acquiring the raft made sense at the time, but years later he no longer had the same need.

When we first started working together, Trevor, 49, had recently been promoted to the executive level of his computer software company. As product director, he supervised several people at the product manager level (a position he'd held for the previous eight of his twelve years at the firm). About eleven months into this transition, Trevor felt stuck. He was excited by his new job, but felt like he was being crushed by his workload and suspected he had not handled the transition into his new role very well. His theme for the future was to move beyond his old role—in which his focus had been to *develop a reputation for excellence*—and now emerge as a strategic director. His new theme was *Leading a team to peak performance.*

Trevor was incredibly organized. He was reliable on a deadline, could estimate how long a task would take and was excellent at breaking down projects into small steps for himself and his staff. He kept an impeccable to-do list, updated it every day, and not one item ever fell through the cracks. But in his case, being organized wasn't enough.

When I helped Trevor inventory the points of entry in his schedule, he instantly pinpointed the biggest obligation on his time: "I spend way too much time doing my staff's work."

Trevor suspected that the fault was not just his staff's dependence on him, but that he was still attached on some level to his old role and had trouble resisting the temptation to get overly involved in their work. Why? Trevor was an expert at the job his direct reports were doing (he'd essentially been in their role for twelve years). He breezed through their tasks with confidence and authority. By doing their work, he was replacing the relative insecurity of his new role with the mastery he'd enjoyed in his old one. (This is a very common dilemma for anyone who makes the switch from hands-on work to management.) Trevor had to release his attachment to the comforts and confidence of his old job in order to succeed in his new one.

2. Time Clutter Can Represent
Misguided Good Intentions

Shirley, 38, was the vice president of a regional bank. Her workdays were poetry in motion—she was focused, able to prioritize, and an excellent delegator. But it was another story when it came to her life at home. She felt like she was coming home to a second job every night. Overburdened with general tidying, cooking, cleaning, laundry, and other household chores the moment she walked in the door until the moment she went to sleep, her role as sole caretaker kept her from enjoying any quality time with her husband or her children. Their family intimacy was suffering. Shirley wanted something different—connection with her family.

We discovered Shirley's underlying attachment to her caretaker role by probing one peculiar task—she mopped the kitchen floor every night. When I asked why, Shirley looked at me dazed and said, "Well, that's what my mother always did." I then asked, "Did your mom work?" Answer: "No." The role of family caretaker represented Shirley's unconscious attachment to being the "perfect 1950s mom," just like her mother had been—except her mother, like June Cleaver, was a stay-at-home mom.

Shirley was doing the wrong task to fulfill a good impulse. She'd gotten caught up doing all the family chores because it was an unconscious way to say I love you. It just happened to be a very, very time-consuming approach—and one that actually did not have the result she thought it would. Her husband and kids actually wished they had a better relationship with her, because she was always so busy and burdened by the housework, she never had time to spend talking or relaxing with them.

How do you know you are taking the wrong approach to the right impulse? It's when your intention feels right, but the activity itself is de-energizing. Shirley did not enjoy doing most of the housework; she did it because it was her duty. By redirecting her love for her family toward a more energizing activity, Shirley was able to open up many hours to put toward her goal of connecting more deeply to her family.

3. Time Clutter Can Represent
Old Comforts

You met Caroline, 41, in the first section of the book. A single woman in mid-career at an investment banking company, Caroline had just changed roles at her firm (and taken a substantial pay cut) as a senior financial analyst to a professional development role. The point of entry in Caroline's schedule was her whole job, which she felt was weighing her down.

Caroline had consistently subdued the more outgoing parts of her personality in favor of a process-oriented, behind-the-scenes position, because that's where she assumed she was adding the most value (even though that wasn't necessarily the kind of work she enjoyed). In fact, the satisfaction she derived from more relationship-oriented experiences often led her to offer extra assistance to colleagues and her bosses—after hours—in any way they needed (helping with budgets, annual reports, and the odds-and-ends of data analysis). As excited as Caroline was to start her new job in the department of professional development and training, she was also anxious about coming out from behind her desk.

Caroline's job change was originally triggered by a conversation with a senior partner during her annual performance review. The partner told Caroline that everyone valued her masterful attention to detail and Swiss-watch efficiency; but *he* got the feeling that she wanted something else (and might actually be more effective and *happier* in a different kind of position). He urged her to pursue a more relationship-oriented role within the company that would put her in a position to leverage her people skills and problem-solving abilities to focus on helping her colleagues full-time.

Yet even with that vote of confidence from a senior partner, the very prospect of front-line work sparked several insecurities. After so many years as a behind-the-scenes operator, she'd grown accustomed to producing great work product anonymously. She rarely received public recognition and came to like that. At the root of her apprehension about a more visible role, Caroline worried that she wouldn't live up to the job. "I knew I would never save the world," she said, "but what if my offering, as a person, didn't make any difference even in my own small sphere of influence?"

Some of Caroline's insecurities also stemmed from what she called a fear of her own personal power. Her parents went through a nasty divorce when she was a teenager, and like many children of divorce, for years Caroline suspected she was responsible. This wasn't true, of course, **SHED**ing uncovered this old belief. Witnessing her parents exercise their personal power to hurt each other (often using Caroline as a weapon during the custody battle) was traumatizing. She feared (albeit subconsciously) that she would inadvertently do more harm than good by using her personal power in a more unrestrained way.

Going Backward Before Moving Forward

Now it's your turn. The key to discovering your attachment to each point of entry in your schedule is to trace it back to its roots—remembering when you acquired the commitment and reconnecting to your original intention.

Use the following list of questions to trace each point of entry in your schedule back to its roots, just as Trevor, Shirley, and Caroline did.

Point of Entry: _____

- *When* did I first acquire this commitment? _____
- *How long* has this task felt so burdensome? _____
- *Why* did I originally take it on? _____
- Have I *already fulfilled that intention* in other ways since? _____
- If I still have that need, is this the most effective way to achieve that goal? _____
- Does this activity reflect an insecurity on my part?

_____

- If so, how can I overcome that insecurity more directly? _____
- If this commitment were gone, what would I miss? _____
- *What* is my attachment to this commitment? _____

What If There Is No Attachment at All?

As with physical clutter, you may not feel an attachment to every stagnant area in your schedule. There are some tasks and activities filling your time to which you will have no attachment at all, that are meaningless to you—you just do them because, well, you've *always* done them. Like grocery shopping on Saturday mornings (when it'd be much faster to go any night during the work week) or continuing to drive the same way to work (even though there's a faster route using a new highway). Simply becoming aware of them is all you need to say bye-bye!

How Do You Know It's a Treasure?

This is the fun part. You get to determine what things in your schedule are worthy of accompanying you on this adventure. What do you absolutely want to have in tow? What would you never want to be without?

Start this process by making a list on paper (just like a packing list you make to prepare for a long trip) articulating what constitutes a time treasure. Remember, treasures should be no more than 10 to 20 percent of each point of entry. If your time point of entry was overseeing your employer's Christmas card project every December (a gigantic logistical hassle, requiring more than 25,000 cards to be signed by hand), the treasure(s) are only 10 to 20 percent of that task. Maybe narrow the list down to 2,500 cards. Shirley, for example, knew that *some* of the household chores did actually belong on her to-do list, because they were relevant to her goal of reconnecting to her family. Her guidelines were short and sweet. Everything else was a candidate to heave during the next step of **SHED**.

- Laundry (excluding dry-cleaning drop-off and her children's sports uniforms her husband and kids could handle)
- Grocery shopping, specifically meal planning, weekly marketing, and shopping for holiday meals

The treasures in each point of entry will reveal something about you—what's most important, what brings you happiness or even helps you see a new path to your vision for the future. As you think through each point of entry in your schedule, consider the story your treasures tell about you.

Treasures Connect You to Your Core Joys

Mari, 44, was ramping up to commit fully to her wedding photography business—after a fifteen-year hiatus—now that both of her children were in high school. Her theme for the next phase of her life was *Flourishing in business*.

The wedding photography business ebbs and flows. Summertime was likely to be the high season (when almost every other Saturday could be booked), while the winter months were always slow. In anticipation of a busy summer calendar, Mari identified her packed social calendar as a time point of entry and started to cull her personal commitments and schedule, including a trip to the city opera house one Thursday evening a month. (She and her husband, Eric, had been season ticket holders for the previous six years— it was one of their standing date nights.) She didn't *really* want to give up their opera tickets, she just felt like she should, since she knew she'd need to invest so much time in her new business venture.

When going through a transition, there is often an impulse to give up the activities we love, so we can focus more intently on making the transition go just right. (In the previous chapter on finding physical treasures, Brooke's initial idea to give up her garden was also born from this impulse.) Mari said the opera had been a "source of joy and creative inspiration for years," as she described the elegant coordination of lights, sound, actors, and design. Ultimately, she recognized how rewarding going to the opera was and decided against canceling their tickets. Nights at the opera were a treasure.

Theme	Flourishing in business
Point of entry	Overbooked social schedule
Treasure guidelines	• Sunday night potlucks with neighbors • Any one-of-a-kind family event (such as shower, birthday party, bar mitzvah) • Going to the opera

Treasures Help You Grow

The biggest point of entry in Trevor's schedule was his tendency to do his staff's work. As discussed earlier, he enjoyed breezing through it with confidence; as opposed to his own work, which was harder and didn't always produce tangible results. As Trevor thought about giving up his staff's work all together, he realized there were a few specific circumstances in which he should remain involved—just on a different level.

He needed to be seen as a mentor and coach without giving into the temptation to actually do the projects himself. He thought it was important to be able to offer support when a subordinate was going to be in a situation for the first time (especially if the margin for error was extremely low). And he would continue to attend any meetings with his direct reports where he had a distinct role to play.

Theme	Leading a team to peak performance
Point of entry	Hand-holding his staff's to-dos
What it represents	Comfort of the familiar
Treasure guidelines	• Prep and debrief time before and after direct reports do meetings on their own • Leading staff meetings • 1 hour of "open-door" problem-solving time per day • Communication and mentorship skills

Treasures Give You Confidence

Caroline was beginning her transition from financial analyst to professional in-house trainer (really, from stagehand to center stage) when we started working together. As much as she wanted her daily responsibilities to include more personal interaction and less number crunching, she'd been an expert number cruncher for years, so it was hard to let go of that old role.

Funny enough, Caroline's first boss, a flower shop owner, told her when she was 14 that she was great with people, but not necessarily detail-oriented. That one comment during a tender moment in adolescence set in motion a pattern of neurosis around details, process, and getting things done. She explained: "I gave away the 'people' side of my personality and started making my contribution through (and hiding behind) my 'work-product.' "

The trick for Caroline was to cherry-pick the treasures from her identity, without holding on to so many that it inhibited her ability to embrace her new public role. Here are Caroline's treasure guidelines:

Theme	Embracing personal power
Point of entry	Attachment to her old job
What it represents	Insecurity about coming out from behind the scenes
Treasure guidelines	• Attention to detail • Willingness to help colleagues and senior staff • Ability to build connections over work projects

Create Your Treasure Guidelines

Put your theme prominently in your mind and take a few moments to revisit each point of entry in your schedule. Remember, treasures can be practical, a specific skill or activity that will help you move in the direction of your theme (e.g., Trevor's mentoring skills); or meaningful (the shot of confidence and joy you get doing something that comes naturally to you, e.g., Trevor's talent for planning meetings). List your treasure guidelines for each point of entry:

Point of entry: _____

Theme: _____

Treasure guidelines: _____

_____

_____

The Essence of Your Personality

The commitments you deem to be time treasures should reflect and express your greatest strengths, passions, and sources of joy. By preserving your time treasures, you maintain the connections that are most rewarding and give you the best opportunity to provide value. You can move confidently into the future with these time treasures safely tucked into your pocket. As one last stop before you move on to Heave, look at your time treasures and see what they say about you:

- Who are you? What skills and contributions are unique to you?
- What activities bring you joy?
- Do you see a pattern in the treasures? What's consistent about them?
- Did you find an unexpected treasure? What is it?
- Are there any new treasures on your list (a new skill, a new insight)? What have you added to your toolkit?

Now that you have analyzed the value and identified the treasures in your schedule, you can jump ahead to chapter 8, Heaving Time Attachments, fully prepared to release the burdensome commitments that are no longer relevant to your life. Chapter 8 will help you manage other people's attachments to your commitments and give you techniques to let them go without compromising the space on your schedule.

Finding Habit Treasures

The best way out is always through.

—Robert Frost

What Is Your Attachment?

Remember the old brainteaser, Which weighs more, a ton of bricks or a ton of feathers? The answer, of course, is that they both weigh the same—a ton. But it's less obvious how hefty feathers can be. Bad habits are like a ton of feathers. They gently float through your day, working behind the scenes to make you pile things onto your schedule until—WHAM—your available time gets hit with a ton of bricks.

Bad habits are behaviors that load your schedule with burdensome commitments, tasks, and responsibilities, forcing you to continue playing roles that are no longer a good fit. At first glance, it's hard to imagine there could be any redeeming value at all in such habits. But there are—and your goal in this chapter is to uncover your attachment to even your worst habits, an essential step in being able to let the bad behavior go. Let me explain with a story about shedding a different kind of bad habit (than the ones we're focused on in this book), but a bad habit nonetheless: smoking.

It's a little embarrassing to write this (and it feels like several lifetimes ago), but I was a chain smoker from the age of 12 until I turned 22. I'd started smoking in seventh grade. Two packs a day every day for ten years. I literally would light one cigarette with the lit stub of another. Of course no one batted an eye at me for this back then. It was an era when most people smoked—both my parents smoked, my older sister smoked, all of my friends smoked.

I eventually grew sick of smoking for a number of reasons—namely, I got winded walking up two flights of stairs and usually smelled like an ashtray—and decided I wanted to quit. I was tired of allowing the addiction to run my life and literally organizing my days around when I could take a cigarette break. Going to the movies or the theater was unpleasant because it meant going two or more hours without a cigarette. For the same reason, long car rides with nonsmokers were out of the question. I was missing out on way too much of life because of my smoking habit—it was weighing me down.

I tried quitting three times on my own. But whether I took a cold-turkey or slow-wean approach, the longest I could sustain my willpower was three weeks. The minute one minor stress or another happened, I'd be lighting up again.

Determined to free up my life and my time, I finally went to a hypnotherapist to get some help (it had worked for a friend, so I figured, why not?). I was completely surprised by her first question, What do you get out of smoking? I'd been so consumed with all the negatives about smoking and kicking the habit that it never occurred to me why I might be holding on to it, aside from my physiological addiction. But as I pondered her question, I realized that there was another reason behind my smoking. I used it to shore up courage. Any time I was confronted with a challenge, however big or small, like writing a paper, walking into a party or a job interview, I'd steal a few minutes, smoke a few drags, and stoke my resolve.

The hypnotherapist then asked what else in my life gave me courage. The only thing I could drum up was the hug I got from my parents as a little kid before I had to do something for the first time (the first day of school, sleepaway camp). In our next session, when she actually hypnotized me, she trained me to respond differently to the urge to smoke. Every time I needed a shot of courage, instead of reaching for a cigarette I'd squeeze my right fist—in effect, giving myself the hug that I needed. And you know what? It worked! I haven't smoked since and releasing that habit was a gateway to a much richer, fully engaged life.

Your job in this chapter is to uncover the positive need the bad habit is serving—in other words, the good reason behind the bad behavior. Trust me, it's there. Once you understand the hidden value of your bad habit, you can begin to let it go, ultimately replacing it with something more productive.

Understanding Your Attachment

When you separate the treasures in the habit realm, understanding your attachment and selecting the treasures happens almost simultaneously (as opposed to physical or time points of entry, where understanding the value must be done first, as a stand-alone activity prior to sorting through the items). That's because when you're dealing with a habit, there aren't tangible items—a to-do list or filing cabinet—to sort through. Once you gain insight about a habit, you can immediately answer the question: How does this habit serve me well? Your answer to that question is the treasure.

We'll focus on five key habits that add bulk to your schedule, taking up substantial amounts of time and energy that could be freed for pursuing your theme. Clients commonly cite these as the habits they would most like to break—but like Bill Murray in *Groundhog Day*, these habit attachments just keep coming back:

1. Mindless escapes
2. Procrastination
3. Perfectionism
4. Chronic lateness
5. Workaholism

If the habit you'd like to detach from is not on this list, you can still use the same process to address it.

1. Mindless Escapes

Understanding the Attachment

Mindless escapes are the habits you do without paying much attention to the activity, while hours fly by—such as incessant TV watching, checking email constantly, surfing the internet for hours, and endlessly playing video games. According to a recent study by Nielsen Media Research, Americans watch an average of 4 hours and 55 minutes of television per day. More than 25 hours per week! Can you remember exactly what you saw on TV last night? What about the night before? Last week? Last month? There is nothing wrong with enjoying an evening by taking in your favorite sitcom or catching up on the news. It's when a night in front of the tube or aimlessly surfing the internet or flipping through catalogs repeatedly usurps your time without your knowledge that an unexpected habit can develop.

In my previous book *Never Check E-Mail in the Morning* I recommended avoiding email for the first hour of every day and instead devoting that time to creative or high-level strategic thinking (that too often doesn't get done). This helps break the email habit and subsequently boosts a person's ability to remain focused and present. Senior management and employees at knowledge-based global firms in every industry imaginable instantly see the advantages of this strategy. Yet everyone admits that it can be a difficult habit to break.

Individuals who have adopted this strategy almost immediately see the benefits. Yet when things get really busy, when deadlines come crashing in or a work-related crisis derails their routine, they find it very easy to slip into the old habit of checking email the minute they wake up or sit down at their desks. When they feel overwhelmed by their workloads, reverting to this habit makes them feel like they are at least getting something done. Feeling connected is satisfying and it alleviates some level of anxiety. Breaking the addiction to the instant gratification of being connected is very, very difficult.

Selecting the Treasures

Rajit, 41, indicated that he checked his email more than 100 times a day—pretty much interrupting himself or whoever he was talking to every six minutes. His habit of constantly checking email had diminished his ability to concentrate on anything. He was unable to be fully present in any meeting (instead, he clicked away on his BlackBerry under the table). He could no longer complete the deep analytic work his job required during normal working hours. He couldn't even get through breakfast with his kids on a Saturday morning without feeling the need to run over to the computer to "connect." He knew he was in trouble when his wife confiscated his BlackBerry the last time they went out to dinner with friends.

We discussed the benefits of his email habit. First, it allowed him to build close relationships with key clients, who came to depend on him because they felt he was always accessible. Second, his colleagues were never stuck waiting for answers, because he was always in rapid response mode. Third, it allowed him to make the most of moments that would otherwise be useless for anything else (time stuck waiting at an airport, for example). Finally, he rarely fell behind in his communications (even though he did fall behind on his more strategic work and the habit infringed on his personal time). We had to find a way to retain these treasures while breaking the mindless habit so he could (re)develop his ability to concentrate.

Interspersed between meetings and other closed-door quiet time, we scheduled six regular email sessions throughout the day, so no one ever had to wait more than about two hours to get a response. As a backup, we trained his assistant to filter his emails while he was off-line and call him with any issue that couldn't wait for his next email session. And we agreed that for (carefully) selected clients and situations, he'd make himself more accessible during non-business hours by distributing a special cell phone number. This allowed him to project a strong image of exclusive accessibility while sending a subtle message that it was for emergency use only.

Name:	Rajit
Theme:	Fewer, better connections
Point of entry:	Mindless distraction—email habit
What it represents:	Feeling of indispensability
Treasures:	Accessibility to VIP clients
	Responsive to colleagues on deadline
	Good use of business travel time

2. Procrastination

Understanding the Attachment

Procrastination wastes time that might otherwise be devoted to activities that support your vision. When we procrastinate, we don't do high-value activities. A procrastinator will do anything to avoid the dreaded task, sometimes even mindless habits like checking email, watching TV, or getting lost on the internet. Regardless of your favorite method of procrastination, it all pads your schedule with fluff.

Jackie, 49, attended one of my executive workshops on boosting productivity. A highly accomplished, brilliant woman with a great sense of self-deprecating humor, she declared herself the world's worst procrastinator.

(Work habits aside, she accomplished an extraordinary level of work—she was in the top 10 percent of management in her company and had the unconditional respect of her peers.) She claimed to be an impossible case, beyond all help; knocking around all day, skirting work at any cost, only getting to it at night or on the weekends. Yet, she added with a laugh, even when she brought work home over the weekend, she wasted all Saturday avoiding the pile (all the while feeling guilty and distracted by her procrastinating ways) before finally buckling down late on Sunday afternoon.

During a follow-up coaching session with Jackie, I asked her about the history of her procrastination. How long had she been this way? Answer: her entire career. What about when she was a student? Answer: ditto. Could she remember a time in her life when she didn't procrastinate? Answer: nope. She'd been this way her whole life, and try as she might, she couldn't identify any particular starting point to the habit. Were there any tasks in her life that she didn't procrastinate on? Answer: again, nope. She was an equal opportunity procrastinator; she avoided home-related to-dos (like buying a new sofa) as regularly as she put off business-related tasks (strategic planning, relationship development calls).

I asked her what was the best thing about her procrastination. With a mischievous smile she confessed feeling a certain victory when she achieved things in a crisis, truly on top of the world. *That* was the value of the habit—it fueled her with a surge of excitement and rewarded her with the victory of having finally gotten something done under extreme conditions.

This was a woman who loved the rush of the deadline. The real cost of procrastination was not the stress of last-minute pressure (she *loved* that), it was the loss of time and creative energy squandered *while* she was procrastinating. We needed to fuel her need for excitement and accomplishment, but find a different way to get there. Jackie had to retain the tight pressure she created on her own around each of her tasks, but eliminate all the time-wasting filler between those tight time frames.

Her motivation was to make the most of every moment of her life and maximize her creative energy. Her theme was *Maximizing every moment.*

Selecting the Treasures

Before completely tossing the habit, I asked Jackie if there were any particular situations when procrastination served her well. She said that certain issues on the job had a wonderful way of working themselves out. In some cases, while her staff was waiting for her to get back to them, they figured out how to solve the problem on their own. Her procrastination often forced people to rise to the occasion and develop their own skill sets.

Moving forward, Jackie decided that on any issue or task where her natural inclination was to procrastinate, she could ask herself, What's the worst thing that would happen if I don't answer right away? If she could live with the consequences, she learned to trust her hesitation. And instead of procrastinating (and not making a decision), she consciously held her tongue and checked in with her staff a week later for a status report.

Name:	Jackie
Theme:	Maximizing every moment
Point of entry:	Procrastination
What it represents:	The thrill of victory over chaos
Treasures:	Low-risk work issues, best handled by staff
	The excitement of tight time frames

3. Perfectionism

Understanding the Attachment

Diane, 46, was a smart, driven, highly accomplished marketing executive who had achieved a successful career in corporate America. Unfortunately, her ambitiousness and job pressures resulted in a life that was woefully out of balance. Married and the mother of three adolescent children, she said, "Between my 90-minute commute, 14-hour days, the zillion and one activities our kids have, time with my husband, and trying to take care of the house, I was constantly out of control. I had no time to tend my own health, or even put on makeup!"

So, in a bold move eighteen months ago, she made a dramatic life change and left corporate America to work in nonprofit as the marketing and development director for a medium-size foundation. She had two goals: one, to regain time to take care of herself, and two, to spend her time on a cause she was passionate about. Her theme: *Healthy balance*.

Within the first few months on the job, Diane realized that most of the staff had been hired more for their passion than for their skill sets. She ended up overcompensating for their skill gaps, driving the organization to raise its performance standards and speed of execution. She insisted on attending every meeting, ensuring that no critical issues were missed, and checked everyone's work three times, generating an excessive workload for herself and her staff. Instead of the nonprofit dialing her down, she was dialing them up.

Even though she felt absolutely crushed by her own self-imposed standards, Diane was struggling to let go of a belief from her childhood that said anything less than perfect is 100 percent unacceptable, and she was the only one who could do it. She alone was responsible for fixing everything.

For habitual perfectionists like Diane, a journey of a thousand miles always begins with fifteen hundred miles—never a single step. Unlike procrastinators, who put off big or complex tasks because they are intimidated to start, people like Diane practically seek the impossible. They turn everything, even the tiniest molehill, into a mountainous challenge, whether it's designing a shopping center or shopping for groceries. As a result, they have little or no time for themselves or family, and no opportunity to just "stop and smell the roses." Ironically, Diane maintained strict boundaries between work and non-work time. This would typically be a great skill to have, but the problem was that Diane didn't spend any time away from the office on her own self-care. Instead, she spent nights and weekends overly burdened and overachieving on household and family responsibilities.

As we searched her past to figure out when her need for perfection started, Diane recalled a childhood where her parents were distracted with many of their own problems. She always had to do everything on her own. As the oldest of twelve kids, she took it upon herself to make sure her siblings had lunches packed and clean clothes. She'd risen to the occasion as a child, and went on to achieve great things, but always on her own, and at the expense of ever having time for fun, or taking care of herself. She *couldn't* relax as a child. And she couldn't relax as an adult.

As Diane pondered this, she realized her sense of over-responsibility may have made sense as a child, but it was inappropriate for her current situation. She is no longer the oldest or by any means the only person capable of fixing problems. Diane in fact is the most *junior* of a team of eight executives running the organization. And if things don't go perfectly well, or she takes time to take care of herself, no one will starve and the world won't fall apart (although that's certainly how she felt as a kid). Diane could begin to relax, trusting her peers at work and her family at home to help tackle the problems and embrace the opportunities they all faced.

Selecting the Treasures

There were some treasures we could pull from Diane's perfectionism. An obvious one was her eye for excellence, a benefit if she could learn to use it selectively (we trained her to do this in Heave). Diane was also very good at quickly assessing other people's talents, even though she never trusted anyone to come through for her. She'd use her eye for people's talents and learn to delegate more effectively at work and at home. Diane also was obviously extremely smart and industrious; she'd apply this drive to planning out a solid regimen of self-care. And she'd let the work go.

Here are the treasures we salvaged:

Name:	Diane
Theme:	Healthy balance
Point of entry:	Perfectionism
What it represents:	Belief that she alone was responsible for everything
Treasures:	Eye for excellence
	Good at quickly assessing other people's talents
	Strict boundaries between work and non-work time
	Resourcefulness and industriousness

4. Chronic Lateness

Understanding the Attachment

The lateness habit places huge time burdens on your schedule in the form of hours spent stressed and worried, doing damage control, apologizing to others, making up for lost time. This is time better invested in pursuing your theme.

Lynn, the mother of four (ages 3 through 15) felt simultaneously addicted to the chaos and yet so weighed down by the stress of her constant lateness, she was convinced her life span would be shorter than normal. "Right now, my heart always palpitates because I constantly feel anxious. If I wasn't late, I'd live longer!" She wrote:

Dear Julie,

It's embarrassing but true; I am late to EVERYTHING! Unfortunately for my friends, employees, spouse, and children. . . . I am generally the last mother to pick my kids up and they are always humiliated and so am I. My employees have to wait (although they are paid to do so) for me to open up the store, and to show up to meetings. I'm late for my own dinner parties, guests arrive and I'm often still out shopping for ingredients! I could go on forever, it never ends! I would love to change this behavior that has been with me since I can remember. Can you help? I am willing to try anything, absolutely anything.

Thank you for your time!

Lynn

When I met with Lynn, she said she didn't understand why she was always late. "Friends tell me I'm just bad at estimating how long things take. But even as I'm racing to a doctor's appointment, I'll call ahead and ask if they are running on time. And if not, I'll stop by Starbucks on the way," she told me. "My dad was always very prompt. He raised me from age 12 on. My mom is quite tardy. It could be genetic. Or maybe I have a mental block."

She continued her litany of the heavy price she and everyone she comes into contact with pays for her lateness. The most painful examples? Consistently bringing her youngest son, Brian, late to physical therapy appointments used to treat a genetic disorder. And being late to her father's funeral. "I was supposed to get there thirty minutes before the wake," she said. "By the time I pulled up to the funeral home, there was already a line out the front door. I was so upset that I didn't have a moment alone with him. I thought, 'This is it. I've got to do something.' But nothing changed."

As I listened to Lynn, it became clear that whatever need was being filled by her lateness was significantly more important than money (she'd lost untold dollars in sales at the store she owns from opening late and paying staff for "wait" time), her family's emotional well-being, or even her own health. Something significant was underlying her lateness, and if she was going to **SHED** it, we had to know what it was.

"I am a huge hypocrite, I'll admit, because I expect my employees to be on time. In fact, I'm insulted whenever anybody else is late. I refuse to wait. Isn't that ironic?"

Actually, I didn't find it ironic at all. Both behaviors (chronic lateness and an intolerance of others' being late) can come from the same root cause: a fear of downtime.

I pointed out to Lynn that she was very much in control of her arrival times. After all, if you're always late by fifteen minutes, then you are obviously showing up *exactly* when you want to. You're not a bad time manager at all—in fact, you are pretty precise. The question becomes, why do you want to be late? Something about waiting brings up deep feelings of anxiety. I asked Lynn if there was any activity in her life she wasn't late for.

"Don't ask me why," she said, "but for some weird reason, I'm almost never late for hair and nail appointments. I think I just enjoy reading the magazines while I'm waiting. It's the only time in my life I get to relax."

This detail caught my attention. While someone might have concluded that this fact indicated selfishness on Lynn's part, I wasn't convinced. I was looking for a more noble reason for the bad behavior. On a hunch, I asked how her mom was about grooming and beauty care. "Impeccable," Lynn sighed. "She's been voted best dressed since high school and at 65, she's still a knockout."

At the beginning of our conversation Lynn had mentioned that her father (her primary caregiver growing up) was always prompt, while her mother (who'd left when Lynn was 12) was perpetually tardy. I wondered aloud if Lynn thought her lateness might be a way of feeling connected to her mom? Lynn quietly absorbed that thought and admitted we were getting close to something.

I probed to find a time in her past when lateness wasn't a problem. College? Late for every class. High school? Nearly missed the prom. Middle school? Long pause. Then she said, in almost a whisper, "That's when my mom still lived with us. I can't remember being late then. Though I do remember waiting for my mom all the time."

Deep recognition washed over Lynn's face. Her attachment to the lateness served two functions. One, it kept her connected to her mom, from whom she was separated at an early age. And two, it kept her from ever having to be left waiting for anyone—a feeling that had been intolerable to her as a child, when she'd always been waiting for her mom. That was why she couldn't stand waiting for anyone.

Selecting the Treasures

We uncovered two treasures in Lynn's perpetual lateness. The first was the connection she felt to her mother. We worked together to find a healthier (less expensive and offensive) way to preserve that connection. The second treasure was the joy Lynn gleaned from a few minutes to sit, uninterrupted, and read a magazine. I suggested she tote a magazine (or two) in her bag and try to arrive to every appointment with ten minutes to spare, time she could use to read.

Name:	Lynn
Theme:	Expanding to her full potential
Point of entry:	Chronic lateness
What it represents:	Anxiety around downtime
Treasures:	Connection to her mom
	Ability to relax with a magazine

5. Workaholism

Understanding the Attachment

Lily, 42, had just won a position at a prestigious graphic design firm in Seattle when we first met. One of the bonus appeals of the job was its location. The city's beautiful site and vibrant social scene, combined with more reasonable hours than her previous job, had Lily hoping for time to devote to her personal life. But after only a few weeks in her new job, she began to feel restless. She felt settled with the firm but floundered in her time away from the office.

She could have joined a hiking club or taken a cooking class (as she'd once envisioned herself doing as a new Seattleite), but suddenly that felt unnecessary and frivolous. To occupy her free time, she decided to take on a few freelance projects for small companies. Working two and sometimes three jobs at a time was a habit she'd developed when she was young. It made her feel good about spending her time on something productive and helpful, rather than wasting away the hours at home. But it wasn't long before she felt overwhelmed. Even freelance work that allowed her to control her own schedule was too much to handle when working a full-time job with a major firm. She didn't need the extra income, but she couldn't justify quitting the additional jobs when she would only be using that time to relax.

There are scores of people like Lily, who live with a deep-seated belief that if they're not working, they're not being useful and productive. Only work, work, and more work makes you a helpful member of society. This behavior is often adopted from parents who demonstrated those values—they worked hard, recognized hard work, and communicated that fun and relaxation were not rewarded. Lily's parents, children of the Great Depression, considered idleness to be the devil's playground. Her waste-not, want-not mentality resulted directly from her upbringing.

Selecting the Treasures

Lily's workaholism landed her a great job with excellent pay and good hours. As long as she continued to produce quality work (given her track record, this was a shoo-in), she had the financial means and freedom to pursue a fun personal life. It wasn't that Lily never enjoyed the benefits of downtime; in fact, she was interested in lots of different things. Once she pushed herself out the door, she actually enjoyed nature, friends, fine food and wine, art, and culture. She always felt she had to sneak those things in, as though they were guilty pleasures. We also concluded that her approach to work was courageous—she was willing to walk into a new situation or project and figure out what it took to succeed. We decided that was a treasure she could transfer to her search for romance and balance.

Name:	Lily
Theme:	Letting love in
Point of entry:	Workaholism
What it represents:	Industriousness is only contribution
Treasures:	Financial security
	Lots of interests
	Brave at starting new things
	Tangible results of job well done

Going Backward Before Moving Forward

As with all other attachments, the key to uncovering the original value of your habit is to begin by tracing it back to its roots and discovering when and why you first acquired it. Take a few moments to ponder your habit point of entry, and place your theme prominently in your mind.

While it is helpful to pinpoint when you started the habit as you think about the past, don't worry if that particular point in time seems a little vague or lacks an inspired "aha" moment. Sometimes habits start when we are so young, we aren't really conscious of the need we are trying to serve at the time. If going backward doesn't lead you to a brilliant insight, what is more important is to honestly and fairly identify what you get out of the habit now.

Use the questions that follow to get at the root of your bad habit.

Point of entry (habit): _____

- *How long* have I had this habit? _____
- *What were the circumstances* in my life when I started this habit? _____
  _____
- *Why* did I acquire it? Why did it make sense then? _____
- Are those circumstances *the same* in my life right now? _____
- *Who else* in my life shares this habit? _____
- *How long* has this habit felt like a burden? _____
- *What* do I gain from this habit now? What positives does it bring to my life? _____
- *Is* my reasoning for keeping this habit still *valid* right now? _____
  _____
- If I were to *stop* this habit right now, what would I miss most about it?
  _____
- *What* is my attachment to this habit? _____

Create Your Treasure Guidelines

The benefits you deem to be habit treasures are payoffs and rewards you will want to preserve as you move in the direction of your theme. Those healthy needs were being inefficiently served by the unhealthy habit. But the key will be finding a more conscious, mindful, and healthy alternative to fulfilling those needs as you move forward. Knowing you will preserve the benefits without the downside of the habit will give you the motivation to **SHED** the negative aspects of the behavior.

Record any benefits of your habit that will serve you well as you move in the direction of your theme.

For each point of entry, list your treasure guidelines:

Point of Entry: _____

Theme: _____

Treasures: _____

_____

_____

_____

With these habit treasures clearly identified, you can move confidently into the future knowing that you are getting what you need, but in a healthy and fueling way.

Take a moment to stop and reflect on your habit treasures before you move on to Heave. Did you discover any unexpected gems in that awful behavior? Do you feel a little better about yourself? It's so nice to stop beating up on yourself and recognize you aren't so bad after all. Just the behavior was bad.

Congratulations. **SHED**ing habits may be the most difficult of all the clutter in your life, but they are also among the most fruitful points of entry, opening up the opportunity to examine, discover, and finally expunge beliefs that are no longer relevant or serving you. You're on your way to finding a more constructive way to serve the needs now filled by the bad habit and to actually heave the habit itself, a process all its own that will be dealt with in chapter 9, Heaving Habit Attachments.

Without change, something sleeps inside us, and seldom awakens.
The sleeper must awaken.

—Frank Herbert

Whether you are **SHED**ing physical, time, or habit clutter, in chapters 4, 5, and 6 you pulled the treasures from each point of entry. With those treasures safely in tow, it's time to lighten your load by heaving; completely and permanently releasing the outmoded, obsolete, irrelevant and dysfunctional.

Most of these decisions about what to heave will be crystal clear and easy; others will be a little harder. Some items you discover in your space or schedule may tickle you, triggering an affectionate feeling or entertaining look back at what used to be meaningful to you or who you once were. Others will shock you by how difficult they are to get rid of. That's OK. It's all part of the process and the excitement of self-discovery that heaving provides. Your goal is to detach your identity from these things that represent your past and clear as much space and energy as possible to move toward your new, vibrant destination.

Regardless of which realm (physical, time, habit) you decided to tackle first, your mission is a rapid, *radical release* of the clutter in each point of entry. In other words, instead of a long, drawn-out process (say, fifteen minutes a day) of getting rid of things in small, conservative, cautious layers, your goal is to clean out completely all of the deadweight in each point of entry and open up as much space in that area as possible as *quickly* as possible. In this way, you will completely detach from the part of the past that no longer serves you. If you're heaving items from your physical points of entry first, flip to chapter 4; if the time realm, chapter 5; or chapter 6 if you are heaving habits.

After creating space in one area, you may find that it spurs your momentum to address a different point of entry. **SHED**ing brings about this cascading effect. You might find clearing out a corner of your home office inspires you to tackle your backlog of to-dos (a point of entry in your schedule). Give yourself over to the process and follow your intuition—always being sure, however, to clear completely one point of entry before moving on to the next. If you leave a point of entry unfinished (even if it's 85 percent of the way there), there's the danger the leftover 15 percent will morph into a new stagnant area.

Heaving requires substantial thought, considerable planning, and lots of self-motivation to keep you going. For each type of clutter, the following chapters will:

- Coach you through the mechanics of a thorough heave.
- Help you determine the best "exit plan" for each item or behavior you're **SHED**ing, based on what you feel is the most appropriate method of disposal (given its condition), the easiest way of doing it (most convenient so it doesn't keep hanging around), and the item or activity that role or behavior represents.
- Help you overcome some of the most common obstacles to getting rid of things *permanently*.

Heaving can be daunting, but it can also be tremendously energizing, fulfilling, and transformative. Even though you are entering this process having clearly defined your treasures, you will still probably find the heaving process to be a little slow at first. But before long (even an hour or two) you will pick up momentum and enjoy the journey, having gained a new perspective on the physical and behavioral clutter you possess, and that has possessed you. You are trading the tangible deadweight for intangible rewards to come.

Chapter 7

(Read in conjunction with Chapter 4)

Heaving Physical Attachments

> *Have nothing in your house that you do not know to be useful,*
> *or believe to be beautiful.*
>
> —William Morris

When it comes to the nitty-gritty of heaving physical attachments, you are likely to encounter three big stumbling blocks:

- **Mechanics.** The actual process itself can be daunting; heaving is a demanding, labor-intensive job. How long will it take? What do you actually do with all of your stuff? Where do you send things you are getting rid of? And how do you manage the logistics?
- **Momentum.** Because it's a big job, you run the risk of losing steam before the job is done. How do you break the workload up into manageable steps? What tricks can you use to sustain your momentum until the end of the job?
- **Emotions**. Because heaving is really a process of detaching your identity from things that represent your past, you are likely to hit some snags—discovering some things are harder to part with than you anticipated, a sudden hesitation to let it all go, a fear of losing an object and what it represented to you. How do you respect these emotions, learn from them, and stay on track toward your goals? This chapter will help you address each stumbling block so your Heave is complete, transformative, and permanent.

The Mechanics

The nuts and bolts of physically removing items from your space can be even more formidable than the emotional aspect of parting with once-beloved possessions. There's the actual hard labor involved in boxing things up for pickup or delivery. Making arrangements for dropping things off or having them picked up. And the BIG question: Where do I start?

As suggested in chapter 4, to see a big change in your physical space right away, begin with the point of entry you identified as the biggest stagnant area during your inventory. By releasing a hunk of treasures in that biggest trouble area first, you will free up not only a significant amount of physical space, but also space in your brain to think.

Physical Clutter—Sample Points of Entry
Start with Your Biggest Area of Stagnation

Books
Magazines and newspapers
Documents and papers
CDs, DVDs, records, tapes
Clothes
Furniture
Electronic equipment
Kitchen supplies
Garage/attic

Gather Your Supplies

The job of heaving your physical attachments can be physically taxing, so make it easier on yourself by gathering all the supplies you need in advance. The specific supplies you will need may vary a bit depending on exactly what you are heaving—is it papers, books, kitchenware, large electronics, clothing, or something else?

If you are heaving papers, have a shredder on hand. Be sure it handles thick bundles of paper such as junk mail and checkbooks. If your shredding job happens to be massive (and by that I mean boxes and boxes of old papers that need eliminating), use a shredding service. To locate a mobile shredding service near you, check out any of the following web sites: www.ironmountain.com; www.AccurateShredding.com; www.shredit.com; www.shrednations.com.

If you are heaving books, clothing, or household objects, you will need boxes and bins. Label boxes by destination if you plan to donate or sell items. Boxes should be sturdy enough to contain heavy items (like books), but don't overpack—remember, it will likely be you doing the transporting! And no matter what the job, don't forget large heavy-duty garbage bags. Clutter can be heavy and bulky; cheap trash bags will tear, slowing you down and adding frustration.

Determine the Best Exit Plan

The people delivering your new sofa or flat-panel TV are rarely willing to cart away the old one (even if you offer them a cash incentive). Charities often can't pick up, or aren't interested in what you have to offer. Without knowing where to dispose of items and making the necessary arrangements ahead of time, you could end up *creating* rather than removing the physical clutter from your life, stockpiling waiting-to-be-thrown-out items in front-hall closets, the garage, attic, or basement, hoping that someday you will want or need these items again. But more often than not, by the time you retrieve them, they are moldy, musty, and even less valuable than before. How do you actually get rid of all that old stuff? There are three exit plans to choose from. You can:

- Trash or recycle it (choose the most environment-friendly option, based on the item's condition and available resources)
- Donate it (consider an appropriate charity, or give it to a friend or family member)
- Sell it (make money or at least off-set costs)

In many respects, just throwing things away is the easiest thing to do. It provides the most immediate result—the stuff is gone—and it requires the least patience. But ironically, it can sometimes cost you more to dump something than to recycle it, once you add up the carting fees, furniture disassembly, etc.

Recycling these days is preferable. It successfully keeps materials out of the landfill by collecting, segregating, processing, and manufacturing used collected goods into new products, making it easier—and more compelling—than ever to give recycling a serious look.

Choose your method of disposal and for helpful tips on resources you can use to start making your arrangements, see the appendix (Resources for Heaving) at the end of this book.

- **Trash, or recycle (when you can):** According to current national statistics, Americans' total yearly waste would fill a convoy of garbage trucks long enough to wrap around the earth six times *and* reach halfway to the moon. At this level of consumption, at least four additional planets' worth of resources will be needed to support earth's six billion inhabitants. These sobering facts demonstrate the difference you, as an individual, could make by recycling those no-longer-needed books, periodicals, old newspapers, clothes, CDs, records, and tapes.

    Call your trash collector to find out how much extra it will charge to pick up an extra load or two (or three or four) of trash and what, if any, restrictions exist as to what he will take. Or, contact your local department of sanitation to determine what days they provide *free* curbside removal of large, noncommercial bulk items (things too big to be discarded in a container or bag). Ask for information about local free city dumping sites—great if you have your own truck, or hire someone with one.

    See the appendix for recycling tips that will get you on the road to going green.

- **Donate:** According to the IRS more than 20 million Americans deduct charitable donations of clothing, books, and other household items every year but many significantly overpay taxes because they undervalue these noncash donations. They might estimate a bag of donated items at $50, when the actual value could be $300 or more. Your tax preparer can give you a list of eligible items for donation so you can ballpark a value to put on them for tax purposes without raising any IRS auditors' eyebrows. If you do your own taxes, IT'S DEDUCTIBLE is a software program that enables you to determine the fair market value (often more than 10 percent of the original price) for all items $500 or less, so you get the full deduction to which you are entitled. Each valuation is determined in strict accordance with IRS guidelines and is backed by an exclusive Dat*Assure*™ Guarantee—meaning, if you get audited, they'll defend their pricing and absorb any legal fees!

Why donate instead of sell? For one, it's less work on your part (no advertising), and the higher your tax bracket, the bigger your deduction. You'll also be giving back by keeping items and materials in use.

Donating can be as simple as giving an item to a friend, posting something on a local community board, or even listing online, on www.craigs list.org. But if you want to get the full tax credit, there are thousands of eligible nonprofits and charitable organizations to choose from.

- **Sell:** The potential financial benefits from selling items are great, but seller beware: this option requires the most effort and expense on your part. Between placing ads in your local newspaper and scheduling appointments, selling your stuff can be a pain, even though the internet (and websites like craigslist and eBay) has made the process more convenient and expanded market reach. If you get a thrill out of bargaining and thrive on advertising, you may have found a new hobby. Keep a few basic things in mind before you get started: (1) putting items up for sale is only worthwhile for higher-value items; (2) sell high-value pieces individually, not bundled; (3) monies received are taxable.

Judging each item's condition can help you determine the best way to get rid of it. Keep it simple by categorizing each item as poor, good, or excellent.

- Poor = anything that's broken, torn, stained, horribly dated, or missing parts (i.e., no one could use it if they wanted to). These items should simply be trashed or recycled.
- Good = any items that work well, that are acceptable looking, usable, and complete. These items can be given away or sold.
- Excellent = anything in pristine shape—either just like new or actually brand-new. These items can be either donated or sold. You (or someone) spent good money on these items, even though they have never been used. Maybe the item is a result of an impulsive shopping trip, a trendy piece of art (you now hate), a fancy organizing gadget that never worked, a gift you already own, or something you just don't want.

Consider, for example, those 30-pound volumes of William Shakespeare's complete works you've been lugging around since college. At one time, they lived in your parents' garage where the roof leaked and they got moldy and wrinkled. As much as you love them, they're practically unreadable now (you can't even turn the pages without tearing them) and beyond repair. Clearly, you would judge their condition as poor. You wouldn't think of donating or trying to sell them. But you also can't bring yourself to just deep-six them with your morning coffee grounds. You could recycle them, however; at least that way they could wind up being turned into paper to produce more books.

Once you've decided how to get rid of each item, use the worksheet below to organize the actual process of disposal for each category of stuff you are heaving. The worksheet will give you a sense of how many pick-ups, deliveries, and other arrangements you need to make so clearing out your space will be as cost-effective, convenient, and painless as possible.

SHED *Heave* Worksheet

Point of Entry_____

	# Boxes/ bags	Name of Resource	Contact Info	When?
Trash/recycle				
Recycle				
Donate				
Sell				

Sustain Your Momentum

Almost all strenuous physical activity (whether it's giving a speech or playing thirty-six holes of golf) requires participants to have perseverance. I've found that one of the biggest obstacles to overcome when heaving physical clutter is that the job often requires several days, or even weeks, to complete; in the case of some of my clients, the work is completed over months. You run the risk (especially when undertaking a large job) of losing momentum before the work is done, which prevents you from achieving the radical release that truly frees you to move forward. It's easy to lose sight of the big picture when you are bogged down in the details of every decision: Do I really want to sell this? Maybe that's a treasure after all. Can this actually be recycled? It's easy to feel overwhelmed, throw your hands up and forget you even tried. There are three basic strategies to employ to make sure you stick with the job until it is complete:

- Maximize the time you have to devote to the task.
- Break large projects into smaller, more manageable steps.
- Make it fun.

First, figure out how much time you can devote to the task, then be realistic about how long you can maintain your focus and keep your decision-making powers humming at full capacity. There's no sense devoting ten hours one Saturday to a project, if you can only stay focused for six of them. In fact, heaving is usually best done in two- to three-hour sessions. Keep in mind that the project will start out slowly; in the beginning you may not get through very much in two to three hours, because you may still be belaboring every single decision. But after some practice you'll be amazed by how much you can heave in a two- to three-hour block of time.

Breaking a big project down into smaller parts makes the task more manageable and gives you the chance to evaluate your progress along the way. We tackled one client's entryway and living room for the first three weeks of a project, just to breathe life into the spaces she encountered when she walked in the door every evening after work. After those areas were cleared, we gave her a month off to reflect and acclimate to her newly empty space before returning to her bedroom and guest room. That took another three weeks. We took another short break, then returned to focus on the kitchen, bathrooms, and linen closets. Working in these different areas of her home gave her the chance to experience the energy generated by open space, one room at a time. The clarity she gained from each area that went through the heave process fueled her commitment and enthusiasm for the next section.

Finally, since each heaving session requires your total commitment and energy, do what you can to make it enjoyable. Your heave should be a fun, energizing, liberating, and nurturing process.

- Pick a time of day when you have a lot of energy (early morning, late night, midafternoon) then choose some fabulous music that sets the right tone and fuels your energy—upbeat, soothing, jazz, or rock. If you are going to be sorting through papers, consider instrumental music (tunes with lyrics can be distracting when sorting through papers and other material that requires you to read).
- Ask a friend to work with you to make it more fun and to help speed up the process. Take his/her availability into account when setting your timetable. You might even offer to help a friend with his own **SHED**.
- Prepare snacks and buy beverages ahead of time to maintain your energy level and to avoid stopping and starting and breaking your stride for a quick trip to the kitchen or grocery store.
- Time yourself heaving items in one point of entry so you can estimate the total amount of time it will take you to clear every area in your physical space. Then set a reasonable timetable within which you can work comfortably and expect to complete the job.

Whenever you feel like you are losing steam, double-check that you are actually doing everything you can to ensure your success. If you are a morning person, but have been heaving for a few hours after dinner every night, consider adjusting your plan. Or, if you have unreasonable expectations about what you can accomplish in a Saturday afternoon (e.g., clean out thirty years' worth of attic clutter), set smaller, more achievable goals (such as, clearing out the holiday decoration collection). You will hit peaks and valleys in the Heave. People who complete the most successful and transformative heaves know how to ride the peaks and keep themselves moving through the valleys.

The Emotional Factor

Besides opening up physical space, heaving is fundamentally about releasing old attachments. It's only natural to feel queasy about some decisions—there will be a strong urge to save once-meaningful items from the trash pile. The trick is to respect these emotions but stay focused on moving forward. In these moments of uncertainty, remember your vision; think of it as your secret decoder ring. When you start to doubt yourself or feel a little squeamish, trust that your vision is helping you chart the right course.

In the process of going through your items you may decide that some items you screened out as non-treasures are worth keeping after all. Recalibrating the balance of the 80 to 90 percent to release and the 10 to 20 percent to keep is part of heaving. It's OK if you find yourself selecting some additional gems—just as long as you don't go overboard and rescue everything, or you'll be back where you started.

Pick up each item and *feel* your reaction to it. Does it make you feel positive, energized, clear, or guilty? Is it something you meant to do, but never took care of? Then ask yourself the two questions below about each item. These questions will help you release your emotional attachment to your stuff.

1. **What is the value of this item for me?** How much space (mental, emotional currency) is this object taking up? Will it help me with my new theme? Does it have true practical current value? Does it have sentimental value? Which has more value—this object or the free space for something new?

2. **Is this the best and most significant reminder of that time in my life or that person I knew?** Jay found several items that reminded him of his late foster mother. The most meaningful item was the set of science encyclopedias she had given him for Christmas one year because she, and those books, encouraged his love of learning.

Jay's experience during the Heave step ended up being one of the most profound of his entire **SHED**. He had been battling the clutter in his apartment (and clinical depression) for years—remember, he was close to giving up and moving—so releasing some of these particularly cumbersome items to leave space for just the gems really was radical. It allowed him to connect to who he really was, *his authentic self,* which had gotten buried under the quantity of low-value items over the years. Jay's deepest desire to put down roots could emerge only if he could separate the idea of having *things* from the actual *meaning* of those things. Before our work together, Jay kept looking for himself outside his home when the clues and symbols of his authentic self were buried in the piles right under his nose.

"As I worked my way through the non-treasures, I came up with the term 'emotional currency' to describe the cost of keeping something versus the loss of heaving it," Jay told me. He said "emotional currency" worked just like real money. "You save it, you invest it, and you watch it grow . . . I realized by letting something go, I would be gaining more of that currency to allocate to other things that were missing—like a love life, for example."

Jay held on to the clutter for so long because he thought he needed it— that it would help him somehow. About halfway through the physical heave process, he became very clear on what the clutter was costing him: the freedom to invite anything else in, including friendships and a real home of his own. "Once the heaving was over and the clutter was gone, I had the energy and the clarity to knock the depression out on my own," Jay said. "It was more effective than years of therapy. Nothing I've ever done has ever been as effective in so short a time."

Wall of Panic

I am not being cavalier about the substantial amount of effort required here, and neither should you. You will need to put in the hard labor (boxing things up, making phone calls and arrangements for dropping things off or having them picked up) and invest your emotional capital in heaving as thoroughly as you can. Creating this new space is the only way you'll be able to move forward.

Once you hit your stride, purging will be fun for a while, and then, about 75 percent of the way through the process, WHAM, you hit a wall. This is a phenomenon I call the *wall of panic.* In this moment, you suddenly can feel the emptiness of space you have created. Without your stuff you might feel lost, uncentered, in unfamiliar territory with absolutely nothing familiar to hold on to. Your nest has been taken apart and it's disconcerting, terrifying, discombobulating. You have to trust the emptiness. Your stuff maybe be gone, but you are never alone—you have yourself, your spirit, and your resources. Trust that the space you have created will one day be filled with things that support your theme.

Remember Alice, from chapter 4, who had accumulated so much clutter after being misdiagnosed with Alzheimer's disease that she was under threat of eviction? About three-quarters of the way through her heave, her apartment was starting to look amazing: the floor was clear, dozens of bags and boxes had been removed, and you could see plenty of open space. Then, suddenly, everything stopped—*she hit the wall of panic.* I found her sitting on the edge of her bed, heels dug in, arms crossed, like a stubborn, pouting six year old. Her whole demeanor said, Who is anyone to tell me how to live? I don't go into anyone else's home and tell them how to live. No one can do this to me.

I was totally empathetic. I just listened . . . and listened. Finally I told her that we'd gotten her place far enough along to avoid eviction. If she wanted to stop at this point, that was fine. The threat of eviction may have been her initial trigger, but Alice needed her own reason to keep **SHED**ing (not anyone else's reason). When we first started, her vision was to resurrect a vibrant life filled with music and books. She could still have that if she wanted to continue the process.

Honestly, I didn't know what she would decide. But to my delight, Alice called the following Monday morning and said, "OK, you can come back." I was stunned. By heaving 75 percent of her stuff, she had really detached her identity from the objects. She just needed a few days to let it sink in and build up the courage to keep going. She had to cross a threshold, shifting her motivation completely away from seeing her **SHED** as a requirement (to avoid eviction) to being her own *desire.*

That's the good news about hitting the wall of panic: the feeling usually doesn't last too long—a few hours to a few days. This wall of panic is the true breakthrough point in the letting-go process. It requires reminding yourself that this process of letting go is a choice, and reconnecting to your own vision for this change.

Once you get to the other side of the panic, the calm and space to think awaits you. That's the experience most of my **SHED** clients have had, including Brooke. "At the beginning of this process, I was motivated to begin, but my attitude was more like the resolve to rip off a Band-Aid than the wild-eyed, endorphin-laced '**SHED**ing' glee I feel now," she told me. "Reduced of its burdens, my house is beginning to breathe again, and more than metaphorically . . . it feels as though the very air is moving better through the rooms now unencumbered by dusty crap!" What Brooke was beginning to experience was the thin line between metaphor and reality. The new space generated psychic space: "I glide through space that didn't exist before feeling I can do anything."

An effective physical heave requires heavers to overcome the daunting mechanics of actually getting rid of stuff, to maintain their momentum, and respect the emotions that are an inherent part of the process without allowing those emotions to send them tumbling backward. You are bound to stumble along the way, but by keeping your vision in mind, you can do a quick analysis of what's more valuable—holding on to the clutter, or creating the space for something more relevant to your theme.

At this point you can jump ahead to the third **SHED** step, Embrace your identity. This next step is designed to help you take advantage of the space you've created, by using it to learn more about who you are, without your stuff.

Heaving Time Attachments

*You can do anything you think you can. This knowledge is
literally the gift of the gods, for through it you can solve every
human problem. It should make of you an incurable optimist.
It is the open door.*

—Robert Collier

In chapter 5 you went through your backlog of to-dos, calendared commitments, ongoing roles and responsibilities to uncover what value these obligations represented on your time. In this chapter, we will look at the mechanics and emotions of heaving the obsolete activities in your schedule that are weighing you down.

Heaving the time clutter may not be backbreaking labor like getting rid of boxes of books and clothes, or moving unwanted furniture out the door, but it is technically more complicated and more difficult emotionally. You also have to decide what you actually *do* with stagnant tasks and activities—do you eliminate them completely, or ask someone else to take responsibility? And then there is the emotional element, because heaving things from your time requires tolerating a certain level of discomfort. You have to overcome the sense of duty and guilt that comes from changing the way you choose to spend your time. Removing obligations from your schedule often involves conversations with other people. What do you do about *their* attachment to a commitment you no longer think is relevant?

When you started to clear out your physical points of entry it was exhilarating to see the newly emptied space open to receive things of greater relevance and importance to your theme. You could also see how those belongings "kept you company." Their release left a space that was both exhilarating and a bit lonely at first. The same is true when it comes to your time. What fills your schedule keeps you company and distracts you—the old, familiar roles (even if they are no longer valuable) and exceedingly large backlog of to-dos gave you the sense that there is always something to do. It is not uncommon to feel a little lonely when you first give up your time attachments. At the same time, the feeling you get from releasing unwanted tasks, activities, to-dos (and the old attachments they represent) is also unbelievably liberating. Some of my clients say it is even more energizing than the rush they feel after opening up their physical space.

Aim for a Radical Release

It helps to think about clearing obligations from your schedule as clearing a physical space. Your schedule is a container, a storage unit with a definite capacity. The trick is to stay focused on tangible rewards (in this instance, the amount of time gained), always looking for the maximum gain possible.

The treasures you selected in chapter 5 represent only 10 to 20 percent of the total time occupied in each pocket of clutter in your schedule. Your primary objective in this chapter is to eliminate—yes, completely eliminate—the remaining 80 to 90 percent of "non-treasure" obligations on your time.

Too often we start out with the best of intentions when it comes to heaving time attachments and then sabotage our own success by adding a little "tail" to our refusal. We start out "Sorry, I can't take on that project right now" and then, out of our own sense of guilt, add a vague soft offer: "But let me know if you get stuck, and I'll try to at least oversee the board." We didn't want to be involved at all, but we offered out of guilt because we got so worried about disappointing someone.

There are three basic kinds of points of entry when it comes to time:

1. Unfinished to-dos and projects
2. Specific scheduled meetings and appointments
3. Burdensome roles and responsibilities

When we dealt with physical attachments, there were four options for getting rid of the obsolete, stagnant items in our lives: trash, recycle, donate, or sell. There are three primary options for heaving time attachments:

1. **Delete.** Cease your commitment to the task, responsibility, or role altogether.
2. **Delegate**. Assign the task or responsibility (or some part of it) to someone else.
3. **Do it (but diminish the task).** If there is no escaping the task, responsibility, or role, figure out a way to do it smarter and faster.

Readers of my previous books who are familiar with the 4 Ds will wonder what happened to "Delay." The 4 Ds were conceptualized for productivity, not for **SHED**ing (a process that may improve productivity as an added benefit but is not the stated goal). "Delaying" is not a radical release because the obsolete burden stays with you. We want these time attachments completely off your schedule and out of your mind, to create space for new activities, roles, and ideas related to your vision. When you face the temptation to "Do, but diminish," remember the goal of a radical release and push yourself to think creatively through delete or delegate first.

Remember, you are **SHED**ing in order to make room to move in the direction of your vision—whether that theme is *Letting love in, Making connections,* or *Leading my team.* Keeping your theme vividly in mind will help you find the courage to do a radical release. Leaving any vestiges of de-energizing commitments in your calendar will keep you bogged down and anchored. Remember the old adage, A ship in the harbor is safe, but that is not what ships are for.

Let's look at each type of time attachment and figure out how you can actually get it off your plate.

Heaving Unfinished To-dos and Projects

When it comes to heaving items from your backlog of tasks, most of these items tend to be promises to yourself, so to heave them you have only yourself to contend with. Getting some of the other items off your backlog may involve a brief conversation with others. Backlogged tasks, even those that don't require a major conversation with someone, can be surprisingly hard to let go of. In some cases, the only way to get something off your schedule is to actually get it done (because there are financial, legal, contractual, or ethical obligations involved). But when this is the case, your job is to look for ways to diminish the scope of the time burden so that you get it done more quickly and completely. Heaving items from your backlog and the guilt that goes along with it often requires a lot of "self-talk," reframing the way you choose to view the situation and the fact that it didn't get done. It helps to look at the potential time gain, why you are having trouble relinquishing it, and then find a new, positive way of thinking about the situation. This frees you to let it go, moving the items off your to-do list, and getting unstuck.

Let's look at three different examples of backlogged to-dos, the attachments they represent, and how you might heave them from your schedule and your life: (1) a collection of business cards for contacts you met at a conference and meant to follow up on; (2) the follies of returning a faulty toaster; and (3) compiling information to file your taxes.

Forgive Yourself

Sometimes the only way to release some items on your backlog is to forgive yourself. See how you might reframe your thinking to make it easier to release them.

Backlog task: Thirty-six business cards you collected at a conference eight months ago, which represent business leads you meant to follow up on, but never did. The cards are still sitting in a pile.

Potential time gain: 6–9 hours (at 10–15 minutes per card)

What it represents: Your own failure to capitalize on business opportunities.

Why having trouble relinquishing: Self-flagellation. Denial. Feelings of failure for not following through. "I'm so bad about this stuff—I blow these things all the time."

Different way of thinking: (a) You are successful—it was because you were so busy pursuing other leads and serving current clients that you did not have time to bring on new prospects. (b) You were under-resourced at the time, which is unfortunate, but understandable and forgivable. (c) It was an overly ambitious, unrealistic task to begin with. Most of the leads were cold—the result of random card exchanging—and probably no more than 2 to 5 percent would have converted to business anyway.

Options for a radical release:

☐ **Delete:** Trust that more current, relevant, and viable prospects or business leads will come into your life if you create the space and mental freedom to receive them. Time gain: 9 hours

☐ **Delegate:** Ask your assistant to do all the data entry and send an opt-in email to everyone to see who is still interested. "We met at the KPL conference last year and we are updating our database. Our company does X and we'd like to know if you'd like to remain on our mailing list." Time gain: 7.5 hours

☐ **Do, but diminish:** Choose 10 percent—that translates to three contacts to enter in your database, call, or send an email to, spending no more than 15 minutes on each. Time gain: 8.25 hours

Backlog task: Return faulty toaster you bought three months ago that has been sitting in a box in your front hall ever since.

Potential time gain: 3 hours

What it represents: Refund of $19.99

Why having trouble relinquishing: It's money down the toilet—you view yourself as being wasteful when it comes to money. You bought it on impulse without having researched the right brand. You almost bought the $79.99 one but thought you'd save a little money.

Different way of thinking: It's not always easy to discern when a bigger price tag means a higher-quality product. Your assumption that a basic model would suffice was reasonable. Beating yourself up over a $19.99 mistake is harsh. Be glad it wasn't a $199 mistake.

Options for a radical release:

☐ **Delete:** Throw the broken toaster out and forgive yourself. You could've spent $19.99 on a meal—a breakfast. Salvage the lesson and toss the errand. Time gain: 3 hours

☐ **Delegate:** Ask your teenager or spouse or friend to return it on their next trip to the mall—and tell them that if they can get the refund, the $19.99 is theirs to spend on whatever they want. Time gain: 3 hours

☐ **Do, but diminish:** Call the store manager and see if you can mail back the item for a refund rather than go back to the store. Copy the receipt and tuck in a brief letter. Or, figure out the store's least busy days/hours so you can get in and out more quickly. Time gain: 2 hours

Backlog task: Assemble receipts and paperwork for extended tax returns

Potential time gain: 8 hours

What it represents: Late penalties and interest, along with legal risk

Why having trouble relinquishing: Task represents resentment of rules and how much your taxes are going to cost you. You are also afraid of finding out you owe more than you can afford.

Different way of thinking: Getting your taxes done and up-to-date provides more freedom than being trapped by the unfinished task. The longer this takes to complete, the more money the government gets from you in penalties and interest.

Options for a radical release:

- ☐ **Delete:** This is not an option, unless you want to go to jail for tax evasion. Time gain: 0 hours
- ☐ **Delegate:** Ask a family member to organize all the information for the accountant. Or send all the paperwork and information to your accountant to sort through. You'll have to pay extra, but it's less costly than extended penalties. Time gain: 6 hours
- ☐ **Do, but diminish:** Assemble the basis of the paperwork but forgo some detailed deductions for this year. Time gain: 3 hours

Keep going through your backlog of to-dos and eliminate as many as you can. Imagine the hours you could reclaim by releasing the rest of your backlogged to-dos and how nice it would feel not to always be busy or behind. The best part of this is that most items on your backlog were most likely put there by you, so you are in complete control of their destiny.

Release the Guilt

Now let's consider how to handle heaving tasks on your backlog that directly *affect other people*. The goal again is to reframe your thinking so that you feel the freedom to release them, looking for the best heave option.

Backlog task: Rose, a social science researcher, was leading her team into new areas of study. Among the many things on her backlog was writing a grant proposal to create a center for the type of work she and her team had been doing for the past five years. Completing the grant proposal would require a full month of writing time.

Potential time gain: 160 hours (5 days per week at 8 hours per day)

What it represents: Validation for the hard work her team had done. A physical and professional representation of two-plus years of strategic thinking and research.

Why having trouble relinquishing: She didn't want to let down the team and ignore their hard work. She was also afraid to pass up the opportunity for professional recognition—it was an idea that had been with her for many years.

Different way of thinking: It might've been nice had she written this grant two years ago when her team was still in the throes of their research. But now that they were doing something different, this grant was not going to be relevant too much longer. It would only tie them to obsolete work.

Options for a radical release:

☐ **Delete:** Completely release the burden and create the space for new research and ideas that could lead to different grant opportunities in the future. Time gain: 160 hours

☐ **Delegate:** Ask a team member to spearhead writing the grant (at the expense of pursuing new research opportunities), giving the lion's share of the labor to someone else while Rose spends minimal hours reviewing the final proposal before submission. Time gain: 140 hours

☐ **Do, but diminish:** Present a bare-bones proposal without extensive citation to show potentially interested parties and flesh out more details upon acceptance. Time gain: 80 hours

Backlog task: Doug was running the family business but had to provide a report to the other family members each quarter. Doug's strength was his intuitive understanding of the industry, watching trends, and knowing which direction to take the company in—but not in writing his thoughts down on paper. Getting them down was like wrestling a bear to the ground.

Potential time gain: 48 hours (6 hours for first draft, 2 hours for edits, and 4 hours for revision—four times a year)

What it represents: His competence and wisdom in running the family business

Why having trouble relinquishing: He knew he had all the information necessary to create the reports and didn't trust that anyone else could express the company vision as clearly as he could.

Different way of thinking: Writing these reports didn't showcase his best talents—his intuitive, no-nonsense business strategy—which was his real contribution to the company. Spending hours dreading the task and then struggling through each draft of the report was not in the best interest of his business.

Options for a radical release:

- ☐ **Delete:** Not an option because the rest of the family needed to be informed about the business status in a formal document. Time gain: 0 hours
- ☐ **Delegate:** Find a freelancer with great listening skills, business experience, and contacts in the graphic design community. For 1 to 2 hours, he could dictate his ideas to the freelance writer, who would then write the report and work with a designer to present the information in a compelling way. Doug could give verbal comments for any revision, if necessary. Time gain: 40 hours
- ☐ **Do, but diminish:** Instead of quarterly reports, draft biannual reports like a periodic company "state of the union." However, this would take buy-in from the rest of the family to receive less information about the company's welfare. Time gain: 20 hours

Disappointment in yourself over some old hope or obligation is really just self-imposed guilt. Instead of seeing these unfinished tasks as failures, reframe them as conscious choices not to continue with a project, idea, or goal that is no longer valuable to you. You have to ask yourself, what's worth more—the attachment to the guilt, or freeing up time (and space) to move toward your vision? What would you say to a friend who insisted on doing something potentially irrelevant just because s/he felt guilty *not* doing it?

Heaving Calendared Appointments and Events

By calendared commitments, I am referring to specific scheduled items such as meetings, events, committees, and appointments on your calendar that you have agreed to attend or host. Whether it's a committee you volunteered for, a task you're saddled with at work (like maintaining the company website), or a commitment to throw a party or host weekend visitors, they all have one thing in common: in hindsight, you realize the commitment is a poor use of your time and irrelevant to your vision. You don't just want to avoid doing them (and *hope* they'll go away): you need to get them off your to-do list proactively and *permanently*.

These commitments represent a huge potential time gain, which is what's nice about them. But they are among the trickiest to get out of because others are counting on us. The key is to anticipate the resistance you will face and be prepared with a script to help you deal with the other person's attachment to your commitment.

We'll explore three common fears you might face in backing out of a calendared commitment, and sample scripts that will help you overcome your concern.

Fear 1: Someone Will Be Disappointed

Nancy had agreed to appear on a study section panel for the National Institutes of Health. Making these appearances is difficult (because of scheduling conflicts), but she knew participating would be good for her career. In light of her various commitments, however, this one stood out as a burdensome attachment. She'd said yes months earlier before her priorities had changed and without realizing how time consuming making the presentation would be. To get out she had to speak with the committee chair, Jane. How did she have the conversation?

She leveled with her in person to express her sincerity: She said, *Jane, this new research I am doing with my team is far more demanding and complicated than any of us anticipated. It's taking triple the time any of us thought it would, but we are on the verge of a huge breakthrough. I thought things would calm down in time for me to participate on your panel, but they are simply escalating. I know how important this panel is to you, and when I took it on, it was to serve your vision and goals. I would not be able to put in the appropriate amount of prep time to make either of us look as good as we deserve. I'll need to graciously bow out for this year. This is more out of a sense of responsibility to what you are trying to accomplish at the conference than disrespect. I hope you understand.*

Fear 2: Someone Will Get Angry

Judith, a corporate lawyer, was asked to attend the marketing department's monthly planning meetings, even though she didn't have a decision-making role. The marketing department needed her for only a portion of each meeting, but they were never sure which part, so they asked her to sit through the entire meeting, just in case. How did she have the conversation?

She said: *I'd love to be available to you all day, but I am already in back-to-back scheduled meetings. I can clear out a two-hour window from 10 A.M. to 12 P.M. and will be at your meeting then. If you steer the agenda to cover my area while I am there, we could make the most of the time I have.*

Saying no doesn't meaning saying NO! You don't have to be blunt or rude when backing away from activities, roles, and obligations, work-related or otherwise. In fact, in a work situation, coming right out and saying no to your boss would likely be professional suicide. Some grace is necessary. And you will want and need to provide an explanation. But if you do it in a straightforward, practical, calm, and persuasive manner, your decision will appear not just logical but also in the best interest of your boss and the company.

Fear 3: Someone Will Try to Talk Me Back into It

If you've decided to say no to a commitment or role, be prepared for people to plead with you to change your mind. They'll weasel and cajole. "Come on, just this once" or "Just until the end of the year—it's hard to get anyone else to do this" or "No one else is as good as you" or "You're our ticket to success."

The temptation will be to buckle and offer to stay involved but on a more limited basis. Don't yield on the spot, unless you were prepared, before speaking with the cajoler, to take on a more limited role. Remember, getting out of a commitment that does not fit your lifestyle or vision is not an admission of incompetence or a signal of selfishness. It's a reflection of your ability to focus on your destination without getting distracted by the scenery along the way.

Here are a few examples of how to say no successfully to some common schedule fillers:

- *I'd love to, but I'm not taking on any new projects until my current ones are complete.*
- *I have a previous commitment. Thanks for thinking of me, though.*
- *That's just not on my focus for this year.*
- *This year, I'm focusing all my energies on family activities.*
- *I'm really flattered you think I'm the right person to handle the job. But I couldn't give it the level of attention that it really deserves at this point in my life.*
- *I'd love to have you visit, but I'm so up to my ears at the moment I just wouldn't feel good about the quality of the time I could give you. And that will make the visit less enjoyable for me.*

Practice saying no to a range of demands on your time in front of a mirror, so you can see how you are coming across. Check your body language and smooth any rough edges.

Heaving Regular Responsibilities and Roles That No Longer Fit

Obsolete roles and responsibilities can be the most challenging time attachments to heave. They represent not just actions but perceptions, and they require you to reframe how you see yourself and how other people perceive you. You need to recognize your complicity in becoming *the* caretaker, *the* go-to person, *the* confidante, and *the* chief cook and bottle-washer in the first place. *You* set things up in a certain way for a reason—at one time there was something you liked about this role. Freeing yourself from large official (or unofficial) roles and responsibilities presents the biggest opportunity for time gain because these tasks usually occupy a significant portion of your schedule.

When it comes to getting rid of a role or responsibility, you will usually have to communicate with a boss, friend, or family member and make the case for why you are moving on. Sometimes you must get buy-in from that person before you delete the activity from your schedule and your life. Occasionally this requires you to demonstrate how the particular role or responsibility would be better handled by someone else. Perhaps you could suggest whom. When removing stagnant roles/responsibilities from your schedule consider how much time you are currently losing to the obligation, your own attachment to the role/responsibility, and other people's attachment to the role you play. Decide which option (delete, delegate, diminish) makes sense in context of your theme, then execute on your plan.

There are quite a few traps to look out for when attempting to permanently heave responsibilities that have become burdens. If you aren't prepared to avoid these traps, any role you try to release may keep coming back to you. Below we will examine five common scenarios that would prevent you from permanently heaving an obsolete role and how to overcome them.

- I didn't realize what my role meant to me.
- I delegate, but tasks keep coming back to me poorly done.
- I just like to help people.
- I don't want to send the wrong signal.
- It's hard to sever ties.

Script 1: I Didn't Realize What My Role Meant to Me

You met Shirley, 38, in chapter 5, a professional working mom who came home every night to what felt like a second job, being solely responsible for all household chores: meal planning, cooking, cleaning, laundry, shopping, clutter control, vacation planning, etc. Her husband and kids had offered many times to help out, but she insisted on doing everything herself. Unfortunately, the time she spent housekeeping prevented her from spending any quality time with her husband and kids. Ultimately she decided she was willing to give up the solo caretaker role, and she identified laundry and grocery shopping as treasures.

Time lost: An analysis of Shirley's time showed that taking care of all household chores was costing her 40 hours per week. (6–11 P.M. nightly, and at least 5 hours each Saturday and Sunday). It really was a second job!

Her attachment to the role: We discovered that Shirley's attachment to the role of doing all the chores for her family was an unconscious way to say I love you. Her mother had been the perfect 1950s June Cleaver stay-at-home mom—and although Shirley was a working professional, she was still unconsciously following that old-fashioned model.

Other people's attachment to the role: Shirley's family didn't feel a strong attachment to her role as the perfect mom. In fact, they wanted to spend more time with her and saw her chores as their biggest obstacle. They, too, were ready for a change.

Heave solution: Here's how she did it: *Hey guys, I want to make some changes in how we spend our time together. Every night, and for most of the weekend, I am unavailable to sit quietly with any of you, to talk, relax, and have fun, because I am always so distracted with household chores. It's not your fault. I have volunteered myself to do all this work and have been afraid to ask for any help. I think I've been trying to be like my mother—showing my love by taking care of the house. But I think we all know that it isn't very effective. You feel neglected, and I miss having any quality time with you. We need a new approach and I need each of you to pitch in and help so the workload is not too much on any of us. How does that sound?*

What else did she do? Shirley divvied up the chores among the family: the kids set the table, fed themselves breakfast and picked up their own toys; her husband dropped off the dry cleaning, washed the kids' sports uniforms, packed their lunches, and handled most of the clean-up after dinner; and Shirley grocery shopped and did most of the cooking and weekly laundry.

Time cleared: 19 hours/week

Script 2: I Delegate, but Tasks Keep Coming Back Poorly Done

Shirley was freed from her role as sole caretaker because she shared household chores with other family members, who were able to complete the tasks just as easily as she could. But what happens when you have trouble delegating effectively?

Nanette's company helped doctors handle their insurance billings. She'd launched the business after her first son was born and it was thriving, six years and one more kid later. Her theme was *Freedom and flexibility*—now she wanted to work fewer hours. The biggest point of entry in her schedule was managing her staff. She did not feel management was her strength, and as a result she felt she was limiting the company's growth. Nanette's underdeveloped delegation skills caused a bottleneck in the business—she wasn't delegating fast enough, and when people turned in work that needed improvement, Nanette found it easier to make the fixes herself than to try to figure out how to coach someone to a better performance. Trying to learn to be a better manager would've taken *even more* of a time investment on Nanette's part (taking classes, reading management books), certainly not moving her any closer to her vision of *Freedom and flexibility.*

Time Lost: 18 hours per week

Her attachment to the role: Nanette felt it was her responsibility as CEO to take on the role of manager, even though it wasn't an her strength boss.

Other people's attachment to the role: Nanette was an easygoing boss.

Heave solution: Nanette's husband was a retired military man who had joined the business to help increase revenue. We agreed she should delegate 100 percent of the staff management to him. Her only hesitation was that he had a very different style; maybe he was a little too direct with the staff. Here is what she said to him: *Honey, I need your help. You are a much better manager than I am. Would you take on my staff management responsibilities? That would free me up to do more selling and customer interacting. One thing, though; I think your style is a little more direct than mine. I think that we will benefit from that, because I tended toward the extra soft and sweet—and we see how far that got us. Sometimes, though, your directness can be perceived as rudeness. Please try to choose your language a little more carefully. The labor market in our town is so small—we want to make sure that our staff not only does the work, but also feels happy coming to work every day.*

Time cleared: 16 hours/week

Script 3: I Just Like to Help People

Many times, we get caught fixing other people's problems, especially in a work environment. Constantly mentoring others through difficult situations can keep us bound to a role we want to relinquish.

You'll recall from chapter 5 that Trevor had recently been promoted but felt an attachment to his previous position. Trevor found doing his staff's work was easy to do and immediately measurable, whereas his new responsibilities—strategic thinking and planning—offered less instant gratification. Sitting at his desk quietly for hours felt a little lonely and disconcerting.

Time Lost: 20 hours

His attachment to the role: Trevor was using old behaviors to mask the discomfort and insecurity he was feeling in his new job.

Other people's attachment to the role: Represented their insecurity about their own skill levels.

Heave solution: Trevor would have to wean himself and his staff off of their mutual attachment to his assistance. Here's how he did it: *You know, you came on board nine months ago, and this was a whole new field for you. You've been an excellent student and have come a very long way. Having me sit in on your vendor calls, which we initially did for training purposes, is no longer necessary. As long as I stay on the calls, the vendor directs their questions to me, and you end up deferring to me, when you could have easily come up with a very viable answer on your own. From now on, I want you to handle these calls on your own. Sure, you'll make some mistakes—we all do, but that's the way we all learn. I'm happy to spend a few minutes with you organizing your thoughts before each call, and then we could spend ten minutes after each call to debrief so we can talk through what worked, what didn't, and what you discovered. That's the best way for you to become a master, and you are well on your way. I have complete confidence in you.*

What else did he do? Encouraged staff to share more information with one another in order to problem-solve on their own. He also set up a chat room on the company's internal website for his staff, which his assistant could oversee. At weekly meetings, staff members presented their work so that other team members were aware of who was doing what. When staffers did need his guidance, he asked them to come to him not only with questions, but also with two or three possible solutions. Then all he had to do was respond to their ideas and guide accordingly.

Time cleared: 15 hours/week

Script 4: I Don't Want to Send the Wrong Signal

Whenever you work with other people, it's easy to become trapped in water cooler conversations that eat away your day and leave you bogged down in nonwork-related details about someone else's life. Getting out of this role can be particularly delicate when you have developed a genuine friendship with the person who corners you with conversation, or when you feel like you're the only emotional outlet for someone going through a difficult time. But remember, relationships are best served by honesty. If you cringe each time your colleague heads in your direction, you're doing a disservice to the relationship by begrudgingly engaging in a tight-lipped conversation at an inappropriate time.

Brenda's longtime assistant, Roxanne, chatted Brenda's ear off with personal matters. Aside from her chatterbox tendencies, Roxanne excelled in every other area of her position. Brenda tolerated the daily banter for years but finally felt like she wanted it to stop.

Time lost: 4 hours/week

Her attachment to the role: Brenda genuinely cared about Roxanne and felt invested in her general well-being. She was afraid to appear rude or inconsiderate by cutting these conversations short.

Other people's attachment to the role: Roxanne counted on sharing her personal stories each morning with her boss. She saw Brenda more as a true friend than as her manager.

Heave solution: Brenda needed to have an honest conversation with Roxanne: Here's what she said: *Roxanne, we have worked together for years and I really enjoy our relationship. It's rare that you work with someone you can also enjoy on a personal level as well. Lately I've been frustrated because I feel overwhelmed by my workload, but I'm also interested in hearing about what's going on in your life. How about instead of taking time away from our workday (because I know we both have a lot to get done), let's make a point to go to lunch together or grab a glass of wine after work at least once a week to catch up. That way we won't feel cheated by having rushed conversations during the middle of the workday. How does that sound?*

What else did she do? Brenda also found other appropriate ways to make Roxanne feel appreciated outside of their routine lunches or drink nights. Brenda made sure to check in occasionally on other "life details" (parents' health, husband, etc.) and always offered to grab Roxanne a coffee (or snack) whenever she ran out.

Time cleared: 4 hours/week

Script 5: It's Hard to Sever Ties

When you work in an environment that values teamwork and face-time with colleagues, it can be difficult to release the "go-to" person role—you don't want to give the impression that you are less committed to your work. Families and groups of friends also have a go-to person—it's the one who coordinates events, plans activities, keeps everyone in touch, bails others out of tricky situations, and listens no matter what. Being the go-to person is exhausting.

Remember Caroline from chapter 5? She was struggling with her transition from a behind-the-scenes role as an analyst to a more public (and social) role in training and development. Encouragement from a senior partner during her annual performance review convinced her to go after a position in a different department. Prior to his suggestion, she'd taken on the role as the go-to person for her boss and about 100 other people, as a way to compensate for relationships she craved and the lack of personal interaction her official job provided. Who had the time to write up a proposal? Caroline. Who could other people call during budget season to run training classes? Caroline. Who knew the exact person running corporate compliance in the China office right now? Not Caroline—but she would spend two hours finding out. She was like the "information desk" at the mall.

Time lost: 20 hours/week

Her attachment to the role: Caroline was devoted to her company and hated the idea of disappointing anyone (even if the responsibilities she stopped taking on were never really hers to begin with). As overwhelming as being the go-to person was, it gave her a sense of self-worth and accomplishment. There was no guarantee her new role in training and development would be able to deliver that feeling.

Other people's attachment to the role: The majority of Caroline's colleagues supported her decision with one exception: her boss. He interpreted her move as a personal betrayal. The moment he learned Caroline was applying for a new position, he called her into his office and reamed her out. "How could you do this to me?!" he roared. "After all this time. This is a bad decision, Caroline; you'll never do as well anywhere else."

Heave solution: Caroline remained calm, despite her roaring boss. Here's what she said: *I have been a loyal member of this department for seven years.*

I've made a solid contribution and have never once shirked any responsibility. It is within my right to pursue career development opportunities in this company and outside of it. I am ready for a new challenge and have every right to manage my own career in the firm. Then she added with great confidence in as constructive a tone as possible, *You have not been the easiest person to work for. You don't have a sense of work boundaries, don't express appreciation for work well done, and you are extremely stressed at all times, which makes our work environment less than rewarding. This isn't my primary reason for moving on, but you should know that it has not been a cakewalk.* To her astonishment, her boss paused, and thanked her for her honesty.

With that, Caroline made a quick exit to the ladies' room and promptly lost her lunch.

What else did she do? Caroline's new job required her to relocate from Boston to San Francisco and in preparation for the move, she switched from being the person to take on all the extra work herself to a more creative, efficient way of supporting her colleagues. She started helping people in a more consultative role—she offered advice and guidance, instead of taking on each project herself.

Time cleared: 20–30 hours/week

Keep Your Schedule Open

You'd be surprised at how liberating, and perhaps disorienting, it will feel to *not* have several hours of tasks, roles, and responsibilities just sitting there waiting for you. It's like driving without the handbrake on or running without ankle weights.

Think back to a time just before you went on a long vacation. In anticipation of two weeks away from the office, you probably zipped through piles you'd been ignoring for months because you wanted to leave town with a clear, unburdened conscience. That worked because you were inspired by visions of vacation. You pictured yourself laying on the beach, trekking through the mountains, meandering through an art museum, or eating a leisurely dinner, and wanted to have your head clear to enjoy the time off. That's the feeling heaving the obligations in your schedule should create on a permanent basis; but visions of vacation are replaced by visions of your theme.

You must be brave to get rid of the things that are no longer serving you and leave space for something of a different texture, consistency, depth, and feeling. At first Caroline felt like there was a gaping hole in her schedule. She panicked—maybe this job change was a horrible mistake? "I won't tell you it wasn't lonely at first, when there weren't one hundred emails waiting for me when I woke up in the morning," she said. "But now, instead of connecting with people in order to make the work meaningful, I feel more connected to the content of the work itself. These days I have only forty emails, but they are actually connected to my job." Everyone who has gone through this process finds their life calmer, richer, deeper, and much more rewarding. You will have less on your plate, but each thing will be far more meaningful to you.

Sit tight through whatever panic you feel and savor the feeling of having an empty schedule and free time on your hands. Don't rush to refill your days with a grab bag of activities—it doesn't allow for surprises or enable you to be open in the moment and ready to receive whatever comes your way. The new flexibility and openness in your schedule just might invite an activity relevant to your new vision. The next step of **SHED**, Embrace Your Identity, will help you imagine how full life can be if you don't *prepack* every waking moment with time clutter—any old volume of tasks, roles, and responsibilities that fill the space but add no true value to your life. You are ready for the next step of **SHED**, where you'll fortify your confidence, reconnect to old passions, and relearn how to take (and enjoy) life as it comes.

Heaving Habit Attachments

A habit cannot be tossed out the window; it must be coaxed down the stairs a step at a time.

—Mark Twain

In chapter 3, you identified at least one time-stealing habit as a point of entry and in chapter 6, you discovered the value in that habit. Your goal now is to expunge this habit from your life permanently so you can use the time and energy formerly devoted to your habit to pursue your theme. Most clients I work with guesstimate their bad habits steal between 30 to 40 percent of their time every day. Gaining 40 percent more time and energy would be a huge win—no matter what your theme is. **SHED**ing habits may be the most difficult realm to conquer, but it is one of the most powerful ways to free yourself to pursue and attain your dreams.

Old Habits Die Hard

Bad habits wreak havoc on our ability to **SHED** because they are often the root cause of our cluttered spaces and overcrowded schedules. Without modifying or breaking whatever the bad habit might be, we are prone to keep falling back into it, succumbing to the temptation to fill up our space and our schedules again and again, winding up back where we started, no matter how much we have heaved along the way. It's like being in a boat with a nickel-size hole—no matter how much water you bail, unless you patch the hole, the boat will keep filling up with water.

While heaving in all three realms involves clearing space to make room for something else more in tune with your vision for the future, the method for heaving habits is a little bit different from that for physical or schedule clutter. Instead of leaving the time (or space) typically occupied by your old habit empty you will fill that space right away, rather than later on. As we learned in chapter 6, bad habits are usually an unconscious indication of a healthy need. By using the urge to indulge in the habit as a "need indicator," you can immediately fill that need with a better choice.

You'd be surprised how much mental energy is currently devoted to worrying about your habit, promising yourself you will kick it, and then beating yourself up for not having the willpower to stop.

As we discovered in Finding Habit Treasures, the first key to breaking a habit attachment is recognizing that there's (usually) nothing wrong with the *need* the habit serves; it's the negative behavior inherent in the habit itself that has to go. In this chapter, you'll learn to heave the bad habit by replacing the need in a more healthy and self-honoring way.

Unsurprisingly, most of the five key bad habits we're dealing with here create time clutter:

- Mindless escapes
- Procrastination
- Perfectionism
- Chronic lateness
- Workaholism

Remember the distinction. Heaving time attachments involves letting go of commitments *already* in your calendar or on your to-do list. Heaving habit attachments involves eradicating the behavior that puts many of those time attachments on your plate. The formula for detaching yourself from each of these—and resisting the temptation to fall into these habits again—consists of the following:

1. Raising your awareness of when the habit kicks in; its "trigger point."
2. Finding a more direct and more constructive replacement to meet the need the habit was serving.

We will apply this formula to each habit, using examples from some of my clients whom you met in chapter 6: Rajit, Jackie, Diane, Lynn, and Lily. We will explore several techniques I call "habit breakers" that have worked in each situation. If the habit you'd like to release is not one of the five discussed here, you can still use the same formula to address it.

How Long Does It Take to Break a Habit?

Most studies agree that it takes about 90 days to form a habit and 30 days to break it. So build enough time into your schedule to give heaving your bad habit a real chance to succeed.

Mindless Escapes

Breaking the habitual dependence on mindless escapes such as incessant TV watching, video games, email checking, internet surfing, shopping, etc., takes a huge amount of will, tolerance, and commitment. These mindless escapes are so insidious, and you may be surprised how much they wiggle their way into your day. That's why breaking your addiction can be a bit unnerving. When taking on a mindless escape, you've got to be brave, and the best approach is cold turkey.

Go on a mindless escapes diet. For thirty days, swear yourself completely off television, computer games, random shopping sprees, internet surfing, and, dare I say it, constantly checking email. One caveat: going cold turkey on email, if you are employed or running a business where people are dependent on you to get back to them, may get you in trouble. Instead, put an auto-reply on your email that alerts the sender that you may be away from email for several hours at a time, and if their matter is urgent, instruct them to call you, providing your number. Then allow yourself only three to four email sessions per day maximum at specifically designated times. No matter how bored or anxious you get in between, no matter how unproductive you feel, stay off email at all other times. The point of this complete break from your habit is that it turns it from mindless to mindful. Within a week of your "fast," you'll begin to find better uses for that time.

Rajit, a senior executive from a software company, who I introduced in chapter 6, was determined to break his habit of checking email every ten minutes, a habit that was preventing him from fully engaging with his design work and with colleagues. And even his family. He tried the modified "cold turkey" approach by establishing four email processing sessions throughout the day. In between, he engaged in other activities, remaining fully focused. He said the first week of implementing this technique actually felt like physical withdrawal. The first couple of days he couldn't get anything done because he was so worried about what he might be missing in his email box that he practically had the shakes. The third day was a little better, but he still felt a little queasy and didn't have much more to show for his day at the office. By the fourth and fifth days, he was able to concentrate on activities other than email, was highly productive, and promised he'd never go back. He described passing a certain threshold, where all of a sudden he remembered what it was like to actually "be in the moment." He found everything he did more gratifying. By heaving his mindless email habit, he went from "instant gratification" to "complete gratification," re-engaging in everything he was doing in a more productive way. He got significantly more done every day, at a much higher level of quality, and completed things more quickly and thoroughly.

Raise Your Awareness Device

Mindless escapes tend to provide instant gratification, an immediate, easy distraction from boredom or anxiety. The first step is to stop yourself in your tracks whenever you feel pulled toward a mindless, unproductive activity. For the thirty days you are focused on breaking this habit, raise your awareness by putting a STOP sign on the device of your vice. Stick a brightly colored Post-it on your computer monitor or tape a note to your remote or video game console. If you tend to use shopping as a mindless escape, put a big red note in your wallet where you keep your credit cards or cash.

When you see the sign, stop and ask yourself, What do I *really* need right now? What am I bored by right now? or, What am I feeling anxious about? Then reach for something healthier to address your need more directly. The goal in heaving a mindless habit is to redirect your energy toward a more mindful solution. Ultimately, like Rajit, you are seeking to replace instant gratification with more complete gratification.

Track your successes every day in your planner, calendar, or journal. Keep notes indicating what causes you to reach for your mindless escape, and see if there is a pattern to the events or circumstances that trigger the need. In this way, your bad habit continues to be of value, because each trigger point moment leads you to more insight into areas you need to address. You may discover that there are certain activities you need to drop because they cause you to reach for your habit, or others where you need to develop new skill sets in order to tackle them with less worry.

Ask a friend or family member to be your buddy and touch base with them every night to report your results. Being accountable to someone motivates you to hold strong and fight the temptations to slip back; you'll want to make a good report each night. It's also fun to have someone to celebrate with and cheer you on when you're making the most of your time. Habits are easier to break with the help and support of a friend.

Mindless Escapes Habit Breakers

Engage more deeply. If you are feeling bored or anxious, challenge yourself to stay put by engaging more deeply in your current activity. Boredom kicks in when we go on "automatic pilot." Listen more closely to the conversation at hand, pay extra attention to the visual cues in your surroundings, notice the sounds and scents of the space you are in.

Replace instant gratification with complete gratification. Figure out what is causing you to reach for your "fix," and then address the need completely. If you are bored, find something more stimulating to do. If you are feeling anxious, do something to alleviate your worry directly (talk to a friend, take a deep breath, go for a walk, write in a journal, read an encouraging quote). See if there is a particular activity that causes you frequent anxiety.

Create healthy alternatives. Decide specifically what you'd prefer to spend that time on, even if these are only temporary replacements, until you find something more permanent to fill the time you free up by heaving mindless escapes. Try listening to music, reading a book, or doing something creative, like drawing, knitting, or working on a crossword puzzle. Unless you are mindful and protective of the open space, your schedule will fill up anyway—likely with the habit you thought you eradicated.

Place alternatives within easy reach. You need to divert your attention quickly from the temptation with an easily accessible alternative. If you've decided to listen to music instead of watching TV, put your top 10 CDs in your stereo system. If you plan to read, write, or do quiet work instead of checking email, decide specifically what project you'll be working on in advance, and make sure you have the necessary materials on your desk or in your briefcase.

Reward yourself. No matter how many tries it takes you to get all the way to 30 days, once you make it, reward yourself. The long-term reward, of course, is the absence of the activity, but also treat yourself to something tangible, like a night out, a spa treatment, or a round of golf.

Heaving Procrastination

Procrastination is all about stalling—putting off starting or finishing something out of anxiety rather than logic. It's also a way of making your life more difficult. Some people, like Jackie from chapter 6, thrive on the adrenaline rush that comes from leaving things until the last minute. It's thrilling to pull victory out from the jaws of disaster. For others, procrastination is born out of worry about their ability to do the job well.

As with most of my procrastinating clients, to break Jackie's habit we needed to work *with* her preference for tight time frames, rather than *against* it. The foundation of this strategy would be to reveal Jackie's "concentration threshold" for each subject of avoidance; in other words, the optimal window of time for each type of task that spurred her to action. Understanding these time frames would allow us to plan Jackie's days in a way that would eliminate all the wasted time in her schedule.

My concentration threshold theory works like this: Give yourself too small a window of time to get something done, you'll procrastinate because unconsciously, you know you'll never finish it. Give yourself too big a window of time, and you'll never get started because you feel like you have all the time in the world.

Jackie and I listed all the types of activities she procrastinated on (there were seven categories in all). Then I asked her to describe how much time she spent on each category of tasks when she was actually up against the deadline. Here's what the list looked like:

Task	Time Devoted When on Deadline
Any writing task	3 hours
Phone calls to clients to touch base	1/2 hour
Strategic planning	1 hour
Mentoring time with staff	3/4 hour
Bill paying	1/2 hour
Household errands and chores	3 hours
Catch-up calls to friends	1–1/2 hours

We structured Jackie's week into windows of time appropriate to each activity. For example, whenever she had a writing task, she would schedule herself only a three-hour window of time. She'd have to get it done in that window, whether it was due in two weeks or tomorrow. She'd spend thirty minutes paying bills, whether it was a week before they were due or the day before she'd get hammered with late fees. These were her concentration thresholds.

By building mini-deadlines into her schedule based on these ideal units of time, her procrastination habit disappeared. And within two weeks of our work together, she finally ordered that sofa (which had been on her to-do list for three years!).

Raise Your Awareness

Since procrastinators will wander into all sorts of activities while they are in "avoidance," a STOP sign on the object of their distraction won't work to raise awareness. There are too many possible distractions! Instead, they can try wearing a rubber band around their wrist or tying a red ribbon to something they use every day (like the refrigerator, their bag, or their planner) as a reminder during the thirty days it takes to break their habit. That physical signal will help keep them mindful that they are on a mission to change something.

Procrastination Habit Breakers

Discover your optimal time frames. Figure out how long you'd spend on something if you were doing it at the last minute. Then give yourself ONLY that amount of time, but schedule it much earlier. Setting aside either too much time or not enough time can make you procrastinate. Tighten or expand your time frames until you find what's right.

Choose the best time of day. Be at your peak energy when you tackle the things you tend to procrastinate.

Create bite-size chunks. Break overwhelming projects down into a series of smaller steps. If it's hard to start a project, try tackling the second or third step first, to get some easy momentum. Delegate pieces you find particularly challenging.

Get expert guidance. If fear of making a mistake or doing a bad job is what causes you to stall endlessly, get help. Reach out to a trusted advisor, talk it through with a friend, do a practice run or first draft, and run it by someone for feedback.

Stop when you say you will. We sometimes procrastinate by not finishing something when we are done, or working on something for an undefined amount of time, which makes it more daunting to get started the next time. Determine how long you'll give something, and stick to it. Set a timer. Give yourself 15 minutes to wrap-up, indicate your next action, and then STOP.

Choose to make your life easy. Putting things off until the last minute is also a way to throw unnecessary obstacles into your own path, making your life more difficult. That's an old belief system. Retrain yourself to believe things don't have to be so hard!

Heaving Perfectionism

In chapter 6, we explored Diane's attachment to perfectionism. Even after bailing from a corporate job to "slow down" and work in nonprofit, she found herself driving everyone in her new organization to reach excessively high standards. Instead of the nonprofit world dialing Diane down, she tried to dial them up.

Diane's biggest complaint was that she was so overburdened she didn't have *any* time to herself. Her perfectionism kept her volunteering to attend too many meetings, spending way too much time checking and revising the staff's work, and investing hours writing long memos to the executive director to appeal for big changes. Although she was pretty good about maintaining strict boundaries between work and home, she overpacked her evenings and weekends going above and beyond with family and household obligations. There were a million and one things she wanted to do to relax, but she never got to any of them. She always felt too responsible for making sure everything went perfectly at work and at home to ever "earn" time for herself.

A chronic overachiever, Diane didn't know how to gauge when enough was enough or how to keep things simple. Whether it was pouring over a program budget or cooking a week's worth of meals for her family, for Diane the shortest distance between two points was never a straight line, but leaping across tall buildings in a single bound. She wanted—*needed*—to kick the habit of making her life so difficult.

Raise Your Awareness

The hardest part about breaking this habit is that perfectionists tend to get so absorbed in what they are doing, so focused on polishing things to a fine finish, that the world disappears and time jettisons forward without their awareness. The first key to awareness is to be on the lookout for common indicators that you have lost your perspective.

One prime indicator is when you've hit the point of **diminishing returns**—where you've been working on the same paragraph, or scrubbing the same tile in the bathroom for what seems like hours. When progress slows to a crawl or when you've begun to glaze over, recognize that moment as an indicator that your perfectionism is kicking in.

Another red flag for perfectionists is the knee-jerk impulse to take over other people's work. Part of the reason Diane felt so exhausted at the end of each day was that she ran herself ragged striving to do the best in her own job, while also taking over other people's responsibilities and tasks the minute she was displeased with their work. Problem-solving sessions with her staff often fizzled into her feverishly working away on their projects while they watched from the sidelines. We trained Diane to recognize those moments as they were happening and STOP. If she felt the need for an impromptu staff training session, she'd have to walk away, come up with a grade teaching plan, and approach them later in the role of mentor, not do-er.

A third indicator that your perfectionism is kicking in is the presence of a certain panic based on the conviction that there is only one acceptable way to solve a problem. That sort of myopic view comes from the belief that there are only two possible outcomes on any issue—perfection or disaster. If you feel that panic rising, you know you have lost your perspective.

People you live or work closely with can help you raise your awareness of your perfectionism. Invite them to call you on your impulse to overdo things. Tell them how to alert you when they think you are obsessing, with a hand signal, a wink, or a line such as "I think there's a simpler way to do this." Then make sure you listen, and be open to alternate approaches to fixing problems. The key is resetting your own internal buttons of believing that there's only one way to do anything.

Perfectionism Habit Breakers

Devise three approaches. Before diving into any assignment, force yourself to come up with three possible approaches to every task— minimum, moderate, and maximum. This puts a conscious check on your impulse to turn every task—big or small, top priority or low priority—into an opportunity to conquer Mt. Everest. Be sure to opt for either the minimum or moderate whenever possible. You can always add a layer of polish after the minimum is done. This technique helps you recognize that there are more than the two outcomes of disaster or perfection.

Rephrase the question *"How* much *can I do?"* to *"How* little *can I do?"* Don't think that you are cheating. You are forcing yourself to think differently, preserving the time saved for other, more enriching activities. Keep a notebook of how you approached various tasks, and periodically look back at each choice you made, noting what the results were.

Drastically shift focus. Train yourself to take a break at the point of diminishing returns, and do something that completely takes your mind off the task at hand. If you were doing a mental task (like reading or writing), try something physical or social. If you were doing something interactive or physical, read something that helps you engage on a different level. If you walk away, but continue to obsess over the project in your mind, it doesn't really count as a break.

Stop doing other people's jobs. Create a sign on your computer or fridge that says "Don't do other people's jobs." Use this reminder to stop yourself in your tracks and ask yourself this simple question, How could I better use this time? Taking over people's jobs sends the wrong signal. Find something better to do with your time, and provide coaching feedback later.

Build in checkpoints. Predetermine natural progress breaks to step away from the work and come back fresh to evaluate it. Run your work by someone else before you get started again. Hearing their feedback can be encouraging, and you may be much closer to the target than you think.

Heaving Chronic Lateness

Like Lynn in chapter 6, the majority of the perpetually tardy are lost in their own web of turmoil and emotions, their lives filled with harried moments, near misses, and guilty apologies. They are so immersed in their own chaos that they rarely realize how inconsiderate their behavior appears to the people left waiting.

Raise Your Awareness

Obviously, the tardy need no tool to recognize they are behind schedule—the clock tells them, as does their racing heart. What they need to become aware of are the unconscious choices that make them late, which usually involve cramming in more to a day, an hour, a moment, than is physically possible. Latecomers are often referred to as time optimists, in that they are always overly optimistic about how much they can fit into a day. They also can get so absorbed in what they are doing, they lose track of the time.

Try the following techniques to raise your awareness of when your impulse to be late kicks in.

Become a time realist. Buy a stop watch and practice time estimating. For a solid month, put a time estimate next to every task on your to-do list. When you execute the task, use your stop watch to see how long it actually takes. Time yourself even for unplanned tasks you decide to shove in at the last minute. For example, if on the way to a meeting or party, you decide to make a quick unplanned run to a coffee shop, thinking "this will only take two minutes," time yourself. Put the actual time next to the estimated time and study the difference. Forcing yourself to examine how long things will take raises your awareness that time is not infinite and positions you to plan your schedule realistically.

Find out what your lateness does to others. The perpetually tardy stay in happy denial about the effect of their lateness on others. Raising your awareness can make you think twice before throwing your own schedule into turmoil. Be brave and invite the people you live and work closely with to tell you the truth. Ask them "What happens for you when I am late?" "How does my lateness effect you?" You may be surprised by what you hear.

My client Lynn was shocked to hear that getting her kids to school late every morning cost the rest of the class close to 40 hours of learning time each year. Her son's teacher explained how challenging it is to get a group of 30 second-graders focused every morning. When Lynn's son arrives late, the other children lose focus, and it takes the teacher another ten minutes to settle them down. Ten minutes per day is close to an hour per week. Multiply that by 45 school weeks, and the kids lose 40 hours of learning per year.

Step outside your own angst for a minute and understand what it's like to stand in the shoes of the people you leave waiting. Invite their honesty, and listen to what you hear. Choose one or two insights to be your key motivation for arriving on time.

Keep track of your successes in a journal. Everyday for a month, write down the number of times you arrive places on time, and the number of times you arrive late. Your goal will be to get to thirty days where you aren't late at all. Watching the "wins" along the way motivates you to keep going. By the end of the month, the benefits you are receiving from arriving on time (appreciative friends and coworkers, less stress, time to breathe) will be all you need to stay on track.

Chronic Lateness Habit Breakers

Arrive 10 minutes early everywhere you go. Instead of cutting it close and arriving just in the nick of time, where any derailment can make you late, plan to get there 10 minutes early to every appointment for 30 days.

Have something great to do while you wait. Fill any time you spend waiting with a highly absorbing, totally engaging task. Plan to get places early so that you can call a friend, catch up on a novel, do some paperwork, review your to-do list, listen to music, people watch, or write in your journal. You don't have to stop being busy. You can still keep a packed schedule if that's how you're most comfortable.

Use your cell phone alarm to indicate stop times. If you tend to lose track of time and forget to get off the phone in 20 minutes, or end the meeting in an hour, which sets off a domino effect on your day, set the alarm so that it goes off 10–15 minutes before it's time to go, reminding you to move on to your next activity.

Penalize yourself for being late. For the 30 days you are actively working on breaking this habit, carry around an envelope with 100 single dollar bills. Each time you are late, pay the person you kept waiting $1 for every minute you kept them waiting. If $1 doesn't motivate you, increase it to $5 per minute.

Change your excuses. Instead of coming up with a dramatic re-enactment of how many things went wrong on your way, state simply "I apologize for being late. I have a problem arriving places on time, and I'm working to improve it. I really don't mean to be rude."

Avoid the just-one-more-task syndrome. What prevents most latecomers from being on time is the tendency to shove in just one more thing—I'll just take this quick phone call before I leave (or marinate the roast, or write a quick thank-you, or clean up the kitchen). Stop! Don't do it. For 30 days, make it a rule that you may not add any new tasks at the last minute if it wasn't on your plan.

Ban all rushing. As you plan your days, or the next couple of hours, or the upcoming hour, if you feel the only way to get it all done is if you rush, and hit no obstacles along the way, you have overbooked yourself. Your sense of needing to rush is the visceral signal that you're trying to do too much. Take one thing out of every rushed moment, and you will give yourself the breathing room you need.

Create a cheat sheet, how long things *really* take. Once you've studied how long things really take (using the exercise under Raise Your Awareness), write common tasks and their actual time requirements on an index card (Get out the door in the morning: 45 mins; food shopping: 2.5 hours; conversation with Mom and Dad: 30 mins, etc.), that you can refer to when planning your days.

Heaving the Workaholism Habit

Workaholics have an internal gauge that indicates to them how much they should work. It's not a formal articulated number, and they are barely conscious of it. It could be a certain number hours (e.g., 14 hours per day) or a set number of days (e.g., 6 days per week), or a general percentage of their time (e.g., 80 percent of their waking hours). One of the keys to breaking the workaholism habit is to establish a "setpoint." Consciously study and articulate your setpoint and then decide to reprogram your number. If you are used to working 7 days a week, change it to 6. If you are used to working 80 percent of your waking hours, shave that back to 65 percent.

Retraining yourself to switch work "off" sooner than you normally would in order to balance out your life is not easy. But it can be done. They key, as always, is to raise your awareness of when the tendency kicks in and replace the need to be industrious with something more healthy.

Raise Your Awareness

Most workaholics will admit that there is a "witching hour," a threshold they cross at the end of the day, between 5 to 7 P.M., when they know they should stop. They've done plenty for the day and should be winding down. But workaholics have a hard time stopping in that moment and making the transition to their personal lives. They tread water for about half an hour, and then find something new to start, an extra bit of reading or writing an email, poking around on a project. And then they're in for several more hours. As a workaholic, this is the moment you have to be aware of. Decide now when your witching hour is and set your computer or cell phone alarm for two hours before that. That alarm becomes your awareness tool, signaling you that you have two hours to wrap up your day and start winding down.

Instead of a red STOP sign, workaholics needs a green GO sign—on their computers, on their briefcases, by the door of their office—that says *GO, do not do any more work, do not check your email one more time, do not start cleaning out files . . . just leave.* Getting out the door is the hardest part for most workaholics. Once they cross that threshold, they are fine.

For the thirty days you devote to breaking the workaholism habit, engage a buddy to call you when it's time to go and make sure you get out the door. My client Lily, who we learned about in chapter 6, charged her assistant with the task of alerting her to wrap up her day. She gave her assistant a $10 bonus for each day she successfully got Lily to leave on time. (And Lily felt responsible for honoring her assistant's efforts to get the reward.)

Workaholism Habit Breakers

Reward someone for helping you leave on time. Whether it's your assistant, a coworker, or your entire team, pay someone to make sure you get out on time for the first 30 days. If you make public your plans to change, several forces will converge to assist you. One, your coworkers will all hold you accountable for following though on your commitment. Two, *you'll* feel obliged to make good on your public promise. And three, the people you work with will learn to stop bringing you assignments at 6 P.M.

Leave with a buddy. Find someone at work who leaves earlier than you do, and make sure you leave when they do. It's better to attach yourself to a person who has no trouble leaving at their designated time than a fellow reforming workaholic.

Set measurable goals for your leisure time. Workaholics tend to find satisfaction in the tangible results they receive from getting work done. Fill your new time off with goal-oriented activities that you can check off a list when complete—seeing four plays or films per month, going to the gym three days per week, learning to play an instrument, mastering the fine art of baking. You may not always need to be so task-oriented in your time off, but this allows you to make the transition more gradually.

Develop yourself in unexpected ways. Trust that if you pursue some interest outside the office (e.g., strolling through a museum, walking through the park, or finding a hobby) you will still be industrious. By becoming an enriched human being you provide a great contribution to the world. It's a slower payoff, but no less meaningful.

Tempt yourself with the familiar joys. You may have high hopes to start all kinds of new activities in your time off, but when you are first trying to break this habit, start with the things that are most familiar and fun. It's harder to sacrifice the things that bring you the most joy than an activity that is unfamiliar.

Make time-specific commitments immediately after work. Arrange dinner with a friend, go to a concert, schedule a trainer at the local gym. Enroll in a continuing education course, spin classes, etc. Anything with a hard start time that will force you to put a cap on your work day. If it's something you've prepaid for, all the better.

Recognize the benefits of recharging. Next time you feel tempted to stay late rather than go home to relax, breathe and slowly count to ten. Picture your kids' faces, your friend's smile, the joy of sitting on the couch next to a loved one and getting a backrub. Give yourself permission to relax, and remember it will make you more productive tomorrow.

Be Generous with Yourself

Heaving habits may be the toughest type of attachments to heave, but they also open up an unimaginable amount of space, energy, and time to pursue your true potential. So give it time, and remember to be extremely generous with yourself throughout this process. Bad habits tend to originate from deep anxieties, insecurities, and fear. As you release them, you will continue to unearth old beliefs that you can examine and expunge. More than any other form of clutter, **SHED**ing habits is the gift to yourself that keeps on giving— offering the opportunity to fortify your self-confidence in a permanent way.

Feeling a little disoriented without your habit? That's to be expected. Turn to part 4: Embrace Your Identity to fortify who you are, without the old habits to define you.

Embrace Your Identity

There is a vitality, a life force, an energy, a quickening that is translated through you into action. And because there is only one of you in all time, this expression is unique. And if you block it, it will never exist through any other medium and will be lost.

—Martha Graham

At the very moment a lobster sheds its exoskeleton or a bird sheds its feathers, the animal is inherently vulnerable, in danger of being preyed upon or suffering exposure to the elements while it waits for new growth to replace the old. That's why its nutrition and environment become even more important; it needs to fortify and protect itself. Humans have a similar experience in this **SHED** process. Embracing your identity is a way of fortifying and protecting your self-confidence while you remain exposed to the world without the comforts of your old "shell." Rather than clutching backward for your old attachments or rushing to fill your space and schedule with objects and activities that aren't quite right, this step will help you stay open in this moment so you can grow.

In many ways I believe that to Embrace Your Identity is an extension of the inside-out philosophy that guides all my work. My approach to organizing and time management exalts the individual. Clean spaces and Swiss-clock efficiency don't motivate me, even if they are sometimes the natural results of the systems I design. My primary goal is to create a system that supports each individual's unique personality and needs. Once a customized program is in place, my clients are free to deliver on their talents and skills; in effect, to be the best possible version of who they are.

Most people feel an odd combination of feelings after Heave. On one hand, there is a sense of energy, hope, and an incredible lightness of being. Newly free of the things that were weighing you down, the anchor has been lifted and you are free to sail. On the other hand, being unanchored brings with it some degree of discomfort—it's not uncommon to feel lonely, anxious, and afraid. You aren't in the same place you were when you started the book, but you haven't exactly arrived at the place where you want to be.

In this moment of ambiguity, it will be tempting to reach back for the things you heaved because those symbols of your past feel more familiar and, therefore, "safe." Don't. You must find the courage to stay empty-handed. You are no longer in the job that once defined you, or your old neighborhood, or surrounded by old objects or unhealthy behaviors—these are the crutches you've outgrown. You don't need those external reminders of who you are anymore because your identity comes from *within*. You generated your old objects, schedule, and behaviors, and you'll create a new environment connected to your new vision, when you're ready.

You may also be tempted to lunge forward, to jump to decisions about what you want to do next. But it's too soon for that as well. You need to give yourself a period of observation where you don't do anything but get centered with yourself. The best thing you can do right now is take advantage of this unhampered moment to reconnect with the things that make you, you, no matter what—your unique character, experience, strengths, resourcefulness, intelligence, and contribution. In this section, I will guide you through practical and introspective ways to uncover and celebrate who you are. Your period of observation can last a few days to a few months, and it is an exciting opportunity to study and strengthen your confidence, discipline, and receptivity to find the best opportunities for yourself as you move forward.

Chapter 10, Trust Yourself, will help boost your confidence by reminding you of the many times you've survived being empty-handed before, uncovering evidence of your ability to achieve your theme and your true personality, regardless of your possessions.

Chapter 11, The Five Disciplines, will guide you through a series of exercises to help you get out of your own way and deliver on your potential.

And chapter 12, Savor the Moment, will help you develop the muscles to stay fully engaged in the present so that you can recognize and enjoy new opportunities.

Embrace Your Identity is the shortest step of **SHED**. It will take between a few hours to a few weeks of concentrated effort to fortify your confidence and feel secure with yourself before you can find your way forward. Once that happens, embracing your identity will be second nature. Use the insight and encouragement you gather in the next few chapters to fall in love with yourself again and to renew your engagement with life. As Brooke crooned, "I feel like I'm ten again!"

Chapter 10

Trust Yourself

*Look well into thyself; there is a source of strength which will
always spring up if thou wilt always look.*
                                        —Marcus Aurelius Antoninus

Woody Allen once said, "Ninety percent of life is just showing up," and I
couldn't agree more. Good things are bound to happen when you show up
and remain open as the most grounded version of yourself—confident, focused, and alive with energy.

But it's not always so easy to access that heightened state of mind. Having
the confidence to trust yourself is always a bit harder when you are without
the comforts of the familiar, floating in the undefined space between your
past and your future. Heave literally required you to clean house. Without
your familiar objects and activities, this new space can be downright disorienting. Instead of stagnating on the what's-happening-to-me feeling, focus
instead on this opportunity to separate who you are from what you do or
own. Have a little trust in yourself.

In this chapter, I'll guide you through three exercises, to reassure you
that:
1. you are resourceful—you've survived unfamiliar territory before;
2. your capacity to achieve your vision for the future is inside you
3. you are a very interesting and unique individual.

Have you seen *Rocky*, the 1976 classic starring Sly Stallone as Rocky Balboa,
the "Italian Stallion"? I want you to get the image of Burgess Meredith, the
actor who plays Mickey (Rocky's coach) in your mind. He's an old, craggy,
curmudgeonly fellow who pokes and pushes Rocky, rooting and hollering—
"Come on, Rock! Go get 'em. Let's go!" Right now, you've got to be your own
Mickey. Find a way to coax yourself off the ropes, into the ring.

You've Got the Resources to Be on This Adventure

The most nerve-wracking thing about any new situation is feeling uncomfortable in your surroundings. Without the familiar symbols, it's hard to tell which way is north. One of the most helpful things to do, whenever you're in a situation like this, is to remember that you've succeeded at new things before, at flying without a net. Let me give you a few examples.

Jennifer, 52, was delivering a keynote address at a major sales conference. She set the notes for her speech on the podium before the audience entered the room so she could bound onto the stage empty-handed, looking all the more confident.

At the anointed hour, the conference chairman climbed to the podium to welcome the audience and introduce Jennifer. He then gathered his notes, shook her hand and exited, stage right. Once at the podium, she launched into an impassioned introduction from memory, drawing the audience in with a few funny stories before laying out her goals and objectives. Five minutes into her presentation, she glanced down to reference her notes only to find that—"uh-oh . . ."—her cheat sheets were gone. The chairman had accidentally scooped them up with his own notes and unwittingly ferried them off the stage.

A moment of pure terror ticked by in silence as she realized her "crutch" was gone. Steadying herself at the podium, she found a well of courage, realizing that she knew the truth of what she wanted to say. Within seconds the feeling of absolute panic transformed into a surge of self-confidence, freedom, and exhilaration. Jennifer continued to speak, pulling it all from within, flying without a net.

Think of a time when you spent hours preparing a cheat sheet or guidelines to support you through a challenging situation, and then couldn't find them, or hesitated to have them in front of you, so you got stuck pulling on what you knew? You can surprise yourself with the knowledge that you have inside you when the crutch you'd prepared disappears.

Everyone has stories of courage, each a little different.

Tony, 49, had a difficult family life growing up. His dad battled substance abuse and his mother was chronically depressed for several years and was never able to hold down a job. Tony knew from an early age that he would have to go it alone. At 16, he sweet-talked his way into a job as a carpenter's apprentice—even though the age requirement was 18—by saying he'd worked with his uncle on construction jobs for years. (This happened to have been a big embellishment, if not an outright lie.) Once he landed the job, he was terrified. But he kept his eyes open, his mouth shut, and learned on his feet. Now, almost thirty-three years later, he owns his own construction company.

Picture the times in your life when you've found yourself in a brand new situation with no roadmap, where you had to wing it, and came through with flying colors?

Here's one more example.

Jacob, 31, had been a rising high school senior when he decided he wanted to combine his two passions: travel and volunteerism. His parents supported the idea and helped him find a nonprofit organization that worked with local authorities and organizations to build infrastructure in rural villages all over South America. It was an entirely new experience for Jacob (he was a city kid from a privileged home), so as his departure date drew closer, he was overwhelmed with fear and excitement: "I hope I can do this," he gulped.

Upon arrival, Jacob was assigned to a bunk in a one-room cabin with another volunteer from the program—Betty, a retired 59-year-old architect from San Diego, not exactly the roommate he had in mind. Besides a backpack stuffed with T-shirts, shorts, a few pairs of jeans, underwear, shoes, a toothbrush, and a book or two, he was on his own. No TV. No cell phone. No computer. Nothing. All he had were his wits, his experience, his (still developing) Spanish language skills, and an open and capable mind and body.

By the end of his three-month commitment, Jacob had assimilated into village life and found a way to make a significant difference. He helped members of the community identify and plant commercial crops, worked with other program volunteers to build a new school, and dreamed up a business plan to generate revenue for the village over the long term.

Think of a time when you felt in over your head, but hung in there and found a way to adjust and succeed despite your inexperience.

Tip: Be Inspired by Your Kids

If you are a parent facing an empty nest and daunted by the new adventure you are about to embark on, gain inspiration by watching your youngsters make their way out into the world with very little but the clothes on their back. That sense of adventure is inspiring and worth mirroring as you embark on your own new exploration.

Exercise 1: Remember Your Resourcefulness

At this stage of the **SHED** process, you've released your old attachments and are moving toward some ambiguous future. You're not sure what you're doing, you have no clear roadmap, and it can be a little scary. Stay strong. Stick with yourself.

Everyone, no matter how young or old, how limited or extensive their life experience, has arrived in a situation empty-handed and succeeded despite their lack of experience, preparation, or creature comforts.

There are plenty of instances in life, remarkable and otherwise, that require us to figure something out on our own. Right now, I want you to identify a point in your life where you walked into a situation unprepared and were required to "just go for it," like Jennifer, Tony, and Jacob. When were you really vulnerable, stuck without your usual security blankets or overwhelmed by the newness of an experience? It doesn't matter what you choose. The only requirements are that: (a) you were unprepared for the experience, and (b) you had to rely on nothing but your own inner resources to get by.

See if answering the following two questions can get you started. Apply each question to your personal life, then to your work.

- The hardest thing I ever did on my own was _____.
- I never thought I would survive _____, but I did.

Many of our most salient memories are from early in life. Look at the list of "firsts" below and see what memories it triggers:

- First day of school
- First time you moved away from home
- Going to college
- First job interview
- First job
- First apartment
- First time buying a house or car
- First client
- First solo trip to anywhere
- First trip abroad
- First time at sleepaway camp
- First time you ever gave a speech
- First time you went on a date
- First assignment at a new school or new job
- First meeting you ever ran all by yourself

Also give yourself credit for any really tough times. Maybe you survived a difficult divorce, beat cancer, or saw a parent through Alzheimer's. Or your most challenging circumstance so far may be work related: an impossible boss, a grueling travel schedule, or unemployment. Take heart in knowing you found a way to get through it, pulling on inner resources you didn't know you had.

Whatever life experience you identified with above, it's safe to assume that the skills you used to get yourself through that situation have served you well in others, too. Think back through the experience and list the things you did really well. The qualities you come up with are just a few that make you, you.

As each of my clients recounted their stories of being in a dicey situation with no predefined script, we reflected on the inherent qualities they had inside them that got them through those ambiguous moments.

Jennifer got through that speech because of the fact that she is inherently knowledgeable, empathetic to audience's needs, naturally funny, and very articulate.

Tony survived the "silent apprenticeship" because he is smart, a quick study, hardworking, has excellent instincts, and knows when to keep his mouth shut.

Jacob was able to make a contribution to a village far from home because of his courage, his perceptiveness on what the true issues are, and because he's resourceful, an excellent listener, and connects well with people.

They each bring these traits to any new, uncomfortable, or difficult situation. This is just who they are whenever they show up.

Reflect on a significant moment in your life where you had to wing it and list the characteristics that got you through it. What skills and talents are inherent that you know you can rely on?

_____

_____

_____

_____

_____

You should keep in mind that your inherent skills will serve you now, too, as you move in the direction of your theme. You may be without the comfort of old, familiar objects and behaviors, but you are not alone. You've got yourself and all of the inherent qualities that make you, you.

Tip: Tell Your Story in the Third Person

Having a hard time identifying your coping skills? Cognitive psychologists have long studied the ingredients that make up an individual's personality, but only recently has the "life story," the narrative people tell themselves about who they are and why, started to get more attention. The results of a 2005 study by Columbia University researchers, published in the journal Psychological Science, _observed how participants reacted to a bad memory, like a difficult task, a bad breakup, or an illness. Based on their data (which included standard surveys administered before and after the recall exercises), researchers found that stories recounting bad memories in the third person were significantly less upsetting than those same stories told in the first person. I'll admit this might seem a little awkward at first, but give it a try. Tell the story of your "first" in the third person, as if it were about a girl named Rebecca or a boy named John. Removing yourself from your story allows you to be more objective, insightful, and empathetic of your experience. You'll likely be able to see more clearly what positive coping skills you demonstrated._

You Have It in You

We've said all along that your vision for the future isn't some random, far-fetched idea beyond your reach. Your desire has probably existed inside of you (however silently) for some time, knocking around in your brain, occasionally peeking through, but repeatedly relegated to the back burner. You are in a better position than ever to fully pursue your vision now that you have released your attachment to the stagnant and irrelevant stuff in your life that was distracting you. But that doesn't mean you won't experience some uncertainty. Actually, most people at this point in the process express a measure of insecurity regarding their vision—they are gripped by some self-doubt, wondering: *Can I really achieve this? Am I crazy to even dream this up?* These doubts are completely normal. But my experience is that our "themes" don't come out of nowhere; they have been brewing inside us all along, because of an innate value, skill, talent, desire that is part of our core being.

I'd be willing to bet that your theme represents something that has been important to you for quite some time. Searching your past to recognize the different shapes and sizes your theme has adopted in previous phases of your life will make it feel relevant and even more within your grasp. If you are wondering whether you can achieve your theme, you can find the answer by doing a memory sweep of your past. What is a memory sweep? It's a guided study of three key phases of your life for evidence of your capacity to express your theme.

Exercise 2: Memory Sweep

For the following exercise, begin by considering the question you are asking yourself: *Can I deliver on this theme?* In other words, Jay would have asked: *Have I ever put down roots?* If your theme is Self-expression, your question would be: *Have I ever been able to express myself?* Then think back through three broad sectors of your life: (1) early childhood (from birth through middle school); (2) young adult years (high school through college); and (3) adulthood (postcollege). For each of these three phases of your life, come up with a memory related to your theme. If, for example, your theme is Finding love, come up with a memory of when you found or felt love in each of those three periods of your life—it could be as innocuous as a third-grade Valentine's Day card or as serious as a long-term relationship in your midtwenties. As always, be specific. In your **SHED** journal or on a sheet of paper, write down your best recollection of that memory or experience related to your theme.

When you are done writing, look back over your stories and consider what made that memory so significant to you. Circle one word or phrase from each story that most directly answers the question, *Can I deliver on this theme?* It's usually the word or phrase that captures what made each memory most distinct or meaningful. Then try connecting the dots. Most times these words add up to an answer that will help to quell any inklings of insecurity you've been feeling about your vision. I've provided a few examples to get you started.

Kate's theme: *Freedom*

You first met Kate in chapter 2. She was considering ending her marriage for a while and finally decided, after seventeen years, that divorce was her only option. She was unfulfilled and unhappy, her personal growth stunted after too many years of accommodating her husband's needs and compromising her own. After so many years of repressing her own ideas about everything— weekend plans, the color of the bathroom tiles, the family car—she was excited to relinquish her role as chief accommodator and focus on her own needs.

Kate had been confident in her decision to divorce, but as she stood on the edge of this big change, she was overwhelmed with self-doubt. Her fear? *Would she know what to do with her newfound freedom?* Would she find a healthy, productive way to use it? Was it selfish of her to reclaim all that space for herself? I asked her to do a memory sweep of any time in her life where she experienced the freedom she was so hungry for. Here's the evidence of freedom she came up with from three different periods in her life.

Early childhood. "I did not experience much freedom growing up. My mom was a strict disciplinarian, full of rules and structure: 'This is what you do,' and 'This is how you do things.' Period. I was a survivor. I always had wells of patience and was able to adapt and be happy in any situation. The one (if only) freedom I had in childhood was deciding what to read. Through books, I escaped to *tons of places.* I went everywhere through books—different countries, different times in history, different characters' lives. I loved it."

High school/college. "I had the most freedom in my life by far during the eight years of high school and college. I experimented with a variety of activities in my teens and early twenties—drama, dancing, piano, softball—and received great feedback from my mentors and coaches in each arena. Every time I took a risk and tried something new, I succeeded. I craved the thrill of the try-out, loved being involved in different things with different groups of people. My biggest aha? My discovery that I had *so many interests* and could actually enjoy and excel at all of them. What happened to those years?"

Adulthood. "After graduating from college, I started out in the insurance industry before settling into my role with a financial management firm, where I manage the assets of high-net-worth individuals. It would have been easy to fall into the money trap—sacrificing my soul, clawing my way to the top, embodying the stereotype of 'the Street'—but I haven't. Somehow, I've managed to stay *true to myself,* evolving into a caring, nurturing advisor to my clients, while still climbing the ranks of corporate America. And when the economy plunged, my clients stuck with me because I've stayed true to who I really am."

Kate's burning question was, *Will I know what to do with this freedom?* We studied her three memories with this question in mind, and three phrases popped out.

tons of places   so many interests   true to myself

Connecting the dots. Though Kate never experienced a significant amount of freedom in her life, when she ever was able to explore and make her own decisions, she made the most of it. She escaped to *tons of places* as a child through her one outlet of books. In high school and college, her one era of true freedom, she marveled at the fact that she had *so many interests.* And even after college, when she began narrowing her choices, she still managed to stay *true to herself.* I had no doubt that she'd find a way to take advantage of her newfound freedom: escaping to different places, exploring new interests, and all while remaining true to herself.

Kate's memory sweep is unique to her, because (quite obviously) she's the only person who has ever lived her life. Even so, there is something universal in her story. A desire for freedom, tempered by the apprehension of being totally untethered, is a common emotion for anyone casting off old responsibilities, starting a new career, moving to a new city, or, like Kate, moving on from an unhealthy relationship. What pieces of yourself do you recognize in Kate's story?

Let me give you another example.

Cheryl's theme: *Self-expression through words*

Youth is a time for self-expression, a time to try on different jobs and roles, relationships and activities, to see what resonates most true. A journalism major in college, by 27 Cheryl had already worked for several community newspapers, a few regional websites, and a small daily paper. She loved telling other people's stories, giving readers an opportunity to connect with one another over a shared experience. But she was bored with her beat, and the daily drudgery of articles about traffic accidents and police reports.

She wanted to experiment with topics of her own choosing, to do something more creative—to express her own ideas, and really explore who she was as a writer and a young African-American woman. She wanted to develop her own story ideas and look for outlets to sell them on a freelance basis. Her theme for the future was Self-expression through words.

During her Heave, Cheryl removed the television, which had occupied a corner of her bedroom, to create space and energy for writing. The TV had been Cheryl's primary tool of procrastination, one of the habits she'd felt was weighing her down. (Every time she sat down to write, she'd turn on the TV to "settle in." Twenty minutes of "settling" often turned into two hours of time wasted.) Now that Cheryl had the space in her room to write—and no TV to hide behind—she was experiencing a terrible case of writer's block. She couldn't figure out what to say, or how to say it, and worried whatever she wrote wouldn't be interesting enough to read. She was starting to doubt whether self-expression through words was even a realistic theme to have for herself. *Do I have anything interesting to say that people want to hear?* she wondered.

Together, we did a memory sweep through three periods of her life, looking for evidence of her theme in the form of any positive feedback she'd ever received about her own writing voice.

Early childhood. "I'd always been a wonderful storyteller; teachers often read my essays aloud in class as an example. In fifth grade, unprompted, I wrote a story about how hard it was to be a mom. (My mother, a single mom, struggled to pay the bills and stay out of destructive relationships.) I remembered my mother's tears upon reading the story, and how powerful and proud it made me feel to be able to elicit such a strong emotional reaction with my words. My mom shared the story with friends and family members, and people kept telling me that my writing was such an *advanced gift*, that I was insightful well beyond my age."

High school/college. "I was the high school yearbook editor and many friends enlisted my editing skills prior to submitting their term papers. During a semester abroad in London, I wrote an essay discussing *The Great Gatsby* by F. Scott Fitzgerald and the American dream. My professor thought my conclusions were thought provoking and a little unexpected, and as the essay was emailed around, it generated buzz among the student body and faculty. Later, as part of my work with my church's college ministry, I wrote a weekly editorial about the Sunday sermon, which was posted on my church's website. One of my pieces was distributed to the entire database (which included an international readership of more than 50,000 people) to great critical acclaim. I received complimentary emails from all over the world, encouraging me to keep inspiring people through my writing. People kept commenting that my ideas *translated well* across ages, nationalities, and life experiences."

Adulthood. "I've written and sold one freelance magazine article so far. It was the first freelance piece I pitched, and I was beside myself when the magazine accepted it. The topic was "overcoming convention" and the piece expressed my own fascination with the exclusionary conventions of religion; how people can feel apart from "faith" because they are uncomfortable with the structure it takes. The editor loved my portrayal of the 'space in between,' and felt the piece addressed a universal need to help people *across great divides* (religion, race, culture, socioeconomic status, politics) catch a glimpse of what it's like to be on the other side."

Cheryl's burning question, as you may recall, was, *Do I have anything interesting to say that people want to hear?* Studying her three memories with this question in mind, the following phrases stood out to me:

advanced gift   *translated well*   *across great divides*

Connecting the dots. Cheryl's memory sweep provided her with a resounding yes, yes, and yes. Her memories showcased overwhelming evidence of her talent and the broad appeal of her point of view. Her advanced gift made its first appearance at a very young age and clearly continued to shine. Her work translated well across cultures, and the things she was interested in writing about—helping people across great divides—had already received commercial recognition. Cheryl was struck by this discovery, "When good things happen, at the time you think that maybe they are random good luck. But looking at it all together, I can see the history, consistency, and presence of my 'self-expression through words.' " She was able to reconnect with the success and positive feedback she'd already received and allow those victories to bring energy and focus to her future work.

> ### Tip: Look Through Memorabilia
>
> To trigger a few key memories, try searching through some of your memorabilia; looking for evidence of your theme in old photo albums, report cards, yearbooks, essays, letters, emails, and journals. What insights do those items trigger?

Cheryl was at the beginning of her career, but her story is no less instructive. She was concerned that the world wouldn't accept (or honor) the theme she established for herself, Self-expression through words. But the memory sweep helped her see that the world had already affirmed what she wanted; she just had to slow down in order to translate the signals.

Here's one more memory sweep.

Caroline's theme: *Embrace my personal power*

You've already met Caroline. She was going through a job transition and struggling to release her old identity as the behind the scenes, "go-to" person. Caroline didn't know if she would be able to have as positive an impact in her new role as she did in her previous position. Her old job was all about output, process, and measurable results. Success in training and development wouldn't be defined by Caroline's ability to write a report or analyze data; it would be contingent on her knack for commanding an audience, communicating effectively, and building strong relationships. Her bosses believed she had those talents, but Caroline wasn't so sure. Her uncertainty about embracing her personal power was made ambivalent by her view of her mother, a powerful figure, who had never used her own power for good (she was a manipulative, negative force in Caroline's life). On some level, Caroline feared her own power would manifest itself in a similar destructive way.

Caroline's worry was: *If I embrace my personal power (my extraverted side), will I have a positive impact?*

She looked to her past for evidence of instances when she had a positive impact by just being her social, personable self.

Early childhood. "When I was a kid I loved to *entertain* a crowd. I was always rehearsing for an orchestra concert or drama troupe performance. I remember telling my mother, at the age of six or seven, that I absolutely had to wear sunglasses at all times. The reason? So my fans wouldn't mob me. I was a total ham."

High school/college. "Like many college students, I refocused my energies to social justice issues. I was attending an Evangelical Christian college in the late 1980s just at the beginning of the AIDS epidemic, and I felt strongly that there should be condoms available on campus (even though abstinence was the administration's preferred method of birth control). I launched a virtual *crusade* to make condoms available, which almost got me expelled. The old dean I bumped into randomly on the street, thirteen years after graduation, told me: 'I've always wondered what you ended up doing with your life. I figured you'd either be president or in jail by now!' "

Adulthood. "Finding a relevant experience in the years after college is harder, because for most of my career I've let my jobs define my power for me. But just recently, my company sent me on a three-week training tour. I visited eight offices in fifteen days and spoke to almost 1,400 people. The feeling that each presentation gave me was very similar to the feeling I experienced as a kid growing up in Christian revival tents, where the atmosphere was all about personal transformation. I was always in awe of the leader's ability to rile up a crowd. Yet, for each group I spoke to, my enthusiasm for the topic caused the audience to *transform* their thinking. Being able to persuade a room of people to change their behavior made me feel incredibly powerful."

Caroline's concern was: *If I embrace my personal power, will I have a positive impact?* The words that jumped out in response were:

entertain   crusade   transform

Connecting the dots. There seemed to be no doubt that left to her own devices, Caroline naturally funneled her innate personal power to have a very positive impact. Her personal brand of power included entertaining others, unleashing her passion and enthusiasm for important causes, and calling for transformation—actions that, added up, would likely do the world a whole lot of good. She felt reassured and encouraged that her personal power was very worth nurturing.

Complete Your Own Memory Sweep

Now it's your turn.

In your journal, first articulate any self-doubt that is coming up for you, as you ponder moving toward your theme. What question are you consumed by?

_____

Now, think back through the three broad periods in your life (early childhood, young adulthood, and postcollege years) for memories connected to your theme. You are looking for any evidence of your ability to fulfill your theme. For example, if your theme is Making connections, come up with specific memories of when you actually made connections in the past: made new friends, asked someone out on a date, or started a new relationship. Once you have written out your memories (one for each time frame) study your stories, and circle one primary word or phrase that pops out, essentially summing up the main emphasis of the memory in context of your question. The words and phrases you use to describe those experiences—the ones that make you proud or ring particularly true—are the words you should pay special attention to. Isolate three different words or phrases (one from each period of your life) and write them down.

_____ _____ _____

Then connect the dots. How do these words relate to one another and to your theme? Like Kate, Cheryl, and Caroline, you should be able to string together a story, summing up positive evidence of your ability to live your theme. It's been there all along.

Look in the Mirror

When feeling vulnerable, one of the most empowering feelings for all human beings is to be recognized and seen for who we are, for our core selves, separate and apart from what we do. **SHED**ing promises to help you connect to your authentic self, and here is a key opportunity to make that happen.

Remember our _Rocky_ analogy? For the majority of this chapter, you've been your own "Mickey," cheering yourself on by reconnecting to the things that make you, you.

But every so often an outside opinion is a good way to broaden your perspective and fuel your self-awareness. Especially when we are embarking on a huge transition, and a little unsure of where we are going, it's centering to know who we really are. It's not always easy to self-evaluate. If you've ever been shocked at the sound of your voice on a tape recorder, because it sounds so different from what you hear in your own head, you'll understand where I'm headed with this next exercise. The way we view ourselves is often a slightly muffled view—we don't really know all of the qualities people notice about us, because we are so focused on how we look to ourselves. And the truth is, most people are pretty hard on themselves. If we want to know who we *really* are, it can be helpful to explore what others see in us. For evidence of your authentic self, I want you to "look in the mirror," and see your reflection based on how other people see you. Asking a few friends, family members, and acquaintances for their impressions will provide insight into the broad qualities, talents, and skills you suspected are there, but doing so will also alert you to talents and characteristics you didn't know you had.

Exercise 3: The Adjective Game

Ask a minimum of six and a maximum of fifteen people from the following list to share three to five words to describe you. (Warning: asking people might make you feel a bit sheepish at first—whether asking in person or via email—but trust me, the payoff is well worth any initial anxiety you feel about asking people to do this.) The objective here is to reach out to a variety of people who are generally positive, who know you in different ways, and see what consistent themes come back to you. Ask for words from:

- Immediate family member
- Extended family member
- Close friend
- Acquaintance
- Coworker
- Boss
- Direct report
- Colleague

- Client
- Neighbor
- Local merchant (dry cleaner, shop owner, landscaper, etc.)
- Community member (church, synagogue, team, book club, etc.)

Assemble into one document the adjectives people send you and look for recurring words. Observe what words are repeated several times. Of the remaining words, group synonyms. For example, words such as *smart, intelligent,* and *wise* might go together, while *gentle, soft-spoken,* and *shy* could be grouped under another heading. Finally, note the unusual words that were mentioned only once but caught your eye—these are the aspects of yourself that someone is noticing but might not be fully expressed all the time.

Added up, these adjectives are a snapshot of you reflected back through the eyes of others. This is who you are, with or without your clutter, a peek into your core self.

Let me give you an example, to show the power of this exercise.

After twenty-two years at home with her kids, Donna, 50, was gearing up to reenter the workforce. She'd worked as a paralegal prior to motherhood and figured a job as a legal assistant in a firm or working in a law school library were her best opportunities for gainful employment. Her theme for the next phase of her life was *Connections*—she wanted to be out and about, see and be seen. But of course breaking out of her shell was a little scary. Donna emailed her request, "If you were to describe me, what three to five words would come to mind?" to eight friends, family, and acquaintances. She felt a little shy with the first email, but then got into it, and was surprised how generous and quick people were with their replies. The very fact that people wrote back so quickly was a burst of love for Donna. Here's how people responded:

Person Asked	Adjectives Describing Donna
Mom	courageous, energetic, generous, charming, sentimental
Madeline (old, close friend)	smiling, bright, helper, wise
Emily (sister-in-law)	articulate, passionate, brave, complicated
Marta (friend)	funny, insightful, warm, smart
George (owner of her health club)	positive, active, persistent
Richard (her son's friend's father)	resourceful, ever-evolving, articulate, caring

Olivia (six-year-old niece)   nice, fun, pretty

Sheryl (hairstylist)   competent, insightful, warm, graceful, charming

Jonathan (husband)   energetic, warm, positive, genuine, beautiful

Once all the responses came in, I advised Donna to consolidate the words and transfer the most common sentiments, as well as the ones she found most interesting (or surprising), to a small index card that she could tuck into her purse. Any time she needed a shot of confidence, she could whip out the card. Here's what Donna's glance in the mirror looked like:

Common sentiments

1. Positive
2. Charming
3. Smart
4. Passionate
5. Funny
6. Energetic
7. Articulate

Interesting mentions

1. Graceful
2. Genuine
3. Beautiful
4. Complicated

What if the words people used to describe you weren't what you were hoping for or expecting them to be? Use the feedback for further reflections. In fact, it's a useful insight. You are what you express—the people you reached out to acted as a mirror, reflecting whatever you send out into the world back to you. If nobody on your list said a particular word, like *stylish* or *enthusiastic*, it doesn't mean you don't also embody those traits. Perhaps you haven't given those characteristics as much expression as you thought, or maybe you need to ask a different set of people—be sure to include a mix of people you know very well along with people you are less close to. We share different parts of ourselves with different people. It's the sum of the images that communicates back what the world sees in you. If you want certain traits to be recognized make a conscious effort to give them louder, bolder expression.

Yup, I Can Do This

By this point, you should be feeling much more connected to your authentic self, and confident and clear about who you are apart from your old stuff.

Armed with memories of past experiences, you know you can handle whatever life throws at you because you've navigated in new territory before. It's easy to pin a couple of victories on "knowing the right people" or just "dumb luck," but when evidence of your capacity emerges again and again, there's no denying reality. Your ability to fulfill your vision for the future is no fluke—you've had it in you all along. And the outside perspective gained from family, friends, and colleagues should have you feeling buoyant and connected to the most ebullient parts of your personality. You don't need a wall of clutter, a packed schedule, or your old bad habits to hide behind. You can stand in this moment, unanchored from your past, heading for a positive horizon. All you need is you.

Next, we'll investigate obstacles to delivering on your unique qualities, talents, and skills, and we'll explore solutions to help you get out of your own way.

Chapter 11

The Five Disciplines

*One's only rival is one's own potentialities. One's only failure is
failing to live up to one's own possibilities. In this sense, every
man can be a king, and must therefore be treated like a king.*
                                                    —Abraham Maslow

The last chapter was about building your confidence and being your own
personal "Mickey." But before you go calling me Pollyanna—always looking
at the positive without acknowledging the full picture of what makes you,
you—this chapter is about getting real and, if necessary, giving yourself a little
tough love. It's one thing to divine your unique qualities, talents, and skills;
it's quite another to possess the discipline to deliver on those core attributes.
Unfortunately, most of us distract and detract ourselves from delivering on
our true potential to one degree or another by diminishing our talents, deni-
grating our experiences, and succumbing to self-doubt. In short, the journey
to personal fulfillment is a process of constant self-actualization, and it's beneficial to know where you trip yourself up, so you can do something about it.

Self-sabotage can prevent you from living as your most authentic self,
which, in turn, makes it even more challenging to achieve your vision for the
future.

Consider this chapter an opportunity to discover what could hold you back
from delivering on your theme, and learn to "get out of your own way."

Self-assessment: What's Holding You Back?

Below you will find thirty statements that will assess your ability to deliver on
a key set of behaviors. Indicate how accurately each statement reflects you by
circling the appropriate number.

1 = Never true
2 = Rarely true
3 = Sometimes true
4 = Usually true
5 = Always true

	Never	Rarely	Sometimes	Usually	Always
1. Once I set a goal, nothing can stop me.	1	2	3	4	5
2. I can tolerate moments of ambiguity while creating something new.	1	2	3	4	5
3. If I don't see results right away, I am patient and diligent.	1	2	3	4	5
4. When I hit an obstacle, I find multiple ways to overcome it.	1	2	3	4	5
5. I'm pretty optimistic—confident that most things work out.	1	2	3	4	5
6. I'm adaptable, able to adjust to many situations.	1	2	3	4	5
7. My home/office is organized—I can find most things quickly.	1	2	3	4	5
8. I keep good track of everything I have to do and don't forget commitments.	1	2	3	4	5
9. I'm a good planner, always looking ahead to anticipate what's coming.	1	2	3	4	5
10. I easily break overwhelming projects into manageable steps.	1	2	3	4	5
11. My space feels calm, nurturing, and comfortable.	1	2	3	4	5
12. I'm realistic about what I can accomplish in a day and I plan well.	1	2	3	4	5
13. I feel relaxed, open, and confident around most people.	1	2	3	4	5
14. I work hard and I feel entitled to extraordinary success.	1	2	3	4	5
15. I avoid getting bogged down in unnecessary guilt.	1	2	3	4	5
16. If I make a mistake, I can forgive myself.	1	2	3	4	5
17. I feel comfortable asking others for help when I need it.	1	2	3	4	5

18. I'm willing to try anything; fear of failure
    doesn't hold me back.   1   2   3   4   5
19. I make healthy choices when eating.   1   2   3   4   5
20. I exercise regularly.   1   2   3   4   5
21. I get enough sleep every night.   1   2   3   4   5
22. I get regular doctor checkups and care.   1   2   3   4   5
23. I never feel victimized; I know my needs
    and get them met.   1   2   3   4   5
24. I pamper myself on a regular basis.   1   2   3   4   5
25. I avoid overcomplicating my life with drama.   1   2   3   4   5
26. I don't let excessive worry or anger consume me.   1   2   3   4   5
27. I feel settled and focused in my life.   1   2   3   4   5
28. I surround myself with supportive, loving
    relationships.   1   2   3   4   5
29. I'm able to maintain my interest in things.   1   2   3   4   5
30. My priorities are crystal clear.   1   2   3   4   5

Scoring

Total your points for each discipline (see below) by tallying your answers to each group of six questions. For example, for questions 1–6, if you circled a 2 + 3 +5 + 5 + 1 + 2, your total score for Determination would be 18. (Note that the highest possible score in any group is a 30, answering each question with a "5—always.") Then read on to interpret your scores.

1. **Determination.** This involves the patience, optimism, and work ethic to see things through to the end instead of being easily defeated. Do you start projects but never finish them, or throw your hands up in the air when the going gets tough? How easy would it be to derail you from your vision for the future?
   Questions 1–6: *Score_____ out of 30*

2. **Organization.** Being organized creates an environment that brings out the best in you, because it allows for a free flow of information between you and the world. Disorganization is limiting, debilitating, and distracting. It prevents you from making the biggest impression you can on the world because you can never find what you need; you plan

your days poorly and never have a minute to think. Are you in danger of being derailed from your vision by your disorganized ways?

Questions 7–12: *Score_____ out of 30*

3. **Self-confidence.** Self-confidence plays a multifaceted role in our ability to deliver on our uniqueness. It begins with trusting our point of view and being willing to engage with the world fearlessly, to learn, absorb, and grow. It continues with the intrinsic belief that you deserve happiness and fulfillment.

Questions 13–18: *Score_____ out of 30*

4. **Healthy habits.** Add impeccable physical, mental, and emotional care to years of devoted training and sheer talent and *bada-bing*—an athlete is positioned to deliver a powerful performance. What do you think you'd be capable of—physically, mentally, emotionally—if you were in peak form?

Questions 19–24: *Score_____ out of 30*

5. **Attention.** Gravitating toward complicated dramas or allowing yourself to be distracted by excessive worry, anger, or unhealthy relationships is a sandbag on human potential and a vision-killer. How would your life be different if you stayed focused on your goals and never gave this other stuff the time of day?

Questions 25–30: *Score_____ out of 30*

Interpreting Your Score

Total of 6–10: Overhaul needed. A score of 6–10 in any discipline means it is a challenge for you, and there is quite a bit of room for improvement. When it comes to delivering the best version of yourself, in this case, *you* are the one holding *you* back. Now that you have pinpointed the areas that need work, you are in a position to improve and change the game. Focus on these disciplines right away, tackling them one at a time, and you will see yourself start moving toward your vision.

Total of 11–20: Getting there. It's common for each of us to land in this middle zone on many disciplines. You've achieved quite a bit in your life but know in your heart that you could be doing much better; you need to get out of your own way. Study the elements of the discipline that tripped you up, and use the tips below to sharpen your delivery in this area. A few incremental changes in each discipline will make your journey more fulfilling and rewarding.

Total of 21–30: Signed, sealed, and delivered. You're doing pretty well in that discipline—good for you. You are a high achiever who gets to most destinations you set for yourself; you have a good handle on this area. Still, you are always ready to get better. Study the disciplines where your score was less than a perfect 30, and make the appropriate adjustments in your life to clean those up. Consistency in your discipline to deliver will ratchet up your experience a notch and make the road even smoother. It'll be fun for you to see how far you could go with no self-imposed obstacles.

Fulfilling your potential allows you to make the contributions only you can make. Consider it a gift to the world. Once you realize and accept your capacity to make a unique contribution, perennial neuroses (like self-doubt and impatience) suddenly diminish in scale and power. Allowing yourself to be consumed by self-doubt seems like a silly, wasteful exercise when you could be giving the world something so much more powerful.

Below you'll find a more extensive description of each discipline followed by tips on how to improve your ability to deliver on each one.

Discipline 1: Drive and Determination

When my father, one of the most determined people I've ever known, had a heart attack, we weren't sure if he was going to make it. As he lay in intensive care, the doctors discovered that he'd also had a stroke—a one-two punch, a devastating blow. I looked at him in that hospital bed, so weak, willing himself to take a breath, and wondered if I'd be able to get myself up if I'd ever been knocked that far back. He hung in there, and within about ten days, they moved him from the intensive care unit to a regular room.

As a result of his stroke, he was unable to eat or walk on his own, the most basic functions to maintaining quality of life. He began physical therapy, but after three weeks, the doctors and insurance company gave up on him, saying his progress was too slow. They moved him out of acute rehab into a nursing home, a profoundly depressing environment that seemed to me like a warehouse where people went to die, not to recover.

But every day my dad did the hour of physical therapy the nursing home offered and even smuggled in a private physical therapist who worked with him an additional hour each day. He did every exercise he was taught; whenever I came to visit, I'd watch him struggle to move his fingers and toes and practice his swallowing exercises. In five months, he got himself home. And once he was home, despite all the experts' predictions, he taught himself to eat, walk, and truly enjoy life again—providing unconditional support and guidance to others, and always making sure people around him were having fun and felt loved.

From a distance, you recognize determined people by their achievements. But if you are lucky enough to be close to a determined person, you know that each achievement is made up of a million different tiny steps. Determined people have an ability to face one moment at a time—to do battle with an individual obstacle as it comes up, without losing sight of the bigger goal. Problem solvers by nature, they are people who can't resist tackling each challenge they encounter.

Determined people are driven by a vision, so with each challenge they face, there is something guiding their efforts. They also appreciate the power of options, recognizing that there are many different paths to their final destination.

Optimism and faith are also behind every determined individual. Never allowing themselves to feel victimized, they trust in the power of the universe (whether that's God or karma or the energy of the human imagination) and the belief that there is always the *chance* for success.

Every time I spoke to my dad in the nursing home I told him he was an extraordinary role model. He'd shrug and say, "I'm just doing what I can for myself and we'll see." He was willing to work on the problems each day, with no guarantee of results.

Determined people work hard, putting in the time and remaining tolerant of the ambiguity that is part of the progress of moving toward any goal. Almost no challenging task ever goes exactly as planned, nor is there such a thing as "instant results." There are moments you get stuck, hit plateaus, run into walls, feel stumped. Determined people wait it out. They don't bolt when the going gets tough because they trust that clarity will come eventually. Working makes them feel alive, gratified, stimulated—indeed, life is a project to be worked through and enjoyed.

How Can I Improve My Drive and Determination?

If you want to boost your drive and determination factor even higher, here are some suggestions:

1. **Surround yourself with determined, successful people.** One of the best ways to learn about determination is through osmosis, and spending time with "determination" role models will demystify the process. You may think success comes easy to those who achieve great things; you assume they have extraordinary talents and skills accounting for their success. But up close, you will witness them wrestling with challenges, getting frustrated, periodically becoming disheartened, but never being discouraged from their ultimate goal. They always get up off the mat with a new idea, looking for another path to their desire.

2. **Seek inspiration in the arts.** Go to museums and study the work of great artists. Read up on their backgrounds and listen to the audio tour. Artists are some of the most extraordinary role models of determination, driven by vision that seems impossible to squelch. Did you know that Auguste Rodin (the famous French sculptor) had several works that were commissioned, then rejected? In fact, his piece *The Gates of Hell* was commissioned by the French government only to be canceled before it was complete. But Rodin was so personally invested in solving this artistic challenge that he kept working on it. For twenty-four more years. Many of his most recognized sculptures—including *The Thinker* and *The Kiss*—were all part of the *The Gates of Hell*. Read biographies of people who interest you. Listen to music, go to see plays,

read novels that will inspire you. Travel. Observe the many ways others approach the world so that you can picture possibilities beyond your immediate point of reference.

3. **Picture success.** Really vividly. Imagine a point ten years from now where you are exactly where you wish to be. What are you wearing, where are you living, who are having dinner with, what's filling your days? Visualize getting exactly what you want, and act as if you're already there. Whatever that is, write it down. Being afraid to say what you want or choosing to downplay your goals—as if you don't really care if you achieve them or not—can derail you from success.

4. **Practice makes perfect.** Pick an activity known to demand determination (like golf, knitting, or crossword puzzles) and go at it. Practicing your ability to conquer with something small will give you greater perseverance when you're dealing with bigger challenges in life.

5. **Boost your optimism factor.** Develop a stronger connection to your own spirituality, personal philosophy, or community, in order to help you step back and gain perspective. Ponder some belief in the power of the universe to support you and reward you for your efforts. There's nothing more reassuring than the sense that you are not alone, that you're part of something larger than yourself.

Discipline 2: Organization

When you're physically organized and good at managing your schedule, you make the most of your time, space, energy, and money. And of course, being organized makes almost anything possible, because all of your resources can be invested in the pursuit of your dreams.

Some people believe organization is about neatness or rigidity or a "one-size-fits-all" solution, but if your system is designed properly, the opposite is true. Organizing isn't about neatness; it's about function. And organizational systems can be as unique to an individual as his own fingerprint. The key is to custom-design your system around your natural habits and the way you think so that it brings out your best self, rather than restricting you. A good system will help you optimize your resources, interests, and passions *and* be easy to maintain. Being organized (in your physical space) is as simple as being able to find what you need, when you need it, and to feel comfortable in your space.

Good time management involves the ability to plan systematically and anticipate your needs. It requires you to know yourself exceedingly well: your energy cycles, natural energy sources, the length of time you can focus on any particular task, and what you are good at. It also involves the ability to adjust your schedule, break down overwhelming projects into manageable parts, and delegate effectively.

How Can I Improve My Organization?

Organizing and time management don't come naturally to many people, but they *can* be learned. When you are ready to apply these tips to your own space and schedule, the key is to think function—not neatness:

1. **Custom-design your system.** Don't copy anyone else's system—not your boss's, your spouse's, or your best friend's. You don't think like they do, so why would you want a replica of their system? Think about your own goals, habits, and style, and design your system accordingly.

2. **Think kindergarten.** A kindergarten classroom is the perfect model for organizing any space or schedule. There are clearly defined zones for each activity—a spot for reading, a place for napping, and an arts and crafts corner. For more information on adapting my activity zone model to your space and your schedule, read my first book, *Organizing from the Inside Out.*

3. **Organize the basics first.** Your handbag, briefcase, and/or wallet are the most frequently accessed reflections of your ability to organize, so get those together first. At home, jump-start your sense of control by tackling your entryway, the bathroom, and your underwear and sock drawers. These are the most frequented areas in most homes, and organizing them will take the least amount of time. Starting with those

key areas will give you a new daily sense of freedom and control. The rewards you reap will likely inspire you to tackle a bigger organizing project later.

4. **Study yourself.** Highly organized people know themselves exceedingly well. Become a nonjudgmental student of yourself and determine your optimal conditions for peak performance. Track your energy cycles, noting the times of day when you have the most/least energy, when your energy starts to fade and what activity (a phone call, chat with a friend, catnap, reading the newspaper, exercising, drinking a glass of water) acts as a natural energy extender. Use a stop watch to time yourself doing routine tasks (at home and work) so you know how long they take. To study more about your personal relationship to time, read *Time Management from the Inside Out.*

5. **Learn your concentration threshold.** What is the ideal amount of time you can focus on reading, writing, paperwork, leisure, cleaning, exercising, or a meeting? Is it four hours or forty-five minutes? Once you know how long you are able to focus on a particular activity, you can set yourself up for success. Plan tasks that won't be either too much or too little for the time you have available. For more tips on how to boost your productivity and mental energy, read *Never Check E-Mail in the Morning.*

6. **Hire a pro or find a friend.** Organizing can be difficult, because you get caught up in questioning your own needs (or changing them all together), so you never even get to setting up your system. You'll have an easier time getting organized if you get an outside perspective. A friend or professional will take your needs at face value and help build a system around them. For referrals to a professional organizer near you, contact www.napo.net.

Discipline 3: Self-confidence

Have you ever been to a party where the group is having a lively discussion and you've got an idea—but you hesitate to speak up for fear that it's so obvious that you'll look like a fool for offering it? And then, of course, someone else says the exact thing on your mind, and everyone thinks he's brilliant. And you kick yourself, thinking, *Why didn't I just come out with it!*

I've always thought Hans Christian Andersen's story "The Emperor's New Clothes" was a tale of confidence. The little boy was the only person willing to speak the truth—*the emperor was naked*—while everyone else claimed they could see "invisible" clothes, for fear of looking stupid or incompetent.

Confidence starts with being willing to be the only person to see something in a particular way and sharing that point of view. Confident people are also willing to take risks and fail, because if something doesn't work out they don't see it as a character failure. They are gentle with themselves and don't beat themselves up unnecessarily over errors or missteps. Confident people are armed with the objectivity to evaluate what is in their control and what isn't and have reasonable expectations. Willing to give themselves credit for trying (regardless of the outcome), confident people embrace the learning opportunity a mistake or failure presents, adding those lessons to their arsenal of skills and tools.

There is a difference between being self-confident and being arrogant or feeling entitled. Confident people are optimistic, believing in their own power to make things happen. But they never hesitate to ask for help if outside input will improve their chances for success.

Confidence as children comes from feeling loved, appreciated, valuable, and deserving. Unfortunately, not everyone grew up in such an emotionally idyllic environment. Even well-intentioned parents may have sent mixed messages caused by their own deficit of confidence. Driven by their own concerns and doubts, they may not have installed confidence in their kids.

When you lack confidence, you are plagued by self-doubt. Self-doubt can lead you to hesitate when it's time to express yourself, articulate what you want, and ask for help. This in turn can keep you from going after your vision, or having the courage to remain empty-handed until your new direction becomes clear.

How Can I Improve My Self-confidence?

1. **Surround yourself with pillars of confidence.** Seek out people who exude self-confidence, demonstrate optimism, and seem to have no

issues over allowing themselves to succeed. Try to find more than one person who meets these qualities. Having a variety of influences will expose you to the common behaviors of confident people, from which you can forge your own style of self-confidence. You are a reflection of the people (coworkers, bosses, friends, family) you spend the most time with, so choose wisely.

2. **Get a pet**. Animals give unconditional love and they have a unique way of absorbing your woes and providing comfort by being just so darned appreciative of you. A pet makes you feel valued, important, understood, and accepted for exactly who you are. It can be grounding. *The New York Times* published an article summarizing several academic studies that documented the benefits of owning a pet. Advantages include lower blood pressure, lower triglyceride and cholesterol levels (than non-owners), and a 3 percent decrease in heart attack mortality—in combination, those factors alone work out to 30,000 lives saved annually!

3. **Volunteer.** Step away from your own troubles and help others in need. Read to hospital-bound children, visit a nursing home regularly, plant a community garden or work the line in a soup kitchen. Making a contribution and feeling a sense of appreciation from others can be a big confidence booster. It gives you a perspective outside yourself and allows you to expand your view of the world and your place in it.

4. **Join a group activity.** Self-doubt often takes over if we spend too much time in isolation, just thinking about our limitations. Get adventurous and join an activity that forces you to interact with others. Take a class, join Toastmasters, sign up for a tour where interacting with others is built into the experience. Being exposed to a wide variety of people helps you put yourself in perspective.

5. **Live an impeccable life.** Low confidence creeps in when you don't feel good about all the choices you've made. It's hard to feel confident if you avoid doing something you know you should do (like writing a

presentation or paying the bills), have told a white lie (perhaps about starting that presentation), or put less effort than you could have into a project or activity. That doesn't mean don't have fun. It means you should follow your inner sense of truth and integrity, always. Don't make promises if you're not sure you can deliver and follow up on everything you say you will do.

Discipline 4: Healthy Habits

When I give speeches on time management and productivity, on average 80 percent of the audience fesses up to suffering from sleep deprivation, lack of exercise, mediocre-to-poor eating habits, and years without a doctor's visit. Of the five disciplines, developing healthy habits, is the easiest to get assistance with (health and fitness is a whole industry, for goodness' sake), yet for some reason, it's not any easier to initiate change.

The moment we get busy, taking care of ourselves is usually the first thing to go. We often put caring for others and job responsibilities first. Many of us take our bodies for granted, pushing ourselves to the limit, basically ignoring our physical and emotional needs until our bodies scream out and demand attention.

Healthy habits begin with physical care: boosting the quality and quantity of your sleep, building exercise into your weekly routine, and eating nutritious foods that are right for your body and fit your lifestyle. Although these activities take time, people who invest in their physical care are usually able to get more done over the long haul than those who push themselves on five hours' sleep, too busy working or caring for others to take care of themselves.

Beyond the basics of physical care, having healthy habits means listening to your body, knowing when it needs to recharge and honoring that need. If you've worked a long, hard week and need a day to yourself just to unwind, do what people who take good care of themselves do; they take the downtime, knowing it will pay off on the other end. And they take vacations, too. Play your body like an instrument, knowing when it needs to work, think, rest, and play. With practice, you'll be able to care for yourself in the ways that bring out your very best self. The payoff? Energy that you can use to do what you love.

How Can I Improve Healthy Habits and Self-care?

1. **Change your relationship with sleep.** Do you think of sleep as the end of one day, or the beginning of another? I've found that people who get too little sleep think of it as the end of the day (which they don't want to end), while good sleepers think of it as the beginning of the next. Good sleepers plug themselves in like a cell phone to recharge for tomorrow. Build relaxation into your evening routine to help yourself wind down an hour or two earlier than you usually go to sleep: listen to music instead of watching TV; read novels or poetry instead of nonfiction or the newspaper; drink a cup of soothing herbal tea and dim the lights.

2. **Get the oxygen flowing.** The federal government, various medical associations and insurance conglomerates recommend physical exercise, and now you'll hear it from me, too. Find a form of exercise you enjoy and start slow, aiming for thirty minutes three times a week: walking, dancing, running, cycling, aerobics, kick-boxing, it doesn't matter. If you haven't exercised in a while, it's hard to get past the inertia to get started. But after a week or two, you'll be feeling so good, it becomes hard to *not* exercise. The idea is to connect you to your muscles and get the oxygen flowing, which boosts your mood and thinking (in addition to all the great things exercise does for your body).

3. **Book all of your doctor checkups *right now*.** Seriously, put this book down and make the calls. Schedule appointments with your general practitioner and/or gynecologist, dermatologist, dentist—and any other medical appointments you keep postponing. Take a couple of personal days and power out all of your checkups at once. Then renew your appointments for the following year. If you don't already have a doctor in any of these specialties, take the next ten minutes to call a friend or colleague and ask for a referral. Go on. Make the call. You'll be that much closer to getting a checkup. I'm waiting.

4. **Master your energy sources.** Be aware of the variety of ways you need to recharge. Every time you feel overwhelmed or confused, figure out what you need to do to right yourself. Social contact? Alone time?

Fresh air? It may sound silly to recommend you think so hard about this, but my experience is that when we get overwhelmed with external responsibilities, the last person we think about is ourselves. We don't even *know* what we need anymore. If you tend to forget what fuels your energy, write it down on a small index card and keep it in your wallet. This card is just a point of reference, like the sticker on the front-left windshield of your car reminding you to change the oil.

5. **Dress the part.** Do you treat yourself to the best-quality products you can afford, or are you frugal to the point of discomfort? The way you treat yourself reflects whether you imagine yourself as an old beat-up station wagon or a Rolls-Royce. My suggestion? Upgrade your self-image to a Rolls. Going a notch above what you usually spend has a re-markable way of communicating to yourself that you are special; you'll quickly begin to feel happier and more productive. So if you are frugal to the point of skimping even on facial tissue to save a few pennies, consider changing your strategy. While staying fiscally responsible, buy the nicest clothing, soap, sheets, and paper products you can afford and when traveling, treat yourself to the nicest hotel you can. It's just a mindset. Even during tight times treating yourself to a few of life's little luxuries sends a message to your soul that you deserve a good life.

Tip: Improve Healthy Habits to Boost Your Confidence

Unhealthy habits and self-care can be a result of low self-confidence. But healthy habits are a controllable, objective factor that can be evaluated as a stand-alone discipline. The benefit of starting here is that getting healthy often boosts your confidence, a double benefit.

Discipline 5: Attention

One of the most devious derailments to being our best selves is getting caught up in distractions that pull our attention away from focusing on our talents, contributions, and healthy interactions with the world. I'm not talking about simple distractions like getting hooked on a popular TV drama (that can be fun, in the right doses). I'm talking about gravitating toward unnecessary time-and-energy-wasting life dramas.

People who are able to maintain their focus resist getting caught up or obsessing over depleting emotions such as excessive worry, anxiety, anger, petty arguments, and general negativity. Instead they stay focused on what is nurturing and healthy. Focused people have clear goals and priorities, which often involve the discipline to actually write goals down and recommit to them regularly (annually, monthly, weekly, and/or daily). Staying clear on what's most important helps them avoid being caught up in trivial distractions, which enables them to deliver the goods.

Highly focused people are also able to extricate themselves from depleting, unhealthy, high-maintenance relationships that leave no energy for them to nurture and invest in their own interests. (Anyone can fall into a relationship like that.) Focused people recognize the problem, and as difficult as it may be, get out of it, in the interest of keeping their focus on healthy pursuits and a positive life.

Some people constantly throw complications into their lives because they love the thrill of coming to the rescue and creating order out of chaos. I call these people conquistadors of chaos, as they thrive on seeing their way through almost impossible situations. Unfortunately, this sort of behavior is a huge distraction from delivering one's unique spark. Conquistadors usually do make headway in delivering on their potential, but they don't get as far, or get there as fast, as they could. It's like always traveling with the handbrake on.

Tip: Overcome Unrealistic Expectations

Setting wildly unrealistic expectations for yourself is a source of unnecessary drama because no matter what you accomplish, you end up disappointed, unsatisfied, and restless, which is discouraging . . . and discouragement is just another form of distraction. Train yourself to set challenging, yet realistic, expectations. When you meet them, take time to reward yourself, enjoying your wins along the way.

How Can I Improve My Attention?

1. **Write down your goals and priorities.** It's natural to be uncertain about our goals at various points in our lives—in fact, one main reason for reading this book is to gain clarity on what's next. But we are sometimes so worried about making the *right* choice, setting the *right* goal, prioritizing the *right* thing that we are unable to choose. Being paralyzed by indecision is a focus-stealer keeping you from making your contribution. Release the pressure by knowing you can make adjustments as needed.

2. **Tie up loose ends.** Take inventory of the unresolved issues in your life and give yourself one to three months (tops) to address them. Ignoring problems, just hoping they will go away on their own, is nonproductive and draining. As long as those issues remain unresolved, they will eat away at your ability to focus and be clear. Once you've cleared the decks, you'll have energy to focus on more productive activities.

3. **Avoid obsessing over negative emotions.** Let go of the little things you can't control. Excessive anger, worry, and anxiety are unhealthy emotions that add no value. So what if someone cuts you off on the highway? If no one got hurt, shrug it off. Ease up on watching too much local news; it only provokes anxiety. And resist the urge to gossip; you'll find yourself involved with and worried about problems that have no bearing on your life. Learn to let these emotions go.

4. **Move toward the positive relationships.** You are a reflection of the people you surround yourself with. If you are in an oppressive, depleting relationship, the energy it consumes will keep you from developing to your full potential.

5. **Ground your expectations with a reality check.** Besides boosting your self-confidence, the best way to set reasonable expectations is to do a reality check with other people in a similar position. Talking to others will give you perspective on what is reasonable and what's not.

Signed, Sealed, and Delivered

Connecting to your authentic self is as much about knowing what you're good at as it is knowing what you struggle with. The five disciplines presented here are reliable companions and enablers on your journey toward your vision. I know that each one requires persistence and hard work to develop—much more than any single chapter could deliver. At least now you are aware of what you need to work on and can work on your discipline to deliver in that area. You might never get a perfect 30 in all five disciplines, but even small improvements will generate a big payoff in your ability to fulfill your potential, get unstuck, and achieve your vision for the future.

Now that you've reconnected to your strengths and cornered your weaknesses, it's time to reap the benefits of your hard work and learn how to Savor the Moment.

Chapter 12

Savor the Moment

To live is the rarest thing in the world. Most people exist, that is all.

—Oscar Wilde

Great figures in literature, philosophy, religion, science, and entertainment have considered for eons what it means to be in the moment. Whether it's about awareness, clarity, a sense of purpose, mystery, or wonder, "the moment" *is a state of being; one that is as elusive as it is rewarding.*

❖ ". . . but upon our perceptions being made finer, so that for a moment our eyes can see and our ears can hear what is there about us always." (Willa Cather, 1873–1947)

❖ "If we could see the miracle of a single flower clearly, our whole life would change." (Buddha, 563–483 B.C.)

❖ "Living in the moment brings you a sense of reverence for all of life's blessings." (Oprah Winfrey)

❖ "The moment one gives close attention to anything, even a blade of grass, it becomes a mysterious, awesome, indescribably magnificent world in itself." (Henry Miller, 1891–1980)

❖ "If I had influence with the good fairy who is supposed to preside over the christening of all children, I should ask that her gift to each child in the world would be a sense of wonder so indestructible that it would last throughout life." (Rachel Carson, 1907–1964)

When you started this book, you were feeling stuck, unhappy with where you were, weighed down, and unsure where to go next. In that state, it's probably safe to say that the concept of being "in the moment" was elusive for you. Distracted by representations of the past and paralyzed by an unclear view of the future, you were either looking backward or forward, knew only that where you were wasn't working. You felt stuck. By this point, if you've followed the **SHED** steps in order, you should be close to (if not already experiencing) living in "the moment." Unburdened and feeling confident about your place in the world, you're now excited to experiment with variations of your theme as it continues to become clearer.

Developing the muscle to be present is important before you Drive Yourself Forward toward your vision because it tunes you in, calms you down, and positions you to experiment with choices that are truly right for you. But if you are worried about the past and what you left behind, or feel distracted by the future and what your next step should be, you're not in the moment just yet. This chapter will help you find your way and give you some techniques to stay there.

What Does "the Moment" Feel Like?

"The moment" doesn't discriminate on the basis of age, gender, income, experience, or life pursuits. Remarkably, "the moment" feels about the same for everyone. It's a universal state of mind that people from all walks of life try to attain. Here's how you know when you're in the moment:

- **All senses are firing on five cylinders.** Your sense of smell, sight, hearing, taste, and touch are extraordinarily keen. You pick up on things (the smell of coffee, the heat of the sun) that usually wouldn't get a second thought. There is a specialness to each thing you encounter that wasn't there before.
- **The world is in high resolution.** Ever sit at a tiny table in a crowded restaurant and feel like you and your dinner partner are the only people in the room? That's precisely what being in "the moment" feels like. The sky looks a little bluer, the grass a little greener, and you notice the details of your everyday environment (street signs, the variety of flowers in your neighbor's flower boxes, the color of your cat's eyes).
- **The little things don't bother you.** Things that usually annoy you (rush-hour traffic, a friend who's fifteen minutes late for dinner, spilled

milk) roll off your back. When you're in "the moment" it's no big deal.

- **Simplicity reigns**. Everything seems simple, including normally complicated projects, tasks, and conversations. Challenging situations still make you work, but they are not painfully hard. You also begin to appreciate the grace of simple things—taking your dog for a walk, going to the grocery store, driving to work.
- **You experience full engagement.** Whatever you are doing commands your complete attention, whether you're at work, at home, with your children, on a date, or at the gym. Outside thoughts don't creep into your conscience as you focus 100 percent on your current activity.
- **Time flies.** This fully engaged state means that time flies, but in the best possible way. There's no anxiety about "running out of time" or "time wasted." Curiously absent is a restlessness that usually keeps you checking the clock.
- **You feel enthusiasm and excitement for whatever you are doing.** When you're in the moment, everything you do is buoyed by a sense of irrepressible enthusiasm. From the smallest experience (mowing the lawn or going to your daughter's Little League game) to the largest (getting married or having a child) is exciting. You're able to be enthusiastic about every moment.
- **You have a sense of purpose for every task and activity**. Nothing you do seems like a waste of time. You give everything your absolute best effort, confident of the payoff; whether that payoff actually results in "success" or a positive recognition of your efforts.
- **You react without worry.** People who are in "the moment" take life as it comes, reacting to each situation with confidence, without worry or regret.
- **Emotions come true and easily.** All emotions—joy and sorrow, elation and anger, love and loneliness—are felt deeply. Being in the moment does not mean to exist without pain; it means that all emotions, good and bad, are recognized as authentic. You are able to sit with whatever emotion you feel, without retreating.

Simply put, being in "the moment" means that you are marveling at the newness and presentation before you. You are reacting, not anticipating or worrying about anything. Being in "the moment" means that you've escaped (at least temporarily) the clatter of voices in your head and you are free of distraction, obligation, or regret. There is an easy, welcome desire to take advantage of each minute, because there will never be another one just like it. How do you answer the questions below?

What percentage of your day do you feel "in the moment"?_____

What benefits do you experience when you are in "the moment"? _____

_____

"The Moment" Is Elusive

If the descriptions above encapsulate what it means to be in "the moment," the next question to ask is where and when you've experienced the moment before. For most people being in "the moment" is just that, a moment, fleeting, mercurial, and difficult to replicate. You tell yourself, *If only I could feel this way all the time!* Here are several situations in which you may have captured "the moment," for more than one minute at a time. Which of the following automatically puts you in the moment?

- **Vacation.** Ah, yes. Relaxation. No worries. Away from the chaos of the work-a-day world with family, friends, or loved ones. You're probably in "the moment" most of the time you're away—with no cares besides selecting what book to read next and what to order for dinner. The minute you start worrying about what awaits you at home (or what you left behind, unfinished) is the minute "the moment" is gone.
- **Natural wonders.** The beach, the mountains, the jungle, and other natural wonders (like the Grand Canyon) have a remarkable effect on our state of being. In awe of the grace, size, and dominance of the natural world, we detach ourselves from uniquely human concerns (money, health, work, kids), gain perspective and just appreciate nature.
- **Wedding day, graduation, and major life markers.** The giant recognition and celebration inherent in these days makes it difficult to think about anything else. You are able to just relax and enjoy.
- **A great date.** Do you remember the first time you ever went on a date with someone you really liked? Whether that date happened in middle or high school, you probably felt absorbed and transported by the sheer giddiness of your crush.

- **A job interview.** An amazing job interview is like an out-of-body experience. Looking your interviewer directly in the eye, anticipating questions and providing answers, there are no awkward silences or flubbed answers. It's like you've been put on earth to do just this. You ooze self-confidence and enthusiasm, knowing you nailed it.
- **A great performance.** Whether it's athletic, theatrical, musical, or professional, there is nothing like the thrill of a great performance: both for the performers and the audience. As a performer, you are in the moment playing with the crowd, just reacting and relishing the experience of being accepted for who you are. As an audience member, having the courage to be open to the authenticity of a performance elicits an involuntary physical reaction: tears, goose bumps, a sly smile.

Two days before Caroline arrived in California she decided to take a six-hour detour to visit the Grand Canyon. "There were literally *no* cars on the road up into Grand Canyon National Park, so the magnificent landscape was on rare display just for me," she said. The natural beauty pushed her into the moment. "The unbelievable size and beauty of the canyon took my breath way. I felt small and new in comparison, as I looked at what the glaciers made over millions of years," she explained. "I found I could really believe that great changes were possible with slow and steady determination and a willingness to chip away at the surface to discover what is beneath."

Not living in the moment isn't so much a failure as a missed opportunity. Going through life on automatic pilot usually turns out fine—you might not take advantage of every opportunity, but it's OK; you're safe. Once you've experienced what it's like to live in "the moment," an autopilot existence isn't enough. That heightened state makes you realize how just going through the motions sands the edges from life.

List three occasions or events that naturally bring out your ability to be in the moment. Are these activities regular occurrences in your daily life (are they replicable), or once-in-a-lifetime experiences (graduation, wedding day, birth of a child)?

_____

_____

_____

What qualities in an experience pull you into the moment? Is it the new-ness or juxtaposition of your everyday life to a different experience? Can you consider that each moment in your life actually has something new to offer if you slow down and look for it?

Slipping into "the Moment"

Author and poet Shel Silverstein said, "You are born with a certain sensitivity, awareness and perception, and I think you have to develop the manual skill." I agree. Being in "the moment" is a muscle that needs to be exercised, a skill that takes practice. Getting to "the moment" can be elusive, and staying there can be difficult.

Some readers may still be struggling with the void in their space or sched-ule left by Heave. The reason that emptiness makes you so nervous is because, as "empty" as it is, it's also "full" of ambiguity. You are accustomed to having that space filled with stuff or busy-ness and will naturally feel compelled to fill the space with something, anything to catapult yourself out of your cur-rent state of limbo into a phase that feels more occupied. Hang in for a little while longer, you're not ready to drive just yet. For those of you still second-guessing your decisions on what you heaved (maybe X wasn't so bad after all . . .), stop. Use that second-guessing as a gateway to access what you are really feeling: excitement, fear, hope, wonder.

Of course, no one enjoys being in limbo. Without direction or a dead-line, you can feel confused, lost, unmotivated, and anxious. All the runners, cyclists, swimmers, and cross-country skiers among you will identify with my next analogy: tolerate the discomfort of limbo like you tolerate the pain of a hard workout. Stay within yourself, be confident that your training (in this case, Separating the Treasures and Heaving) is ample preparation, and push yourself to find the gift in the unknown.

It's extremely challenging to exist in "the moment" at all times, even for the most Zen among us. As powerful as mastering "the moment" can make you feel, it's a tenuous state. Stress at work, a bad night's sleep, a lover's quar-rel, or a bad mood can easily snuff it out, sending us out of the moment into worry about the future (*What's going to happen now?*), or regret about what we just said or did (*Why did I say that?!*).

How do you transform the remarkable lightness of being you've only been able to sustain for a short period of time into a constant state? Whenever you feel yourself slipping, use the following techniques to get yourself back on track.

- **Proclaim a period of observation.** Commit one to two weeks to nothing but the conscious study of yourself. Observe your reaction to the world around you. What do you notice? What do you daydream about? Take advantage of the empty space to evaluate different ideas, but don't pressure yourself to decide anything.

- **Reconnect to your vision.** Whenever you are distracted by thoughts of the past or future instead of focusing on your current situation, reconnect to your vision or theme. Get the words of your theme in your mind's eye and ask yourself what the gift of the current moment is in relation to your theme. Reminding yourself that you are moving in the right direction is soothing, and experiencing the moment in context of your theme will ground you very quickly.

- **Start every day brand new.** British nun-cum-author Monica Baldwin (1896–1975), wrote, "The moment you first wake up in the morning is the most wonderful of the 24 hours. No matter how dreary or weary you may feel, you possess the certainty that, during the day that lies before you, absolutely anything may happen. And the fact that it practically always doesn't, matters not a jot. The possibility is always there." I couldn't articulate it any better.

- **Accept your feelings as authentic.** Getting to this point in the **SHED** process required a vigorous effort on your part to uncover a more authentic version of yourself (assuming you've read the chapters in order). Trust that hard work now. Know that whatever emotion you are feeling is authentic and pay attention to it. What clues do your feelings give you about the fulfillment of your theme?

- **Find your own meditation.** Traditional meditative practices (prominent in many Eastern religions) use breathing techniques to calm the mind and body. But traditional meditation isn't for everyone; many people don't have the training or the patience for the exercise. So find your own form of meditation. What calms your mind and body and helps you tolerate the ambiguity of a moment? Maybe it's something physical, like jogging, or it could be something less active, like listening to music or repeating a simple mantra to yourself.

- **Listen**. When you fall out of "the moment" you stop listening. Instead of listening to the person you're talking to, halfway through their end of the dialogue you start thinking about what you are going to say next. Get yourself back in "the moment" by concentrating on your partner and taking in their every word; then figure out your response.

- **Do a sensory check.** One of the surest ways to reconnect to your immediate surroundings is to do a quick sensory check. Slow down and look around. What do you see? What do you feel? Smell? Hear? Taste? Use all five senses to connect to details of your current moment. The act of slowing down and forcing yourself to take in the situation, sense by sense, will put you back on track.

Knowing what pushes you out of the moment, combined with a plan to counteract those situations, can help you stay in it. Name two or three things that kill the moment for you every time, then list what you do to keep from straying too far.

Moment Stealers

_____

_____

_____

Moment Grabbers

_____

_____

_____

Carpe Diem — Seize the Day

Living in "the moment" is an optimal state of being; once you know what it feels like, you can practice staying there. Why develop this muscle? Because living in "the moment" results in the fullest, most textured life experiences. It's only possible to achieve (and maintain) once you've embraced your identity. By this time you should be feeling more grounded. If you've applied the recommended practices and exercises in this section, you have connected to the core essence of yourself, totally separate and apart from the objects, activities, and habits that used to define you. It's an amazing feeling to need nothing *but you*. Throw a net around this feeling; capture and savor it!

Brooke, our college English professor, relished living in the moment, a state that came naturally to her after she'd tackled a few points of entry. "I feel ten again! Remember ten?" she explained. "I remember before boys, and before hormones, I felt invincible. I loved my girl buddies and we had an adventure every day. I have no memory whatsoever of walking on eggshells to please someone else—we lived authentically, as ourselves, strong and bliss-ful." Her keen sense of awareness and engagement with life cascaded into her work. "While others seemed to be agonizing over administering a program's details, I was having a great time," Brooke said. "By the end of the meeting we were all laughing—one of those 'life is too short' moments—and I keep having them."

Using the techniques described above, spot-check yourself during a meet-ing at work, while running errands, or on a Sunday morning with your fam-ily. Do the characteristics of being in "the moment" (simplicity, no worry with the little things, full engagement) apply? If they do, great. If not, tune out the background noise and make adjustments until you are there. With enough practice, you can live in "the moment" most of the time. Flex your muscles!

The sensation you are experiencing right now is the interplay between confidence and openness—confidence in who you are and openness to the possibilities before you. You are game for life's adventures. From this new position of power, you are finally ready to explore the future, trying different opportunities and deciding what stays and what goes, gradually filling your space with items and activities that support your theme for the next phase of your life.

Don't forget this feeling. It is the essence of life at its fullest. You will continue to draw upon it as you drive toward your vision. As you experiment with new choices for your life, and choose what is right and not right for you, you should always be able to come back to this feeling of centeredness. Because if you are comfortable with the moment—savoring everything about the here and now—the journey becomes a joy.

Congratulations, you are back in control. Are you ready to drive?

STEP 1

Drive
Yourself
Forward

The purpose of life is to live it, to taste experience to the utmost,
to reach eagerly without fear for newer and richer experience.

—Eleanor Roosevelt

By now you have separated your identity from your old attachments and feel confident, open, and ready to move forward toward your vision with courage and anticipation. Congratulations.

Although I suggest you read these last three chapters in order, they are not intended to function sequentially. The purpose of each chapter in this section is not to lead chronologically from one step to the next but to work together, in tandem, helping you move steadily toward your vision. The benefits you derive from each chapter will help you practice your ability to "stay in the moment" and maintain your momentum.

Chapter 13, Break Your Mold, challenges you to try things that are totally unrelated to your theme in order to expand your view of yourself and see the world through a different lens. Encounters that are off the beaten track and out of character will dislodge you in unexpected ways. You can transfer these lessons to pursuits more related to your theme.

Chapter 14, Experiment with Your Theme, will move you more directly toward your vision as you explore activities that are specifically connected to your theme. You'll see what you like, what fits and what doesn't.

And chapter 15, Beware of the 30 Percent Slip, will keep you on course by showing you how to check in on yourself periodically. It will help you to continue making progress toward your theme, assess if your vision has changed, and determine when something in your life has gone stale and you need to **SHED** again.

The state of mind each chapter triggers is valuable and enriching. The spaces left temporarily vacant after your Heave will slowly fill up again, little by little, with experiences more relevant and connected to your vision. As you complete the exercises in these chapters, you'll find yourself unencumbered and able to take these new journeys. And with each step, your theme will become clearer and clearer, and you'll move to your new destination.

How long this final step of the **SHED** process will take you is absolutely unclear—because the end itself is unclear. When does transition stop? When we feel comfortable in a new environment, with a new set of activities and focus. But it is human nature to evolve, which is why **SHED**ing is an ongoing process; the need for it never goes away, as long as you feel the need to grow.

The good news is that this is the enjoyable part. You are driving your own adventure, and it is enriching, rewarding, and downright fun. You've moved beyond the anxiety that being in limbo can elicit and are fully engaged in the process of exploration and discovery. Life is good, vibrant, exciting, and real.

Chapter 13

Break Your Mold

What is traveling? Changing place? By no means.
Traveling is changing your opinions and prejudices.

—Anatole France

And Now for Something Completely Different

I started taking gymnastics on a whim last August at 47 years young. My 21-year-old daughter had been begging me for six months to take a gymnastics class: "Mom, it's awesome; you jump up and down and do flips and handstands! Doesn't that sound fun?" Sure it sounded like fun if you were 21, but I believed I was simply too old for that: *It's just not something a person my age does.*

But my daughter persisted and I finally relented, just to put the topic to rest. Within the span of a single one-hour private lesson, Randy, my extremely gifted gymnastics instructor, completely shifted my self-perception. I went from being convinced I had no business on a trampoline to true believer. *Wow, I can do this!* I thought as I bounded out of the gym.

I've been going about once a week ever since and can now do a one-armed cartwheel, back flips (on the trampoline) and front handsprings (on the mat). What I've discovered is that gymnastics is as much a *mental* exercise as a physical one—maybe even more—because I am constantly working against my preconceptions about what is possible. Doing a back roll into a handstand, for example, requires that you shift your center of gravity. This takes intense concentration and yes, some courage. And I'm always amazed when I am able to do it.

As I continue to explore and develop my life "empty nest," pursuing my theme *Connections*, the carryover effect of my gymnastic lessons has been remarkable. Now, when daunted by the newness of an activity closely related to my theme in my personal or professional life, I'm less inclined at first to believe it's not doable. I stop and think to myself, Hey, if I can do a back flip, why can't I do this?

Taking gymnastic lessons was a real stretch for me (forgive the pun, I couldn't resist). But that's the point. It was an activity completely outside my comfort zone that "never in a million years" would I ever have imagined myself doing, let alone succeeding at or enjoying. Gymnastics became an unexpected source of self-discovery and empowerment that fuels my courage daily and translates into very tangible rewards directly related to my theme. In the years since my nest got empty, I moved into the city, renovated my home to be conducive to entertaining, hosted several gatherings, took on business partners, and enriched many professional and personal relationships. Life is rich, and vibrant, and exciting, and I feel very much on the other side of my transition.

Your objective here is to break out of your mold, remove the blinders and give those sensory muscles of yours a workout so they'll be ready for the "main event," achieving your vision. By tackling something new, you give yourself the sensation of succeeding at something you never thought possible. Whether it's a social activity like joining a book club, an artistic activity like taking a pottery class, or an athletic one like gymnastics, doing something totally out of the ordinary at this stage of **SHED** plays an important part in changing your self-perception.

The Pressure's Off

It's liberating to try something "out of the box" because you don't have to be the best, or even remotely good, to gain value from the experience. In fact, if you decide to do something new that's already within your comfort zone, you defeat the purpose, running the risk of putting pressure on yourself to be an expert and fall into that pass/fail, good/bad mindset.

Let's say you're an accomplished guitarist who decides to try something outside your realm of experience but is still within music, like learning how to play the saxophone. Because you are a professional musician, you will put pressure on yourself to learn how to play the sax like Kenny G. But if you're, say, a research scientist, saxophone lessons are probably far enough outside your daily experience *and* comfort zone, and you'd be happy just to learn how to play your favorite song, or even to produce a note that doesn't sound like a wounded duck. You wouldn't be going for the gold or going for broke; you would be trying something brand new *just for the lessons you may learn*—a mind-set with no self-imposed risk of failure.

Tip: Choose an Ongoing Activity

Skydiving would definitely qualify as an "off-track" activity for many of us. And you could try it if you like, but for most virgin skydivers, the experience is a one- or maybe two-shot deal—unless they get really hooked. Strive to experiment with an off-track activity that will provide an ongoing, longer-term learning experience, not just a short-term adrenaline rush. I recommend to my clients that they pursue their "off-track" activity (activities) for six to twelve months for the best results.

Here's what two of my clients did to push themselves into new and uncharted waters.

Ekatarina, a 29-year-old college graduate and aspiring fashion designer, decided to leave her comfortable suburban life and good job (with benefits) in Southern California and move cross country to New York City to pursue her passion. To push herself outside her comfort zone during the last few months of California living and have some fun (with the added bonus of doing community service), she and a few friends started volunteering at a homeless shelter in the Skid Row area of downtown Los Angeles.

"It was incredible and absolutely terrifying," she told me. "Skid Row is the kind of place where you get out of your car and pray you don't get killed crossing the street. You're never quite sure if your car will be where you left it when you're ready to go home."

She told me that every Wednesday night, in the heart of Skid Row, a group of about 100 to 150 homeless people gather at a local church for a night of free karaoke. "I was amazed at some of the talent possessed by these people," she said. "They have no inhibitions and some of them had voices that would put any musician with a record deal to shame. I didn't expect the experience to affect me the way it did. I thought I was going there to be a good Samaritan; you know—do my part for humanity and make a positive change in the lives of these otherwise neglected people. But when I left, I was the one who was truly changed."

The experience expanded her rose-colored suburban view of the world by showing her the cruel reality of the American poor, but it also rocked her perception of herself. "Surprisingly, sharing the stage with the homeless each week was as invaluable to my new life on the East Coast as the time I spent working on my portfolio," she said. "Having the gall to sing—an act of reckless abandon for me—in the midst of a dangerous environment unveiled some reservoir of courage and fearlessness I never knew I had. The experience gave me confidence I could transform to my fashion career. When I got to New York, I felt I had the resources to get myself through any situation."

Here's Raymond's tale of true grit's breaking his mold:

A 37-year-old sales manager in a financial services firm, Raymond loved his job and exuded competence. But when his firm merged with another, a dramatic culture shift took place within the company (as often happens in such circumstances) that left him feeling unappreciated, unhappy—even incompetent. He and a number of his colleagues who felt the same way took the buy-out option offered them and left, rather than struggle to hang on.

Raymond didn't know for sure what he wanted to do next, so he decided to take three months off before even looking for a job, in order to relax and regain his self-confidence. A self-proclaimed homebody who seldom ventured anywhere for more than a long weekend or so at a time, Raymond decided to go to Peru for four weeks, enrolling in a Spanish language immersion experience. He asked a neighbor to water his plants, canceled his daily newspaper, and took off to another country for a month of travel and study. His experience was extraordinary—the country was beautiful, he expanded his horizons, and he acquired a surprising level of fluency in a new language. The four weeks flew by, and he developed a new view of himself and an appreciation of the world beyond his usual routine. His experience boosted his confidence to new career horizons and being able to figure things out as he went.

When Raymond returned from his travels he began to explore job opportunities. He didn't limit himself to the financial services industry, because he had made the decision (and had the flexibility) to not take any job just for the sake of being employed. He wanted to continue to feel the sense of vitality he'd experienced in Peru. During a networking lunch with an old colleague, he heard about a start-up opportunity (a business that partnered with universities and corporations to broker student loans), which caught his interest. An entrepreneur at heart, he'd always fantasized about one day owning his own business, but had expected to stay in corporate America for at least ten more years to build his financial nest egg. The opportunity tugged at him, though, and after some serious soul searching, he decided to jump in, rather than wait several years for another chance to come along. He attributes the leap of faith he took into running his own business in part to his courageous trek through Peru.

Like Ekatarina and Raymond, you too should shoot for unleashing that wild and crazy guy or gal inside by doing something totally new, totally unconnected to your vision and way off the beaten path from your normal interests and activities. It doesn't have to be "dare-devilly"—in fact, if you've always been a daredevil, try something more sedate and provincial that draws on another part of you. Choose the thing you *can't* picture yourself doing.

Command Your Total Concentration

Whatever new and unfamiliar activity (or activities) you choose to pursue for this exercise, make sure it is one that will *command your total concentration,* just like my gymnastic lessons and Ekatarina's volunteer experience. Gymnastics demands my full focus because I previously had no idea how to do flips and cartwheels (and because I don't want to break my neck in the process). Similarly, Ekatarina's karaoke on skid row adventure took her completely outside her own head, and this total concentration on "something else" helped her fully engage in the activity and compelled her to look at the world through an entirely different lens.

This is central to learning how to open yourself up, the benefits and lessons from which can then be applied to other parts of your life and vision.

What follows is a list of possible off-track activities for you to consider that I've picked up from working with clients over the years. I have separated them into three categories—artistic, athletic, and social—to stimulate your thinking in different areas. Don't be afraid to go outside your comfort zone; in fact, *go for it*. If, for example, you're an intellectual or artistic type, consider an athletic activity. The key here is to take off your blinders and open yourself up to new adventures by seeing yourself and the world through a different lens.

Tip: Choose the Least Likely Option

If you tend toward the artistic, choose an athletic or intellectual activity. If you love sports, try something artistic. Be bold. Be different.

These are just idea starters. Brainstorm other possibilities and talk to friends and coworkers to come up with more on your own.

As you ponder the many activities listed here, I hope you feel excited by how much there is to learn. It's energizing to realize that no matter how old you are, or how much you've done, the world you know is only a tiny part of a much bigger universe of experience. And it's all yours for the taking. Here's a chance to have some fun. Choose something that breaks your mold.

Artistic

- **Community Theater.** Ever had a yen to play Stanley Kowalski in *A Streetcar Named Desire* or Eliza Doolittle in *My Fair Lady*? No? OK, then this could be the perfect activity for you to break your mold. Or consider the many possible backstage roles you could tackle for a community theater production—from wardrobe, makeup, and props to lighting, scenery design, and directing. A typical community theater production takes about three months from casting to opening night, and most community theaters put on between four and six productions a season. So there's plenty of opportunity for you to stay involved and fresh by tackling a different responsibility each show. And who knows, maybe one day you'll even cut loose and make your debut onstage!

- **Cooking.** If you are typically a distracted cook—you only know your food is done by the smell of a burnt pan—this could be a great unexpected activity for you. Discover your inner Mario Batali and explore different cuisines. Try out different recipes. Cooking nurtures the desire to experiment. It demands your full focus, requiring you to slow down and pay attention to details, which can be eye-opening and rewarding when you are not the detail-oriented type. Have dinner parties. Enjoy good food, good wine, and good company, cooking with love year-round!

- **Crafts.** Is taking up painting, sculpting, or woodworking as foreign to you as the idea of walking on the moon? Good! Then taking up one or all of them is ideal for this exercise because everything you learn will be new to you—a different perspective if ever there was one—and who knows where what you learn may take you. Many community colleges as well as local artists and craftspeople offer classes on everything from pottery making to iron making, from sketching to watercolors, to help get you started. You'll see the world through a different lens.

- **Flower arranging.** Check with a nursery in your area to see if it offers classes. If not, stop at a local flower shop and ask if the owner might have time for a few private lessons. Developing the art for mixing colors, shapes, heights, and styles in a vase could be unexpectedly eye-opening. And if you want to take an online course, visit www.online-education .net/courses/floral-design-courses.html.

- **Gardening.** One of my clients is a news photographer, a high-pressure job if ever there was one. It's go-go-go all the time, capturing footage of the day's events (often very unpleasant ones). In complete contrast to his workday, he took up gardening a few years ago and now spends his leisure time tending to and expanding the English garden he has created in his backyard. He finds gardening to be a relaxing and rewarding activity full of surprises and challenges, one that trains his mind on something far removed from the pell-mell world outside.

- **Knitting and sewing.** They're not only useful skills to have but cost-efficient ones, too! You can add new sweaters to your wardrobe and even make some of your own clothes, having fun while cutting down on expenses in the process (you can then apply the money you save toward other activities you never dreamed of doing). Check out www .learntoknit.com and www.sewing.org for tips, resources, patterns, and leads on classes nearest you.

- **Model building.** It's a big world out there—but also a miniature one. Turn your imagination loose creating your own miniature universe full of scale model planes, trains, automobiles, and ships if you've never had the gumption, stick-to-itiveness, and eye for detail to try it before. Kits are available at your local hobby shop, or check out www.scalemodel.net (for all kinds of model building) and www.nmra.org (for model railroad building) to get more information and tips on how to get started.

- **Music.** Think of yourself as being less than musically inclined—in fact, tone deaf? Then c'mon, live dangerously and open yourself up to a really new experience: learn to play an instrument—*any* instrument. No matter what your age, you're never too old to try. A client of mine took up the piano at 40 and revels in playing Christmas carols for his family during the holidays. He doesn't do Beethoven or Bach, and he can barely keep up with his 10-year-old daughter (who's been taking lessons since she was 6), but it doesn't matter; he's having fun, and it helps break him of his "No, I could never do something like that" thinking.

- **Performing arts.** If you aren't quite ready to take up an instrument, this is still an opportunity to expand your musical horizons. Virtually every city in America offers a slew of year-round concerts of every kind, performed by all kinds of groups, from imported world-renowned orchestras to hot local bands. Take in a symphony, groove to a jazz concert or experience an opera. Transport yourself to a different world each time.

- **Photography.** It wasn't so long ago that this activity was too daunting to most novices because of the technical savvy involved. But today's digital cameras allow even the most amateur shutterbug to produce quality photos (or eliminate the not-so-quality ones on the spot). All you need (apart from a camera, of course) is the willingness to try, some patience (especially for nature photography), and a reasonably good eye that you can train to get even better by reading photography books and magazines, or even taking a continuing education course in photography (or videography) at your local community college or photo shop.

- **Scrapbooking.** You know all those boxes of photos and other family memorabilia you haven't sorted through, much less *enjoyed*, in years? Take them out, dust them off, and start building a family history scrapbook (or scrapbooks!). Everyone loves sharing the memories sparked by looking through these special items, and younger folks can learn more about you and the family in "the old days." You'll end up sharing a very special time with your family—and have a keepsake to be shared for generations. Check out www.scrapbook.com for tons more scrapbook ideas, bulletin boards, learning and information centers, and supplies.

- **Quilting.** A colleague of mine was determined to find something outside her teaching job that would impact her life and boost her self-esteem. Impulsively, she volunteered to make a picture quilt for her mom and dad's fiftieth anniversary. As a complete quilting novice she was counting on a friend who quilted regularly to walk her through every step and even do some of the more technical stitches to get her through. Then her friend's dad fell ill and the assistance she was so counting on went poof—*gone*! She panicked and wanted OUT, thinking that there was no way she could do this without her friend's help. She hadn't even selected the fabric and couldn't begin to explain what kind of design she would try to create. But she had "volunteered," so she pressed on bravely and got the quilt done—and not just done, either; her parents, family, and her husband (who had watched her struggle) were very impressed. She was so brimming with self-confidence from the quilt project that a year later, when a local college offered her the opportunity to teach a college class (after years of teaching high school), she had no misgivings whatsoever about grabbing it. She trusted her ability to learn.

- **Writing.** Like to write but never thought of yourself as a writer? Start out small with poetry, short stories, and autobiographical sketches. Writing is like a muscle; the more you exercise it, the stronger it becomes. Once you've got something down on paper that you like, show it to family or friends. Who knows where this long-dormant talent and interest of yours may lead?

Jay

When Julie told me to try doing something new and completely different from my experience—something totally outside my vision—the first thing that hit me was cooking. I certainly had never seen myself as a cook, and I wasn't alone; no one else had, either. Sure, I could boil water, but make enough food for a dinner party? Forget it! So I got a cookbook and just started learning how to make pasta, scallops, beets—and saw the benefit of this exercise right away. It took me out of myself. I wasn't afraid to mess up (and trust me, I did!). Now I cook all the time—one-, two-, even three-course meals. I never would have believed it was possible, and I'm starting to see how I can apply my cooking lessons to activities more related to my vision.

Jay's theme: *Putting down roots*

Athletic

- **Bicycling.** You can strengthen your body, stoke your energy, and take in some eye-opening scenery along the way. Pedal on your own, with friends, or as part of a tour group. There's no end in sight to the different routes you can take and the different experiences you can have, which you can apply all your life. Visit your local bike shop or www.backroads.com for individual, group, or tour information.

- **Bowling.** Join a league and give those tenpins a roll. A game of accuracy and power, bowling keeps you on your feet and moving several hours a game, circulating the blood and offering plenty of hearty fellowship. (It's also fun to wear those silly shoes.)

- **Camping.** Get someone to explain the basics—building a fire, pitching a tent, purifying water, storing food—then head for the hills. Especially if you're an indoor person, communing with nature is a great way to widen your horizons (in this case literally) and learn how to take in the great outdoors.

- **Dancing.** OK, maybe it's not purely athletic, but it's a physical activity all the same, and a whole lot of fun if you take classes with a group (where you can meet new people in the process). There are many different dance classes available, ranging from tango, Afro-Caribbean and Haitian folklore to Greek, line dancing, and swing dance—pretty much everything to keep you hopping year in and year out.

- **Golf.** This is an activity, hobby, passion you can take up as a youngster and play well into your senior years without ever worrying about becoming an expert—because no one ever does. Even Tiger Woods will tell you that with golf there is *always* something new to learn and *always* something old to revisit and improve upon—just as in life. In fact, as an anonymous sage (probably a golfer) once put it: "Golf *is* life," because it teaches many transferable life lessons (among them, "stay out of the rough" and "be patient"). Check your local sporting goods store or any area golf course for information about learning to play.

- **Hiking.** By yourself or with a group, you can set your own pace and stop whenever you may choose to just smell the roses and absorb all of Mother Nature's marvels that you come across as you breathe her clean air. Visit www.trails.com or www.americanhiking.org to find some of the best trails in your area.

- **Kickball.** Start a league with friends or join one and make new friends while getting back in touch with your inner child. This elementary school sport is catching on like wildfire among adult Gen-Xers all across the country.

- **Pilates.** This widely popular exercise is designed to help stretch and strengthen your muscles and teach balance and control of the body—knowledge and skills that can be translated to many other areas of your life. Ask about classes at your local gym, Y, or community center. You can also buy Pilates exercise DVDs if you prefer a workout (à la Jane Fonda or Richard Simmons) you can do at home at any time.

- **Qigong.** Say what? If this sounds suspiciously like a martial art, that's because it is. Qigong is also an ancient approach to health care that combines physical training with Eastern philosophy and relaxation techniques to connect you to your core strength. You can practice standing, sitting, or lying down. Other forms may also include structured movements and massage. It takes time, commitment, patience, and determination to learn Qigong, making it an ideal long-term experience.

- **Rock climbing.** For an ongoing off-the-beaten-path challenge where you are constantly discovering something new around you *and* about yourself, you can't beat this never-in-a-million years' activity, because there is no end to the number of rocks (in all sizes, shapes, and locations) to climb. Climbers will tell you that the activity demands your full concentration and will yield many valuable—and broadly applicable—insights into your personal potential and authentic self. For more information about the activity in your area and nationwide, check out www.rockclimbing.com.

- **Running.** If you're the type of person who believes the only reason to run is to escape the large and unpleasant thing chasing you, actually trying this activity may change your point of view. Whether you do it on a treadmill or on the open road, running is a great aerobic exercise that can improve your health, stamina, and determination and goal-setting. Runners World (www.runnersworld.com) has great advice for newbies.

- **Skiing and Snowboarding.** Downhill or cross-country, the variation is yours with these popular winter sports. Skiing is the perfect off-track activity for those who live where it snows and usually prefer to spend the winter months hibernating. Get out and play in the snow.

- **Softball.** It's a pretty good bet that your employer has a team because softball is probably the most popular after-hours team activity in most workplaces. It promotes bonding between coworkers and a little friendly competition. Never thought of signing up? Here's your opportunity.

- **Water sports**. Swimming is one of the best forms of exercise available on a year-round basis. From swimming you can gravitate to even more adventurous water sports like surfing, snorkeling, scuba diving, or even sailing, which thousands of beginners tackle every year. If you're a land-lubber, make these activities your annual vacation!

- **Weightlifting.** Burn up calories, get yourself in shape, and learn how to focus your mind on achieving a set goal. Staying in "the moment" is never easier than when there's a 100-pound weight dangling above your skull. And there's no need to become muscle-bound to realize the benefits.

Social

- **Book club.** Create a group with friends or join one through your local library. Local book clubs and reading groups are in these days. Tackle a genre you've never tried before to expand your taste to other categories. Enter the actual world of authors by visiting the spots where they lived and worked. For example, you can tour Henry David Thoreau's famed Walden Pond, a beautiful Massachusetts park reserve (www.mass .gov/dcr/parks/walden/), explore Ernest Hemingway's homes in Key West (www.hemingwayhome.com) and Idaho (www.svguide.com/hem haunts.htm), or take your youngest readers to see where Laura Ingalls Wilder lived during the pioneer days (check online for information at www.lauraingallswilder.com/homesites.asp).

- **Indie movie club.** If you don't consider yourself a social butterfly, a movie club is perfect for pulling you out of your shell. As film studies becomes more mainstream in colleges and universities, more and more of these clubs, which are modeled on the book club idea, are sprouting up. Each member of the group takes a turn choosing a documentary, foreign, or independent film on DVD to view at each meeting. When the movie ends, the discussion and social interaction begin. Go online for festival ideas at www.documentarychannel.com, www.ifilm.com, or www.undergroundfilm.com and for links to other sites for more screening possibilities.

- **Foreign languages.** Ever been abroad? It seems that everyone in the world speaks at least a some English, while Americans are infamous for speaking no language but their own. Expand your cultural education by taking up a foreign language. Most colleges offer a diverse range of after-hours education courses in the always popular French, German, Spanish, and Russian to the increasingly popular Arabic, Chinese, and Japanese. You can also teach yourself at home via language courses on CD or DVD. Or learn online by checking out www.rosettastone.com, which provides interactive learning software in twenty-eight different languages.

- **Public speaking.** Does the thought of standing up and speaking in front of a group of strangers practically make you break out in hives? Then it's a ready-made new adventure to open you up to new possibilities—not to mention overcome your fear. You may even discover it's not as frightening as you thought. Toastmasters and Dale Carnegie Training are two of the biggest international organizations aimed at helping anybody who wants to explore their public speaking skills. Check out their websites for a location near you at www.toastmasters.org and www.dalecarnegie.com.

- **Travel.** If you're retired with plenty of time or have a few weeks of vacation time banked, use it to see the world! There is no more eye-opening new experience, because there's a lot to take in and all of it's different. Travel with friends. Take a tour with a group. Or rent a car and travel the roads at the pace you choose. If you've always been the stay-at-home type and overseas travel is too far out and far off a first step (or too expensive), then see the United States instead. You've got fifty states to choose from, beginning with your own.

- **Volunteer.** Donating your time and skills to a good cause is a great way to see the world around you through many different lenses. Go behind the scenes and volunteer at your local library, museum, hospital, or nursing home. Each of those places can use the help, and the rewards you'll get in return from the knowledge you'll gain will be tenfold. You could also volunteer to assist your favorite candidate in a local, state, or national political campaign. And if you're a retired executive with a desire to give back, use your experience to provide free business counseling to America's entrepreneurs. You can do it in person, by phone, or online through SCORE (go to www.score.org/volunteer.html to learn more).

Those are my suggestions, but they're just the tip of the iceberg. What do you want to do? Savor that feeling of taking off your blinders and the joy of carefree experimentation.

Fly Toward Your Theme

The purpose of breaking your mold is to shift your perception of yourself and what you are capable of. You may never be a master of your new activity, but it has expanded your vision of yourself and what is possible.

Now that you've wriggled out of your cocoon and taken on challenges you never thought possible, you're ready to experiment with your theme head on.

Remember, these activities were only precursors to the real adventure, designed to widen your blinders. So get ready to take all that you've learned about yourself through free-flowing experimentation and channel it toward that foggy vision you've seen in the distance. Let's get purposeful!

Chapter 14

Experiment with Your Theme

*When you follow your bliss . . . doors will open where you
would not have thought there would be doors; and where there
wouldn't be a door for anyone else.*

—Joseph Campbell

In the previous chapter, Break Your Mold, you learned about the benefits
of opening yourself up to activities that are outside your normal purview.
Now it's time to start proactively filling the empty spaces left by your Heave
with activities and objects that are more directly related to your vision for the
future. All the work you have put in so far brings us to this point—finally,
that specter of "there's something more, but I don't know what it is" is ready
to assume a more precise shape. With your space cleared of clutter, most
people are bursting with new ideas about how to realize their theme and just
need a gentle push in the right direction. The key is engaging in specific ideas
on proactive exploration, rather than passively standing by.

Experimenting with your theme is a process of trial and error in which
you directly explore ways to develop your theme. It is a fluid experience that
will give you the opportunity to pursue many different paths to your vision.

If your theme for the future is *Connections,* now's the time to sign up for a
new theater club or upload your profile to an online dating service. (Whereas
in the last chapter, you would've tackled something totally unrelated, like
flower arranging or Qigong, to expand your perceptions about what you are
capable of achieving.) But don't feel pressured to get it right the first time. If a
new activity doesn't fit, you don't have to make a commitment. This is a time
for experimentation. You are unstuck, moving toward your goal.

It could take a month, a few months, or maybe a year or more to pick
and choose what will (or will not) be part of your new life. You'll play with
what works and what doesn't. And you should expect to make some bad
choices—that's what the trial and error aspect of any experiment is all about.

Don't pressure yourself to figure things out quickly. Trust your intuition—if an activity feels right and brings you energy it stays, if it doesn't, it goes. In that way, your space will fill up naturally, over time, with things that bring you joy and truly connect to your vision.

One word of caution: *Be wary of allowing your old attachments to creep back into the empty space.* If you are not actively pursuing ideas related to your theme, it's easy to slip back into your old patterns and activities.

Get the Ideas Flowing

Generating a list of specific ideas to pursue your theme is a great way to move beyond just *thinking about* your vision and into proactively exploring. Turn to a new page in your **SHED** journal, or take out a piece of paper, and start brainstorming ideas of ways to pursue your theme. Begin with a list of at least five ideas.

Many clients find that at this point in the process, opportunities and possibilities for pursuing their theme are in abundant supply. They feel brave and able to generate many innovative ideas to pursue. The beauty is, you don't feel the need to grab at every idea that comes to you. You can give some ideas a whirl, let some things simmer, let some things go. It's a joyful experiment.

Go beyond the usual—be creative, explore new ideas and ways to achieve your theme that you may never have tried before. Once one idea pops into your head, zillions more will follow. Don't censor yourself or belabor your decisions. Let each experience take you where it will, always with your vision in mind.

Once Jay cleared the physical clutter from his life, he was surprised how much more room he had to think. Without the layers of clutter "crowding out" his thoughts and dreams, ideas had room to bubble up, evolve, and deepen. His mind was constantly generating possibilities, some of which he pursued; others he contemplated for a while and then easily tossed.

He explained, "I'm meeting girls; I have friends. People are randomly stopping by to visit. I'm finally finished with my demo. It took me years to finish a demo! I swear I could never finish one. And in reality, it took only a couple of days. The ideas just flowed! I had room to think.

"Over time, a week or two, I started thinking more and more about school. I always had the idea of going back to school buried deep inside me, but now, suddenly, I started thinking of steps to make it happen. I'd leave it alone for a couple of days, then find myself wondering if NYU had some kind of seminar that could help me figure out the financial aid process." He went online and to his delight, they did.

Jay carved out the time to attend the orientation and learned about a program that offered tuition reimbursement if he worked for the university; all he had to pay was the taxes. "You know, I never focused on any of this stuff. I never thought about tuition reimbursement or seminars that could help me find financial solutions to my education at NYU. Never. And I've wanted to go to NYU the whole four years that I've been in New York, but I'd just been dealing with my mess the whole time. It helps to have room to think."

Expanding the range of activities you're willing to try opens you up to opportunities to pursue your vision in new ways. Jay never even considered working at a university, but getting a job on campus was an open door to the education he wanted. As you start experimenting with new activities, keep the same level of open-mindedness you had when you tried salsa dancing or started that book club. Even though you're getting closer to your theme, you're still breaking out of your shell and experimenting with something new.

Finding Your Sweet Spot

I can't tell you what specific experiences and activities to experiment with, but I can guide your process by helping you clearly identify what excites you. When you make a conscious effort to connect to what you are passionate about, it's much easier to recognize an activity (or object) worthy of a place in the next phase of your life.

The most rewarding aspect of my business is getting to work with so many interesting people. I believe each individual has a unique contribution to make to this world. You are the only one who sees things the way you do, who thinks the way you do, who possesses the particular combination of passions and skills, insights, and values that is you.

Whether we go into public service, own a successful business, pride ourselves on being a wonderful husband or a great mom, each of us has an opportunity to leave our own little mark on the world. What is yours?

Whatever (or wherever) we choose to make that contribution is our sweet spot, the place where we feel most comfortable, most alive, and most special. We want to be the most prolific in that area. Yet finding that sweet spot isn't always so easy.

We get distracted by what other people think we should be. We get anxious being in limbo and may be tempted to leap at the first idea that comes along, by simply fulfilling other people's definitions of what we should be doing. We get caught up "fixing ourselves," making comparisons to other people, trying to become more "like him" or "like her," "like this" or "like that," and end up ignoring the things that light a spark in our eyes. But if we take the easy way out, we fool no one but ourselves. As Ralph Waldo Emerson said, *Insist on yourself; never imitate. Your own gift you can present every moment with the cumulative force of a whole life's cultivation; but of the adopted talent of another you have only an extemporaneous, half possession.*

It's always been my experience that the people who know themselves well, those who are clear on what interests, pleases, and energizes them, create the most fulfilling and productive lives.

Getting to know yourself is, of course, a lifelong process. There are several well-respected assessments and personality tests out there—Myers-Briggs, Disc, the Oxford Analysis. Those tests have merit, helping people gain insight by assigning them to different "types," certainly helpful information when going through a career change or assessing the compatibility of a potential employee. But that's not our objective here. I want you to rediscover your inherent passions and values, so you can evaluate future experiments on your theme and recognize what is right for you.

Enthusiasm = "The God Within"

At this point in the **SHED** process, my primary role with my clients is to be a sounding board, helping them think through and evaluate ways to pursue their theme. I can usually predict with relative accuracy what will be a fit for them, and what won't. My clients are often amazed at how quickly I *get* who they are.

I'll let you in on a little secret. What I am paying attention to is their enthusiasms—what lights up their eyes.

The word *enthusiasm* is defined by Webster's dictionary as "a strong excitement or feeling." Its Latin root, *enthios*, literally means "the god within." By studying your enthusiasms and accepting them, you will gravitate toward the light, and find the best, most natural, most organically satisfying ways to pursue your theme.

Interspersed throughout this chapter is a series of self-reflective exercises for tuning you into what lights you up. These exercises in self-reflection bring an additional layer of awareness to the process of rediscovering your most authentic self. As you explore your new theme, it will be easier to select the objects, activities, and behaviors that are truly *right for you*.

By looking at your inherent drives, your passions, and your values, you can often come up with unexpected ideas that resonate with your most authentic self. Use the insights you gain through these exercises as a springboard to generate new ideas and also as a filter for considering what might be a fit. For each possibility, ask yourself if it speaks to "the God within"; is it something you can feel enthusiastic about. You might need actually to try it on for size to be sure.

The assessments you did in chapter 10, Trust Yourself, were designed to give you the confidence that you *can* do it; i.e., you should be on this journey. The exercises here are designed to help you explore the right direction, suggesting *how* and *where* you may find your bliss.

Exercise 1: What Are My Natural Strengths?

As you are well aware by now, **SHED**ing involves releasing obsolete objects, roles, and activities to make room for something new. Yet no matter how much **SHED**ing you do in your life, there will be certain core actions and strengths that stick with you no matter what. These actions and strengths bubble up over and over because they are a part of your core identity, just as the core personality traits that you uncovered in chapter 10 are always with you.

How do you find them? Study the types of tasks and roles you have gravitated to during your life. Look over the following list of words, which are all verb related to some type of strength. Even if you don't consider yourself a master of any of the actions listed, you should still gravitate toward a few words that point to where your talents and skills inherently lie. Circle eight to ten words that describe something you enjoy and have done with frequency in the last year. The words you select should generate *only* positive emotions: excitement, interest, joy, curiosity, and passion. Look over the following list of verbs (defined as things you can do with your body and mind). Identify the ones you've spent a lot of time doing and enjoyed. You should feel yourself gravitate toward a few words that point to activities that are a natural fit for you.

Adapted

Administered

Arbitrated

Audited

Budgeted

Built

Collected

Communicated

Composed

Computed

Conceptualized

Constructed

Coordinated

Coped

Counseled

Decided

Diagnosed

Discovered

Dissected

Dramatized

Drove

Edited

Empathized

Evaluated

Experimented

Filed

Financed

Fixed

Founded

Guided

Handled

Helped

Hypothesized

Illustrated

Imagined

Implemented

Improvised

Influenced

Inspired

Installed

Integrated

Invented

Judged

Maintained

Managed

Mediated

Memorized

Mentored

Motivated

Nurtured

Operated

Organized

Oversaw

Painted

Presented

Questioned

Reasoned

Reconciled

Reduced

Represented

Researched

Resolved

Restored

Risked

Served

Shared

Sold

Solved

Spoke

Taught

Trained

Translated

Traveled

Unified

Wrote

Let's look at how you might use the words you chose as a springboard to generating ideas to pursue your theme. When I took Anne, 58, through this exercise, she already had a pretty good idea of the direction she wanted to experiment with. After years of putting her own career as a playwright/screenwriter on hold in order to raise her family, she was anxious to get back to her craft. Anne's vision for the future was *Making my mark*.

The words Anne circled were: *wrote, edited, empathized, traveled, unified, solved, mentored, discovered,* and *communicated*. I asked her to review her verb selections and use them as a springboard to generate possible ways to pursue her theme. It's likely that any pursuit she came up with that includes some combination of these strengths would feel like a natural and satisfying fit.

Here's the list she came up with:

1. **Mentored/communicated:** Consider teaching a screenwriting class at the community college in her town. (The director of the arts program at the college was an old friend, who had been trying to convince her to teach a night class for years.)

2. **Discovered, unified:** Commit one night every two weeks to seeing a community theater performance with a group of girlfriends.

3. **Wrote, edited:** Write five two-minute "shorts" (mini-scenes) a week, just to get her writing muscles firing.

4. **Empathized, discovered, communicated:** Take an improvisation class to connect to others in the community and spark ideas.

5. **Traveled, wrote:** Go on the one-month solo trip to Spain she'd always dreamed of, and write a play related to that experience.

This list of five ideas was by no means meant to be limiting for Anne. She could start with these five, and see what grows from there. Using the list as an idea generator and filter helped her separate out what might resonate for her and be close to her sweet spot from what might be less satisfying.

Exercise 2: What Topics Capture My Imagination?

There are as many ways to view the world as there are people walking this earth. Each of us notices something slightly different among the many riches of the world. Scientists see molecules, while actors see emotions.

Three people can all walk down the same New York City street and each notice something completely different. One person may be captivated by the faces of *people* on the street, imagining what type of home they live in, how each of them started their morning, what their lives are really like. Another might be mesmerized by the city's *architecture*, noticing small details on buildings others would miss, inspired by the creativity of centuries of architects. A third person might be charmed by the bustle of *commerce*—curious how each business owner from the street pretzel vendors to high-end shop owners manage the cash flow to keep their enterprises operating profitably.

It's in our unique points of view, what we notice in the world where our enthusiasms lie. That is where we have an opportunity to find our sweet spot.

What fascinates you? What do you pay attention to? What catches your eye? What big categories or concepts consistently excite you whether you're directly involved or just taking notice of them in the world around you? The particular combination of things you notice is a unique blend—which can lead to insight into your sweet spot in the world. Circle a few things on the list below that represent what catches your eye in the world. This goes beyond hobbies; we are looking for what fascinates you, where you will notice details others may fail to see. If you think something is missing from this list, add it in yourself. What topics inspire passion in you?

Civil and human rights	Human behavior	Philosophy
Great writing	How things work	The great orators
World cultures	Government	Social justice
Artistic expression	Religion	Home environments
Medical science	Fashion	Commerce
History	Invention	Food and wine
Cultural expression	Human perseverance	Economics
Mechanical processes	Business models	Ecology
Visual arts	Sociological trends	Natural resources
The human form	The solar system	Sociology
Education and learning	Scientific research	Entrepreneurship

If you were walking down the street, or perusing a bookstore, or thinking about life, what issues would you be ruminating on? Think about your theme, and look at the topics you circled. Do they stimulate any ideas for creative ways to link your theme to your passions?

Matthew was a law partner who'd grown accustomed to working 14-hour days and being on the road for business more than 150 days per year. In pursuit of his theme *Fulfilling personal commitments,* he left the law firm and took a different job that would give him time and stability to create a life outside work. But spending leisure time with friends and family was so foreign to him, he wasn't quite sure how to drive toward his vision.

The more enthios-related activities Matthew added to his life, the more likely he would stumble on the right things to help him achieve his vision. Matthew was a guy with a ton of interests, so we explored all of his areas of passion.

From the list on the previous page, Matthew chose the following soul-fueling topics: history, scientific research, travel and culture, food and wine, and nature. The question was, How could Matthew's topics of interest spawn creative ways to *fulfill his personal commitments?*

Here's Matthew's list of possibilities:

1. **History:** Start a Don't-Know-Much-about-History club with friends, gathering at one another's homes every other month, reading and discussing the ideas of great philosophers through time.

2. **Food and wine:** Host a major family holiday (Thanksgiving, Christmas, or Easter) next year.

3. **Science:** Buy a season pass to the Museum of Science and commit to visiting at least once a month.

4. **Nature:** Help organize a week-long ski trip to Montana with his two brothers and their families.

5. **Travel and culture**: Create a list of friends who live in other parts of the world, and commit to planning two purely leisure visits a year to see them.

The list Matthew came up with was a place to start off his theme exploration. Some ideas would pan out, others would dissipate or evolve into more refined ideas. The key was for Matthew to actively experiment.

Take a moment and look over the list of interests that you identified. What imaginative ways can you come up with to link your enthusiasms with driving toward your theme? Get creative. Seek input from friends and family members. Do a Google search or go to a library and peruse books related to your topics of interest.

Who knows what would happen if you were to combine your areas of interest with your new theme? One thing is for certain. Studying the topics that fascinate you can lead to your one-of-a-kind imprint on the world, because you are the only one who sees what you see. It's easy, especially if you are leaving behind an entire way of life (like working all the time), to trick yourself into thinking you are actively "experimenting" on your vision when really, you're only "thinking about" experimenting. Obviously, there's a big difference. Perusing the topics that fascinate you is a great way to make yourself be more specific because each enthusiasm will lead you to a different set of activities. Identify the broad categories that get you excited now, and later you can link these enthusiasms to new activities that will fuel you.

Exercise 3: What Qualities Do You Cherish?

Engaging in activities with others who embody your core values is deeply fulfilling and energizing. All seems right with the world when we are living our values—and things definitely seem "uncentered" when we are compromising our values in any way. Take a moment here to define your values.

It's important that any new experience you add to your life matches up with your core values, otherwise it won't last over the long haul. There are times during your transition that you may be tempted to just stick with an idea because you are antsy to speed through the process, feeling, "all right already, enough, I just want to get there." Selecting an experience that doesn't mesh with your core values is a mistake. Before long, it will feel like an attachment that is weighing you down because it doesn't quite fit. Take a moment to think about the qualities, traits, and characteristics below. Circle the ones you find attractive in yourself and other people.

Honesty	Optimism	Sense of humor
Intellect	Spirit	Warmth
Logic	Hardworking	Laid-back
Confidence	Self-deprecating	Cautious
Risk-taking	Joyful	Reserved
Curious	Gregarious	Thoughtfulness
Caring	Sympathetic	Empathy
Respectfulness	Genuine	Helpfulness
Commitment	Maverick	Ambition
Contentment	Introspective	Aggressive
Competence	Loving	Generosity

Forgiving	Tough	Organized
Sweet	Enthusiastic	Polite
Fearless	Calm	Good listener
Practical	Dreamer	Loyal

You first met Kate in the early chapters of this book. She finally decided to divorce her husband after seventeen years and was pursuing a theme of *Freedom*. In Kate's case, this "values" exercise was critical. For too long, she had compromised on her core values for the sake of accommodating her husband. She'd given up a lot in order to keep the peace. Interestingly, the one place Kate refused to compromise was in her career. A Wall Street asset manager, she'd managed to steer clear of the backstabbing culture notorious to her industry and stay true to herself. Now she had to apply the values that had guided her career to her personal life.

The words Kate selected from the list above included *joyful, gregarious, empathy, caring, curious,* and *fearless.* She took those qualities and brainstormed activities related to her theme, *Freedom,* to experiment with.

Here's her list of qualities that inspired ideas she came up with:

1. **Fearless:** Taking rock climbing lessons
2. **Caring/empathy:** Volunteering at a cancer center
3. **Joyful:** Joining a community choir
4. **Gregarious:** Taking African drumming lessons
5. **Curious:** Traveling to Alaska

Look at the qualities you are attracted to in yourself and in others, and use them as a springboard to coming up with ever more interesting avenues for pursuing your theme. Free association works very well here; don't be afraid of anything that doesn't seem to make sense. You may find some interesting information about yourself based on the qualities you chose that don't seem to line up. Remember you're just experimenting. You're a scientist in observation mode. Don't rush to classify yourself. Just collect information. Studying your enthusiasms is the shortest route to discovering your core self, and finding experiences that are likely to stick.

For at least the first six months of his retirement, Max submerged himself in the process of *Embracing his identity*—being fully in the moment, with no agenda, no need for structure, and no need to know where he was headed. During our periodic check-in calls, Max would share his excitement and joy, tell me about all the books he was reading, the blissful moments sitting in the park, or looking out at the bluffs beyond his kitchen window. "I have no idea where I'm going, and it feels so good to not worry about that," he said. Max was reconnecting with his core self.

About eight months after retiring, Max received a call that presented him with an opportunity to pick up a dream deferred. He'd been an actor in his youth and had left that career on the side of the road for the security of a teaching job. This opportunity seemed to show up on his doorstep. There was a tiny theater just up the street. The director was an old friend, and he called Max and asked if he'd be willing to audition for a show they were producing. Max hadn't been looking for this, but it triggered some old, deep desire in him and now that he was retired, he certainly had time to devote himself to the task.

He went in with a complete openness, open most of all to discovering that this was something that might not work out for him. Having spent months embracing his identity, Max was perfectly willing to discover he neither had the talent nor the interest in picking up acting again. But he was perfectly willing to experiment on vision, and see where it might lead.

 Max

Acting was a joy in my youth but it was a gift and set of skills that had gone off over the years. I was picking up a dream deferred. It was exciting and terrifying, but it was the only game in town. A chance to test some skills that never were fully developed in my youth—to find out if this could be, on whatever level, a reality for me. I was willing to accept any outcome. I was not constrained by crippling expectations, positive or negative. And I was willing to follow it anywhere it might lead me.

Max's theme: *Self-discovery*

This particular experiment went well. Max was able to learn his lines, reconnect to what it feels like to open yourself up to a character, and share your most vulnerable self with an audience. Three roles later, he continues to explore this path—to become an actor. In his words, "Having just completed a run as Willy Loman in *Death of a Salesman*, my journey continues, splintering into many alternative routes, detours, pit stops, blind alleys, etc. It is easily the most personal and fascinating trip I have undertaken in my life."

The Thrill of Adventure

Once you have an initial list of ideas for your theme, just get started. You may pursue some ideas and not others, and any choices you make will lead you to more discoveries, pathways, and tributaries. This is about exploration, interacting with possibilities, and moving toward the realization of your vision.

You are standing at the doorway to possibility. You will experience a tremendous lightness of being—an energy you haven't felt for a long time—and the thrill of adventure all around you. Let yourself enjoy the release and the shifts in priorities. There is a sense of vitality, of owning your identity—and choosing your life. You will begin to come up with more ideas about what you want, because now you have space to think. And ideas will have time to develop, because you are no longer distracted with piles of "stuff" or bad habits that you are fighting on a daily basis.

Every client who has gone through **SHED** reports the same sensation that Max described: as they experiment with their theme, they don't feel the need to attach themselves to any single idea just to fill the space. You won't feel that need, either. That is the direct result of work done in the first three **SHED** steps: Separate the Treasures, Heave the Trash and Embrace Your Identity. Comfortable in your own skin, and more attuned to what feels energizing to you, you are empowered to experiment until you find the activities and experiences that truly feel right to you. And the picture will start to take shape, like a photograph coming into focus in a darkroom.

Turn to Mark Twain whenever you start to feel uncertain: "Twenty years from now you will be more disappointed by the things you didn't do than those you did. So, throw off the bowlines. Sail away from safe-harbor. Catch the wind in your sails. Explore. Dream. Discover."

Chapter 15

Beware of the 30 Percent Slip

*Living is a form of not being sure, not knowing what next or
how . . . We guess. We may be wrong, but we take leap after
leap in the dark.*

—Agnes de Mille

Are We There Yet?

Transitions are long and often complicated processes. Unlike an organizing project, which has a clearly defined end point (e.g., you can organize your garage or office in a weekend), **SHED** is an evolution. Instead of tackling one specific trouble spot in your home or your schedule, **SHED** works by creating space and generating movement, which helps to fuel sweeping transformations. This means the "end" of **SHED** is harder to define. How do you pinpoint the exact moment a transition (or a transformation) is over? You might not even be able to isolate when it began! The finish line, in this instance, comes unannounced: you know you've arrived only by a measure of how energetic, authentic, and excited you feel about your life.

There's no doubt you have dislodged yourself from that heavy state of paralysis you felt when you started this book. And by now, you should be feeling the payoffs of your new situation, whether it is a new home or neighborhood, a new job or career, a new role, or a new relationship. Over the next weeks and months, enjoy the sensation that your transition is in full swing, and don't worry so much about the destination. Remember the old adage Life's in the journey, not the destination. Let thoughts and feelings come, hover, and move through you; you're relishing the adventure, excitement, and discovery as you make headway toward the future. Keep reflecting on your new situation, brainstorming new ways to experiment with your theme, and experiencing the joys and confidence inherent in living a fully engaged life as your most authentic self.

As a general rule, once you are consistently devoting 80 percent of your time and energy toward achieving your vision for the future (even if your vision is still evolving), the bulk of your **SHED** is complete. You haven't made any final decisions yet but are still excited at the prospect of what may be around the next turn, and it all feels *s-o-o-o-o-o right*!

Here is how our principal cast of characters knew they were arriving at the end of **SHED**.

SHEDing Gave Me New Energy

Remember Brooke, the 53-year-old English professor who was figuring out the next phase of her life as an empty nester? She wanted to **SHED** in order to expand her audience as a writer. Six months into the process she knew she had reached a turning point. She wrote, "I have to tell you again how profoundly **SHED** has changed my direction and frame of mind. I feel so incredibly confident and renewed. I am heading into the next phase of my life and it happened when I made space for it. For now, the writing is just beginning to blossom, but I am filled with joy of simply valuing that part of me. The greater effect is that I am enjoying life." Far from the empty nester she was at the start of her **SHED**, Brooke felt an energy and fullness within herself.

"As I finished my year as president of the local chapter of Zonta—a wonderful service club promoting the status of women—I couldn't believe how many of the members told me I had changed the energy of the club. One young woman wrote in a card: 'I aspire to be a woman who knows her way in life—and can confidently and assuredly lead others in accomplishing great things—all qualities I saw in you as president!' I was a little blown away by it all, but I hear in it how my **SHED**ing has helped me focus my energy."

SHEDing Empowered Me

When you first met Caroline, our 41-year-old investment banking professional, she was struggling to embrace her personal power by **SHED**ing her old behind-the-scenes role. Eight months into the process she felt centered;

the change she made put her back on target for the first time in more than a decade. She said, "What a difference to be relaxed, focused, and present in my life. This is a great way to start a new job in a new location, and the momentum I have created is an excellent way to keep myself inspired going forward."

I had dinner with Caroline not too long ago, almost one year to the day we started her **SHED**. She was full of light and energy and enthusiasm, clearly coming into her own both professionally and personally. She told me her new job "is what I was meant to do." She is traveling all over the world for both business and pleasure—spending time with friends, using 100 percent of her vacation time, and is always off on a new adventure. She feels invigorated, alive, and excited.

Caroline has been awed at the positive impact she's been able to have now that she has unburdened herself and unleashed her personal power. As she put it, "Embracing my personal power made me powerful and unapologetic. And being real and authentic is an instant bonding mechanism for other people. Now, everywhere I go, people say 'Please don't leave; we need you here.' And it isn't because of to-do stuff—it is much more about the energy I bring." She reminded me how afraid she had been early on to come out from behind the curtain (and relinquish her anonymity), because she wasn't sure she'd be able to have as positive an impact in a more public (and less process-oriented) role. In **SHED**ing the old role and behavior, she was able to alter that belief system. Now she realizes how to exercise her power in a totally different way. She's a woman on fire, and I'm personally looking forward to watching her continued evolution.

SHEDing Encouraged Me

Twelve months into his **SHED**, Max, our 60-year-old theater professor, is also on the verge of coming into his own. Moving through his process at a relaxed pace, he was making significant strides. On the trek for self-discovery after leaving his nearly forty-year run in academia, he shared these observations with me: "I am in a position to discover something about myself, for myself, with myself. I'm uncharacteristically bullish about preserving this position, no matter what. My selfishness is a sort of life preserver."

His bullishness was paying off. Here's a snippet from a review: "Fading salesman Willy Loman is an iconic role for older actors. And veteran performer Max Johnson . . . gives a fine performance. Johnson shows us the tired, pathetic guy returning from a fruitless trip—but also locates small, positive traits that make Willy's wife's devotion to him credible. That, in turn, gives moral grounding to the wife's lectures to her sons, begging them to help their faltering father. Here is a Willy worth saving. Which makes . . . the end all the more tragic." Max was nominated for an award for this role.

"After all these years," he said, "indeed, after a whole other life and career—it seems I can do this after all."

At the time of completing this book, Max had received a call from a well-known film actor who was seeking Max's coaching on the biggest role of his life. Another unexpected opportunity, Max at first did not know quite how to approach it, or if he could provide value. But again, he took on the challenge, applying the principles of just trusting who he was, and showing up. Max was able to draw on his own personal experience as both an acting teacher *and* an actor. The coaching sessions went extraordinarily well (I wasn't surprised), and I have the distinct sense that Max is well on his way to another vibrant career—this one being a more complete expression of his true core being.

SHEDing Gave Me Stability

Jay, our 32-year-old composer, was hoping to get back in life through the **SHED** process. Eighteen months after he started, he wrote me to say his creativity had blossomed and he was feeling settled for the first time in his life. "My music career is going very, very well and I've had some wonderful things happen. I took a BMI seminar and out of sixty musicians who participated, BMI chose my song to produce. I now have regular space in a full-fledged production studio outside my apartment. Before, I had a portable recording studio which I carried in my backpack—because at the time, my home was not a place I was comfortable in. As a foster child my life was always mobile, so even after I had finally gotten myself a nice apartment, I was still in mobile mentality. Now, my home is fully functional and I've been extremely prolific with the composing, churning out song after song."

After years of feeling disconnected, Jay was finally able to throw down his anchor and plug into his life for the first time. "Now I feel settled in for the first time in my life in a place of my own that feels nurturing. I feel rooted."

Beware of the 30 Percent Slip

In any evolutionary process like this one, it's normal for progress to stall at various times. You may feel a lack of forward motion or enthusiasm, or like things are getting a bit more routine (and less fresh) than you'd like. You may even feel complacent, like you've slipped back into your old ways, just a bit, by allowing your old attachments and bad habits to weasel their way back in. I call this the "30 percent slip."

Recognize that what feels like slippage is often just a matter of having made significant progress in one area but not in others. Stalling is actually a way to give yourself a break before tackling your next big point of entry, which could be even more intimidating than the areas you've already addressed. Sometimes, we need to recharge between growth spurts.

Caroline, for example, decided to pursue her vision of "embracing her personal power" by changing jobs first, but about seven months into the process, she realized she needed to more consciously apply her vision to her day-to-day work life. She said: "This new job has the potential to bring together skills I've developed over the many years of my career, with talents that have been long buried deep inside me. And things I didn't even know were in there. Yet, I feel the danger of getting dragged into a behind-the-scenes role again—becoming the planner, the project coordinator, the researcher behind the desk, rather than the leader, out in front with the troops. I'm feeling about 30 percent derailed."

She said the realities of her work life (like getting policies written, meeting deadlines, and fulfilling last-minute requests) had a way of making her yield to old habits and roles. Caroline was slipping into what was known and comfortable, taking on work outside her responsibility.

Caroline knew this leadership role was the place where she could make the greatest contribution *and* be happy. She wanted to avoid falling back into tasks that drained her energy (like crunching numbers and doing project plans), which she could do perfectly well but were neither fun nor easy to pull off.

Jay had the exact opposite problem. A year into his **SHED**, he'd made great strides on getting back into life on the professional front but hadn't put that same focus toward his love life. It just happened to be the way his **SHED** evolved—his identity as a music composer came first. "I'd say I'm at about 70 percent, which I think is still pretty good," Jay said. "I've been dating here and there but not putting enormous effort into it and so nothing has really developed," he explained. "I still occasionally bump up against the issues that led to the former mess, but now I see the correlations between the mess and my internal emotional state. They feed off each other. Sometimes it's the messiness of the apartment that can tip the cycle. Other times, it's the opposite. Usually it's the bathroom that's the first to go, or the kitchen. I don't stay on top of those areas when my remnants of depression resurface. When I'm feeling that way, it becomes harder to stay disciplined, and easy to let the mess build up. When the apartment is clean, I feel stellar, bright, and energetic; but the minute the clutter creeps in, even a little bit, the space feels so stale and futile. That's when I start using it [the clutter] as a convenient excuse for not going out on a date or having female friends over."

So, if and when you find yourself regressing, don't worry—it's normal. Allow it to be what it is. A big change, like the one you've been going through, is extremely stimulating. You may need to slow down, rest, recharge, and then leap forward again. Any parent is familiar with the growth and regression cycles a kid goes through—one month they run off on their own, only to be clingy and "childlike" the next, then they grow up a bit more, only to take a few more steps backward. This situation is similar. Don't beat yourself up for needing a little break—**SHED** isn't a race.

What Do You Need to Get Back in Gear?

How can you tell if you're beginning to slip and, most important, what can you do to get yourself back on track? I've created this Back on Track diagnostic to check in on how you're doing. Answer each question as honestly as you can. Then use the scoring mechanism at the end to determine what step (or steps) you need to revisit in order to reinvigorate your efforts and keep charging forward.

Back on Track Diagnostic

1. T F My calendar has filled up with new obligations that feel wrong for me.
2. T F The burdensome responsibilities I **SHED** keep coming back to me.
3. T F I'm feeling lost without my old, familiar stuff and behavior.
4. T F I am rushing into decisions about my future that don't feel exactly right.
5. T F My physical spaces feel less "vibrant" than when I first **SHED**.
6. T F My storage areas have become overstuffed again.
7. T F I am battling some self-doubt about my abilities to fulfill my vision.
8. T F I'm having a hard time making decisions about what I want.
9. T F Some troublesome time wasters have made their way into my life.
10. T F Items I meant to heave are still sitting in a corner of my house or office.
11. T F I keep allowing myself to get distracted from my goal.
12. T F I've run out of ideas on how to move toward my theme.
13. T F Portions of my physical spaces remain untouched and stifling.
14. T F There are obligations I was supposed to get rid of, but never did.
15. T F My life feels disorganized and chaotic. I can never find things.
16. T F It's hard to imagine getting everything I am hoping for.
17. T F There are burdens in my schedule I haven't yet **SHED**.
18. T F I've reverted to old habits that I tried to get rid of.
19. T F I'm getting a little complacent, operating on auto-pilot.
20. T F I've stopped tracking my progress in my journal.
21. T F My bad habits drive me crazy, but I can't imagine letting them go.
22. T F I'm unable to make a dent in my backlog of to-dos.
23. T F I'm not taking care of my health the way I should.
24. T F I am stagnating on moving toward my goal.

Scoring

Now, tally up your answers to see which section of the book can help you get back on track. If you answered "True" to questions:

- 1, 5, 9, 13, 17, 21

Revisit Separate the Treasures (chapters 4, 5, or 6). You might be having trouble deciphering the treasures from the trash.

- 2, 6, 10, 14, 18, 22

Revisit Heave the Trash (chapters 7, 8, or 9). Remember, you can only create change if you have the space and energy to do so. Make sure old physical, time, and habit clutter haven't wriggled their way back into your life.

- 3, 7, 11, 15, 19, 23

Revisit Embrace Your Identity (chapters 10, 11, or 12). You might need another shot of self-confidence or a refresher on how to get out of your own way.

- 4, 8, 12, 16, 20, 24

Revisit Drive Yourself Forward (chapters 13 and 14). Resist putting pressure on yourself to decide *exactly* what shape your vision takes and instead allow yourself to experiment with what works and what doesn't.

Here's a brief summary of each **SHED** step to help you remember where you need to refocus your efforts.

The 4 SHED Steps at a Glance

Step 1: Separate the Treasures. A process of self-discovery that enables you to identify what to preserve from the past and bring with you into the future.

Step 2: Heave the Trash. A time of practical action, in which you release physical and time attachments that are weighing you down, freeing up space to pursue your vision.

Step 3: Embrace Your Identity. A moment to build your self-confidence. Enables you to discover your authentic self, pulling your identity from within, in context with your theme, rather than attaching it to external "stuff."

Step 4: Drive Yourself Forward. A time of proactive exploration, which enables your "something more" to come into focus and finally start taking shape, filling the space left vacant by your Heave with new stuff connected to your theme.

Starting Over Again

Now that you've cleared a significant portion of the physical, time and habitual clutter from your life and are moving toward your dream, remember that the **SHED** process is something you can naturally keep coming back to, to keep renewing your life and staying fully engaged. Some of the people you met in **SHED** are already doing this, and because they see the process as a way of life, they have started applying it to other stagnant areas in their lives.

SHEDing is cyclical. Just when you think you've reached the end, a new opportunity to **SHED** presents itself. And you keep getting more excited, and freer, and more fully engaged in life. Each time you begin to feel complacent in your life, you will use this technique to reinvigorate yourself.

Max wrote me, "I am becoming convinced that there are only three stages in life: pre-**SHED**, **SHED**, post-**SHED**—then back to pre-**SHED**." He's right. Start viewing **SHED** as a way of life, striving to free yourself of anything that weighs you down and stifles who you are.

In this book, we've focused on applying the steps of **SHED** to the most tangible areas of your life—physical space, time, and habits—as a gateway to releasing less tangible burdens, like old belief systems and insecurities. But once you understand the steps of **SHED**, you'll find you can apply the framework to larger and more esoteric aspects of your life. **SHED**ing works for a relationship, a way of thinking, or any old attachment that you need to release. With each thing big or small that no longer feels relevant, you can Separate the Treasures, Heave the Trash, Embrace Your Identity, and Drive Yourself Forward.

When you make **SHED** a lifestyle, the anxiety around whether or not you're "done" growing will dissipate. "The beauty of this process," Brooke wrote, "is that I never have to worry that I might not have gone far enough. Like my big old golden retriever, Bailey, each day brings me the opportunities to **SHED** some more. **SHED**ing makes him more comfortable, and quite clearly as long as he keeps growing hair, he is never going to be finished. Likewise, as long as I keep walking in the door with more—as George Carlin would put it—'stuff,' I am going to keep culling out what I do not need. **SHED**ing really does make me feel like I have a new haircut!"

Caroline says, "I am beginning to see the full actualization of my vision, and it is thrilling. Getting out of the rut I was in at my old position has allowed me to see how much I have invested in the company, and how much I value it, and how much passion I have for helping shape its future."

Don't be afraid of setbacks; focus on how far you've come. When you start to slip back into old habits or the clutter builds around you, start from the beginning. Jay said, "When I started this process, I honestly wasn't sure I was going to make it this far. I was in such a bad place; I mean, I was ready to give up. **SHED**ing has given me an apartment that feels like home, a career booster, maybe the chance to go to NYU. I'm able to tolerate the sadness and loneliness that comes and goes with my depression, without letting it get the best of me and my space (at least not for too long). I might keep struggling with these issues, but now I have a solid battle plan."

No two **SHED**s are the same. Jay's breakthrough came from recognizing that there were gems buried in his clutter, while Caroline's came as she reconnected to her core personality traits. Brooke bloomed at the idea she could establish her *own* vision for the future and Max came to life at the prospect of trying new things. Those differences, I think, are what make this process so fascinating and unique. **SHED** is a customized, respectful, and permanent solution that can help any individual, in any situation, seize a change as an opportunity for transformation.

I wrote at the beginning of this book that if organizing is like putting down anchor, **SHED** is the equivalent of setting sail. As you continue your journey through whatever transition brought you to this book, you will begin to feel ready to anchor down again. And you should. Such is the cycle of life. But the moment you feel anxious, restless, or that your life could be something more, take heart in knowing you've been in that place before. Then it's time to **SHED** all over again.

Appendix

Resources for Heaving

The resources identified here will help you target your items to specific outlets for trash or recycling, donating or selling. I've provided you mostly with national programs, but there are many more regional options out there. If there's a charity or organization in your area that you care about, call and see what options are available.

Trash or Recycle

If the items you have **SHED** are in bad shape, seek the appropriate way to discard them. Some resources that will help:

- **1-800-GOT-JUNK** (www.1800gotjunk.com) is a national service that will cart away just about anything—old furniture, appliances, office stuff, construction debris, yard refuse, and general household trash. If it's a nonhazardous item that two people can lift, they can take it.

- **Reuse Development Organization** is a national partnership of organizations dedicated to promoting reuse as an environmentally sound, socially beneficial, and economical means for managing surplus and discarded materials—including, but not limited to, clothes, building supplies, art scraps, medical supplies, and electronics. Visit their website, www.resuse.org, to search by state and find the reuse center nearest you.

- **Earth 911** is the largest environmental recycling and conservation database for locating a recycling or reuse center near you on, well, *earth*! Go to their web page (www.earth911.org), input what you are disposing of and your zip code, or call the Earth 911 hotline (1-800-CLEANUP) to locate centers in your area. Earth

911 also has a sister site you can link to for recycling and environmental information specific to business materials and the locations in your community.

- **GreenDisk** (www.greendisk.com or 1-800-305-3475) will help you responsibly and securely dispose of all your computer-related waste, spent supplies, and obsolete accessories, such as used ink cartridges, old disks, CDs, and so on. And what do they do with your old stuff? Make products!

- **Antron Carpet Recycling and Reclamation** (www.antron.net), a division of DuPont, recycles commercial carpet. DuPont's recycling program began in 1991 when the U.S. Department of Environmental Studies revealed that Americans were tossing up to two million tons of used carpet into landfills every year. DuPont collects and processes about 1.5 million pounds of used carpet a month, which is shipped to one of DuPont's eighty processing centers, where carpet quality and recycling value are determined.

- **The Peanuts Hotline** is *the* national reduce, recycle, and reuse program for plastic packing "peanuts." To find the collection center nearest you from one of the 1,500 sites nationwide, go to their web page (www.loosefillpackaging.com) or call 1-800-828-2214.

- **The Alliance of Foam Packaging Recyclers** (www.epspackaging.com or 1-401-451-8340) can also direct you to a recycling center in your area for disposing of Styrofoam package filler.

Books and Magazines

Who doesn't have books they could donate! Each of the places listed here are not simply spots to dump your unwanted literature. Most organizations have fairly strict standards for what they'll accept (based on the physical condition of the book and sometimes even content), so make sure to check that your donation meets the qualifications. Many used book dealers may accept books as donations. Check the Yellow Pages or www.smartpages.com under Books, Used and Rare for a listing of these locations in your locale. Magazines are more difficult to give away. If they are less than three months old, your local library or senior care center may take them. But here are some other major resources for donating books, as well:

- **The Global Book Exchange** (www.bookexchange.marin.org) is a nonprofit organization committed to fostering community-based literacy initiatives all over the world. Since its founding in 2000, it has delivered hundreds of thousands of books, textbooks, and journals to communities in Africa, the Caribbean, and other developing areas.

- **The Darien Book Aid Plan** (dba.darien.org) is a nonprofit, all-volunteer organization that donates books in response to specific requests from Peace Corps volunteers, libraries, and schools all over the world. Books are also donated to libraries, prisons, hospitals, and Native American and Appalachian groups in the United States.

- **The International Book Project** (www.intlbookproject.org) sends donated books to developing countries and parts of the United States. You can send the books on your own via UPS, or the United States Postal Service, which offers a service called **M-Bags**, where large amounts of printed material can be mailed to other countries for about a $1.00 per pound. See the following link (www.usps .com/global/mbags.htm) for information on how to send **M-Bags**, or arrange shipment with the project for a fee, currently $3.00 per pound of books sent.

- The mission of **Adopt a Library** (www.adoptralibrary.org) is to keep used books out of the landfill and get them to people who need and could use them by encouraging donations to libraries, schools—even prisons—in the United States and around the world.

- **New School University—Journal Donation Project** provides current subscriptions and back volume sets of English-language scholarly, professional, and current events journals to needy libraries and other organizations. Visit their website at www.newschool.edu/centers/jdp.

- **ESL Podcast—Donate** (linguapod.com/eslpod_blog/donate) accepts donations of magazines (and books, too) for use by teachers and professors in teaching English as a second language throughout the United States.

- **BookCrossing** (www.bookcrossing.com) is the world's biggest book club. It's based on the practice of leaving a book in a public place to be picked up and read by others, who then do likewise.

- **NovelAction** (www.novelaction.com). If your shelves are full of books you've already read, join the nation's only online book exchange store. Select any books from the site and send in an equal number of your books in exchange. With flat rate shipping and no transaction fees, it's the perfect site for avid readers who want to keep the contents of their bookshelves vibrant.

Clothing, Housewares, Cars

- **Salvation Army**. Donating here couldn't be easier. All you have to do is visit their website (www.satruck.com) or call 1-800-95-TRUCK (1-800-958-7825) to schedule a pickup in your location when you're ready.

- **Goodwill Industries** is a member organization in the United States and Canada (in addition to 45 international associate members in 34 countries) similar to the Salvation Army in the variety of items it will accept as donation, such as your old books, CDs, and clothing. For delivery locations in your area, visit their website (www.goodwill.org) and type your zip code in the space provided.

- **Donate to Charity** (www.giftsforsight.org) will take almost anything, from cars and boats to time shares, for use in befitting the blind and seeing-impaired. Once you choose from a listing of member organizations, giftsforsight.org offers to collect the item at no cost to you.

- **The National Furniture Bank Association** (www.help1up.org or 1-800-564-0774). Furniture banks in America provide used furniture to more than 100,000 families in need each year. Typical clients of furniture banks are victims of natural disasters such as Hurricane Katrina, mothers and children escaping domestic violence, and working families living below the poverty line. The organization currently has 11 member states and is growing, with 35 to 40 active furniture banks around the country. Every donated item must be structurally sound, and upholstered items cannot be ripped, torn, or stained. Other household items (small kitchen appliances, flatware, drinking glasses) can also be donated but will be accepted only in combination with a piece of furniture. In most cases, you, the donor, will be expected to pay for removal.

- **Dress for Success** (www.dressforsuccess.org). Dedicated to promote the economic independence of disadvantaged women by providing professional attire, this is a network of support and career development tools to help women thrive in work and in life. Each Dress for Success client receives one suit when she has a job interview and can return for a second suit or separates when she finds work.

- **ExcessAccess** and **Inkindex.org** (www.excessaccess.org and www.inkindex.org) are websites with national reach that connect potential donors with the organizations who need their items. Based on a simple search by area code, each site will provide you with a list of organizations and the specific items they need. You can choose the organization you care about most, and contact them directly to arrange your donation.

- **National Vehicle Donation Program** (www.auto-donation.com) accepts used cars and gives them to organizations in need.

- **The Loading Dock (TLD)** (www.loadingdock.org). TLD is a self-sufficient nonprofit organization for the reuse of building materials. TLD facilitates and coordinates the reuse of building materials for low-income housing production across the country. Materials handled include lumber, toilets, nails, paints, carpeting, and more.

Computers, Cell Phones, and Technology

- **Students Recycling Used Technology (StRUT)** (www.strut.org). The StRUT program teaches students to evaluate and repair donated computer equipment, which is then contributed to local schools.

- **Learning and Information Networking for Community via Technology (LINCT)** (www.linct.org). Using computers donated by businesses, LINCT provides computer training, teaches individuals to refurbish computers, and allows them to earn computers through community service.

- **Materials Exchanges** (www.epa.gov/jtr/comm/exchange.htm). Many materials exchanges accept electronics. The Southern Waste Information Exchange (SWIX) has developed a materials exchange specifically for electronics at www .ElectronicXchange.org.

- **PCs for Schools.** Dedicated to providing low-cost alternatives to teaching technology, www.pcsforschools.org is an organization that will accept donations of all quality used (or unused) computer equipment for refurbishing. Call 1-800-939-6000 for more information.

- **Carpel Video** (www.carpelvideo.com). Carpel Video purchases used videotapes for reuse and video duplication and sells them to smaller organizations such as smaller television markets.

- **GreenDisk** (www.greendisk.com). GreenDisk is a company that accepts outdated, unused software packages, computer disks, and compact disks from across the country. The company cleanses, tests, erases, and reformats the disks for resale to consumers as blank high-quality disks.

- **Computers for Schools** (www.pcsforschools.org). Computers for Schools is a nonprofit dedicated to providing a low-cost alternative for achieving technology in the classroom. Computers for Schools offers certified refurbished computers to schools and nonprofits at about a third the cost of new.

- **The Wireless Foundation—Call to Protect** (www.wirelessfoundation.org/Call toProtect/) Call to Protect is a national program sponsored by Motorola, the Wireless Foundation, participating telecommunications carriers, and the National Coalition Against Domestic Violence. This program invites consumers to donate used wireless phones to be refurbished and distributed to domestic violence shelters. The mission of the program is to protect tens of thousands of potential victims by donating preprogrammed wireless emergency phones and airtime to organizations working to combat domestic abuse. These phones allow victims to call for help in threatening situations, enabling police to respond immediately, and they also serve as valuable tools for caseworkers and advocates.

- **Computers 4 Kids** (www.cfkidaho.org) is a nonprofit organization working to close the "digital divide" by providing youngsters with older, obsolete home PCs on which to learn and increase their educational opportunities. Without help from CFK, the future for these kids would look bleak. Unable to purchase a home PC because of economic reasons, they would, in all probability, fall behind in their assignments, which require internet-based research. Call 208-345-0346 to receive authorization prior to shipping (which is also tax deductible!) or delivering your equipment.

- **The National Cristina Foundation** (www.cristina.org) provides computer technology and training in order to give people with disabilities, students at risk, and economically disadvantaged people the opportunity to lead more independent and productive lives. NCF matches the donated technology to one of its partner organizations (located in fifty states nationally, and internationally). They offer pickup service in some areas, but they will accept shipped donations. Call 1-203-863-9100.

- **World Computer Exchange** (www.worldcomputerexchange.org) provides computers and support services in education, environment and economic development to help connect more youth to the internet through its 422 formal partners in 61 developing countries.

Selling Your Excess

If your items are in top-quality condition, and you'd like to recoup some of their value, you can look for sites like eBay or craigslist to sell your items. Here are some additional resources to consider:

- **The Advanced Book Exchange** (www.abebooks.com) is an online marketplace for selling your used, rare, and out-of-print books.

- **Auction houses/antiques dealers.** If your items are high end, contact a professional appraiser to assess the value of your used books and records (those old LPs are making a big comeback). Who knows, you might be sitting on the winning lottery ticket! Once you know their worth, contact your local auction house, previously owned music dealer, or antiques dealer and see what they offer (most are honest and will propose a legit price). You can also try placing an ad for the items in a local newspaper or magazine geared to collectors.

- **Online sales/auctions.** With the advent of eBay, this is one of the most popular options, especially for lower-end and commercial items, such as books, music, clothes, and even magazines—if they happen to be collectible, like *National Geographic* or old movie magazines. Rules and regulations vary between sites, but the general idea is the same. Sellers post items for free (or as little as 1 percent of the total sale price), then buyers start the bidding wars; www.ebay.com, www .auctiondawg.com, and www.missionfish.org (which will arrange to donate a percentage of the proceeds from your sale to a nonprofit of your choice) are secure sites with good reputations. So are www.sell.com and www.ioffer.com, where you can either fix the price of your item or let potential buyers make an offer, which you can then accept, reject, or bicker over in email exchanges. Craigslist.org has expanded to more than twenty cities worldwide—you can sell (not auction) items there easily and keep the power to pick your buyer.

- **Consignment stores** are a great option if you have large amounts of stuff in good-to-excellent condition. Don't be surprised if some shop owners are fussy about what they are willing to sell (wool in winter, linen in summer); contact them beforehand to discuss what you want to bring in. Consignment terms and length will vary between stores, but most offer 50/50 profit splits and 120 days to sell your piece. Be sure to ask about pickup services, and if you're consigning antiques, try to make an appointment with their resident expert before you come in.

- **Garage sale.** These are a lot of work, but if you've got the time and a lot of items in good-to-excellent condition that you'd like to turn into some ready cash (just don't expect to get rich), they can also be a lot of fun—especially if you live in a populated area where you can expect a fair number of bargain hunters to drop in. Make sure items are clean and clearly priced, preferably with color-coded tags to avoid confusion if you are teaming up with a friend or neighbor to have the sale. Get the best price you can but be fair and reasonable. Aim for 25–30 percent of the original price on older items, depending, of course, on their condition. Remember, you can always negotiate down, but never up. Last but not least, have enough singles, quarters, dimes, and nickels on hand to make change for people—about $25 ($20 in singles, $4 in quarters, $1 in dimes and nickels) should get you off to a good start.

- **Garage Sales for Charity.org** (www.garagesalesforcharity.org). Have a garage, yard, or flea market sale. Clean out your excess stuff, simplify your life and help your favorite charity. Make a commitment to donate a minimum of $50 or 10 percent of your sale proceeds to your favorite charity. It can be any local charity, food shelf, church program, national organization, etc.—wherever you feel it will do the most good. The choice is entirely up to you. After the sale, send your donation to the charity of your choice, making a notation on your donation indicating GarageSalesforCharity.org to make them aware how the idea came about.

Acknowledgments

Every book is a bit of a miracle. It starts with an impulse, an idea, a notion, some goals, and through the diligence, devotion, insight, encouragement, and pure hard labor of a virtual village, the book comes to life. I am surrounded by a phenomenal team, each of whom has his or her hand, and heartprint, in this book. Buckets of gratitude to:

Joni Evans, devoted friend and sage advisor, who spearheaded this project and provided invaluable input, wisdom, and encouragement from concept to completion.

Suzanne Gluck, my literary agent, for being my greatest advocate and ensuring I had the time, space, and opportunity to make this book a reality.

Michelle Howry, editor extraordinaire, for bringing such passion and skill to this book, shaping the pages with an impeccable eye, crystal-clear vision, and the deepest respect and enthusiasm.

Cloe Axelson, book midwife and collaborator, for taking this journey with me, for "getting me" better than I get myself sometimes, and for brilliantly helping me translate my thoughts, voice, and soul to the page.

John McCarty, book foreman par excellence, for steadfast commitment, flexibility, diligence, and uncanny skill for getting the manuscript done on schedule and clean as a whistle!

For *inspired* contributions that appear throughout the pages of this book, deepest gratitude to Linda Jacobs, Ric Murphy, Beth Meyers, Corinne Johnson, Will McAvoy, David Maue, Lisa LaVecchia, JJ Miller, Judy Wineman, Rhonda Morgenstern, Monique Kuschel, Steve and Sue Morgenstern, David and Sonia Morgenstern, Eddie and Shirley Fonarow, Gary Greenfield, Robin Goldfin, Deborah Kinney, Gail Koff, and Bud Libman. Your insights, ideas, feedback, and encouragement made this a richer book. And to my dad, who found a miraculous way of being a part of this book and coaching me on the content from afar.

To my team at Simon & Schuster—Carolyn Reidy, Mark Gompertz, Trish Todd, and Chris Lloreda for being behind the book. To the production team, including the very fast and agile copy editor Josh Karpf, Allison Brennan, Kevin McCahill, Jan Pisciotta, and jacket designer Cherlynne Li: thank you for helping me produce a beautiful book. And to the greatest publicity team in the world—Marcia Burch and Kelly Bowen—thank you for being such true believers, and genuine movers and shakers. It's wonderful to be working together again.

To my family at FranklinCovey—Debra Lund, Jeff Anderson, Sara Merz, Kent Frogley, Tomasso Cardullo, Lisa Gee, Cherell Jordan, Lacey Pappas, Jason Frederick, Gordon Wilson—for your vision, talent, enthusiasm, skill, and help in building my brand and for creating a partnership made in heaven.

To my all-star team at the William Morris Agency—Brian Dubin, Strand Conover, Andrew Muser, Cara Stein, Lisa Grubka, Jason Hodes, and Irv Weintraub—thank you for being so solidly in my corner and for your many years of impeccable support. And to Faith Hamlin and team at Sanford J. Greenberger Associates, for being there from the beginning.

To my amazing team at Julie Morgenstern Enterprises. First and foremost, to Herve Jolicoeur, my devoted partner, for being the Rock of Gibraltar, watcher of the ship, and man at the helm—keeping the business going and growing while I was off writing.

To Chanel Graham, my multitalented assistant, who kept every area of my life organized while I was on deadline, and also contributed editing and writing talent at key points along the way.

To Emily Dreisen, my "coach" assistant, who picked up the baton with gusto and confidence and helped launch the book without a hitch.

To Joanie Johnson, Lauren Podber, Natasha Davidian, Bob Frare, and Valerie Norvell, for your talent, enthusiasm, skill, and passionate contribution to the enterprise every day. To Ellen Kosloff, for years of being a pillar that granted me time to think, to dream, to create. To Bob Muller, the sharpest, wittiest, and nicest of accountants on the planet, and Urban Mulvehill, chief counsel, business advisor, and patron saint of Julie Morgenstern Enterpises from its inception.

To Koray Memisoglu, Sam Rosenthal, Lisa LaVecchia, Jill Hiat, Peter Lorring, Maria Reitan, Emily Small, Erin Brennan, Clark Nesselrodt, Katherine Madison, Mark Kargl, Chris Wire, Betsy McFaddin, Carol Crespo, Lee Harris, for always being there with practical support. And to the extraordinary talent behind the Julie Morgenstern **SHED** community: Laurie Lohner, Corey Spencer, Rico Celis and Gordon Hofheins at Wifi5, for your creativity and passion at the speed of light.

To the talented team of organizers, coaches, and facilitators representing JME globally: Deborah Kinney, Ron Young, Sue Becker, Chris Frazier, Fern Silvernagel, Marcie Singer, Gary Greenfield, Charlie Daniels, Allison Blankenship, Margie Gozdiff, Rebecca Herrera, Matt Horoff, Ed Robinson, Anita Berg, Linda Birkinbine, Ronnie Burnett, Jane Carroo, Kristi Constanteles, Mary Donovan, Bonnie Everdeen, Melanie Haack, Jeanine Hanson, Connie Johnson, Meg Kaminski, Deborah Lloyd, Judy Lubowicki, Linda Olsen, Linda Radford, Barbara Ricketts, Standolyn Robertson, Liz Tully, Jill Weaver, Janet Williams, for bringing so much integrity, joy, and commitment to what we do everyday.

To Lisa Kogan and Julia for keeping me grounded, encouraged, and centered.

To the girls—for cheerleading me every day of the writing.

To Randy—for convincing me I could do a one-armed cartwheel.

To Jessi—for being the greatest treasure in my life.

Index

clutter as representing old comforts, 87–88
as connections to core joys, 90–91
effectiveness of, 50
and emotions, 125
and essence of personality, 93
finding, 79–93
and finding treasures, 79–94
as giving confidence, 92
and goals, 82
and going backward before moving forward, 88–89
guidelines for finding, 82, 83–84, 92–94
and guilt, 125, 126, 130–32
and habits, 145, 151
and heaving the trash, 125–43
as helping growth, 91
and identity, 92, 143
and insecurity, 85–88
meaningful, 84
and measuring time clutter, 50–52
options for heaving, 126–27, 136
organization of, 191, 192
and physical objects, 52, 119
points of entry for, 42–43, 44, 45, 79, 80, 84–88, 89, 90, 91, 92–93, 126, 137–38
practical, 84
questions about, 88–89
and radical release, 126–27
and roles and responsibilities, 126, 135–42
sample burdens of, 43
and saying no, 134–35
and scheduled meetings/events, 132–35
and steps of SHED, 9
and themes, 50, 81, 85, 90, 91, 92, 93, 127, 137, 138
and unfinished projects, 126, 127–32
and volume of busy-ness, 80–84
and where to find clutter, 41
See also backlogs; calendars; to-dos
Time Management from the Inside Out (Morgenstern), 12, 192
to-dos
backlog of, 52, 80–84, 110, 126
and finding time treasures, 80–84
and heaving time trash, 110, 126, 127–32
and measuring time clutter, 50, 51, 52
unfinished, 126, 127–32
Tony, and trusting yourself, 166–67, 169
topics, that capture the imagination, 234–37
transformation, 14, 20
transitions, 10–12, 23, 46, 90, 212, 241. See also change
trash
resources for disposing of, 251–57
selling your, 115, 117–18, 257–59
trashing/recycling of, 115, 116, 251–57
See also habits: and heaving the trash; heaving the trash; physical objects: and

heaving the trash; time: and heaving the trash
travel, 226
treasures
and attachment, 15
clutter mistaken for, 75–76
as defining you, 70–72
as empowerment, 72–73
finding habit, 15, 94–108
finding physical, 15, 61–78
finding time, 15, 79–93
guidelines for identifying, 15, 68–77, 89–92
and inventories, 56
mixed feelings about, 71–72
and online SHED profile, 16
overview about, 15, 58–60
and separating treasures as step in SHED, 9, 58–108
Trevor
points of entry for, 51, 55–56, 86, 91
theme for, 51, 85, 91
and time treasures/trash, 51, 85–86, 91, 92, 138–39
triggers
for habits, 145, 148
for memories, 176
trusting yourself
and achieving your vision, 165, 171, 182
and being an interesting and unique person, 165, 178–82
and confidence, 165, 172, 182
and connecting the dots, 172–78
and driving forward, 163, 165–82
and embracing identity, 165–82
exercises about, 165, 171–78, 179–82
and memories, 171–78, 182
overview of, 163
and resourcefulness, 165, 166–70
and self-evaluation, 179
and themes, 171, 172
Twain, Mark, 144, 240

unclutter. See heaving the trash; attachments, understanding

values, core, 232, 237–40
Vicky, and forced change, 37
vision/dreams
and being in the moment, 207
and determination, 188
and driving forward, 212
editing, 29
and experimenting with themes, 212
and looking to past, 31
and naming your theme, 29, 30
reconnecting to, 31
staying connected to, 212

About the Author

JULIE MORGENSTERN is an internationally renowned organizing and time management expert, *New York Times* bestselling author, and corporate productivity consultant and speaker. She is a contributor to *Redbook*, solving readers' problems by creating order in their lives. Julie has been a guest on many TV and radio shows, including *The Oprah Winfrey Show*, *The Rachael Ray Show*, the *Today* show, *Good Morning America*, and National Public Radio. She is quoted and featured regularly in a wide variety of publications and has been seen in *The New York Times*, *The Chicago Tribune*, *The Wall Street Journal*, *Bottom Line Business*, *Best Life*, *Martha Stewart Living*, *Better Homes & Gardens*, *Woman's World*, *Fitness Magazine*, *Men's Health*, and *Cosmopolitan*.

Julie has served actively on the Board of Directors for The National Association of Professional Organizers (NAPO) and was honored with its prestigious Founder's Award in 2002. Julie is also an award-winning member of the National Speakers Association (NSA). In 2003, she was honored by the Small Business Administration with an Outstanding Woman Entrepreneur Award. Additionally, Julie received the Best Organizing Book Award at the 2006 Los Angeles Organizing Awards.

Julie is the author of *Organizing from the Inside Out* and *Time Management from the Inside Out*, both of which have been made into popular one-hour PBS specials. Julie and her teenage daughter Jessi Morgenstern-Colon co-authored *Organizing from the Inside Out for Teens*. Her latest book is now available in paperback, *Never Check E-Mail in the Morning*. Since 1989, Julie and her staff have worked with clients such as American Express, Microsoft, FedEx, Bear Sterns, GlaxoSmithKline, the Miami Heat, NBC News, New York City Office of the Mayor, Sony/BMG Music, Medicare/Medicaid, Viacom/MTV, and Victoria's Secret. She is also the creator of the Julie Morgenstern Collection of organizers, totes, and leather accessories, designed in partnership with FranklinCovey.

Visit Julie at www.juliemorgenstern.com.

OTHER BOOKS BY JULIE MORGENSTERN

Available at fine bookstores everywhere.

For information on all of Julie Morgenstern's services and products, and for media interviews, visit www.juliemorgenstern.com or call (212)586-8084.

To book Julie Morgenstern for a keynote speech, visit www.juliemorgenstern.com/Speaking.php

For corporate training, workshops and consulting, visit www.juliemorgenstern.com/Corporate.php

For personal organizing and time management, visit www.juliemorgenstern.com/Organizing.php

To register for classes in Julie Morgenstern's coaching methods,
visit www.juliemorgenstern.com/Organizing_institute.php

To read Julie Morgenstern's blog, visit www.franklincovey.com/getorganized

To purchase products from the Julie Morgenstern
Organizing Collection by FranklinCovey,
call 1-800-819-1812,
or click www.franklincovey.com/julie to order
or find the FranklinCovey retail store nearest you.